The Most
Important
Place on
Earth

The Most Important Place on Earth

What a Christian Home Looks Like and How to Build One

Robert Wolgemuth

Foreword by Nancy DeMoss Wolgemuth

W PUBLISHING GROUP

AN IMPRINT OF THOMAS NELSON

Published in Nashville, Tennessee, by W Publishing Group, an imprint of Thomas Nelson.

Published in association with the literary agency of Ann Spangler and Company, 1420 Pontiac Road, S.E., Grand Rapids, MI 49506.

Thomas Nelson titles may be purchased in bulk for educational, business, fund-raising, or sales promotional use. For information, please e-mail SpecialMarkets@ThomasNelson.com.

Unless otherwise noted, Scripture quotations are taken from the New King James Version®. © 1982 by Thomas Nelson. Used by permission. All rights reserved.

Scripture quotations marked NLT are taken from the *Holy Bible*, New Living Translation. © 1996, 2004, 2007, 2013, 2015 by Tyndale House Foundation. Used by permission of Tyndale House Publishers, Inc., Carol Stream, Illinois 60188. All rights reserved.

Scripture quotations marked NIV are taken from the Holy Bible, New International Version®, NIV®. © 1973, 1978, 1984, 2011 by Biblica, Inc.® Used by permission of Zondervan. All rights reserved worldwide.

Scripture quotations marked KJV are taken from the King James Version. Public domain.

Scripture quotations marked TLB are from The Living Bible. © 1971. Used by permission of Tyndale House Publishers, Inc., Carol Stream, Illinois 60188. All rights reserved.

Scripture quotations marked PHILLIPS are from J. B. Phillips, "The New Testament in Modern English," Revised Edition. © J. B. Phillips 1958, 1960, 1972. Used by permission of Macmillan Publishing Co., Inc.

Scripture quotations marked ESV are from the ESV® Bible (The Holy Bible, English Standard Version®). © 2001 by Crossway, a publishing ministry of Good News Publishers. Used by permission. All rights reserved.

Scripture quotations marked GW are from *God's Word*®. © 1995 God's Word to the Nations. Used by permission of Baker Publishing Group. All rights reserved.

Italics added to Scripture quotations are the author's own emphasis.

ISBN 978-0-7180-8806-4 (repackage)

Library of Congress Cataloging-in-Publication Data

Wolgemuth, Robert D.
The most important place on earth: what a Christian home looks like and how to build one / Robert Wolgmuth.
p. cm.
Includes bibliographical references (p. 257–66).
ISBN 978-0-7852-8032-3 (TP)
ISBN 978-0-7852-6026-4 (HC)
ISBN 978-0-7852-6776-8 (IE)
1. Family—Religious life. 2. Family—Religious aspects—Christianity. I. Title.
BV4526.3.W65 2004
248.4—dc22
2004014206

Printed in the United States of America

16 17 18 19 20 21 RRD 6 5 4 3 2 1

To our family's next generation of men and women who are—or will be—building their own most important places on earth.

Andrew & Amy Bordoni

Steve & Beth Guillaume

Jon & Angie Guillaume

Josie Guth

Rob & Rebecca Wolgemuth

Kristin Fitzgerald

Jon & Missy Schrader

Brent & Katie Johnson

Christopher & Julie Tassy

Emily Wolgemuth

Mark & Jamie Wolgemuth

Andrew & Chrissy Wolgemuth

Tim & Elizabeth Wolfmeyer

Michael & Molly Grace Bornfriend

Taylor & Laura Birkey

Erik & Kendal Wolgemuth

Noel & Robyn Birkey

Chris & Alli Horst

Marshall & Anne Marie Birkey

Scott & Georgia Godfrey

Mookie & Betsy DeMoss

David DeMoss

Nate & Kathryn Scheibe

Brad & Madison Brizendine

Emily DeMoss

David Fonseca

Deborah Fonseca

Sarah Fonseca

Esther Fonseca

Daniel Fonseca

CONTENTS

CONTENTS

FOREWORD

R obert Wolgemuth and I first met in 2002, when a mutual friend recommended his literary agency to represent my book-writing ministry. During this time I became acquainted with Robert's family and was quickly drawn to their tender hearts and their love for the Lord and for each other.

Several years later I interviewed Robert and his wife, Bobbie, along with their two daughters and one of their granddaughters, for a *Revive Our Hearts* broadcast. We talked about the value of singing as a family. Then I recorded a conversation with Bobbie and the girls about nurturing your child's heart.

On one occasion the Wolgemuths and I were involved in ministry in the same city and went out together for a meal. As we drove back to our hotel from the restaurant, I remember being spellbound as they sang hymns together in beautiful harmony. It was obvious there was something special and unusual about this family.

In 2012, Bobbie was diagnosed with Stage IV ovarian cancer. Over the next two and a half years, Robert and Bobbie openly shared their journey with many friends who were lifting them up in earnest prayer. In the midst of this trial, they were eager for Bobbie to be healed; but more than that, they wanted God to be exalted, and they were committed to trust Him and to embrace His plan for their lives.

When Bobbie went home to be with the Lord in 2014, I had the privilege of watching her memorial service by means of live stream. It was a beautiful celebration of a life lived for the glory of God. Several weeks later we aired a two-day broadcast honoring this faithful woman of God.

In the course of time Robert reached out to me, and we began communicating. Eventually he asked if I would be open to continue developing a friendship to see where the Lord might lead us.

I had grown to respect Robert from a distance and through our professional relationship. But I wanted to know more about his heart, his walk as a husband and a dad. Without his knowledge, I picked up *The Most Important Place on Earth* and started to read. (At the same time, apart from my knowledge, he began reading my book, *Lies Women Believe*!)

How I savored the up-close, personal glimpse this book gave me of its author. I read it eagerly, highlighting sentence after sentence, paragraph after paragraph.

Yes! So true! So good! I thought. *If this man lives half of what he's written in this book, he would make an amazing husband!*

Robert's perspective and insights on the Christian home brought to mind these words from the Old Testament:

> Blessed is everyone who fears the LORD,
>   who walks in his ways!
> You shall eat the fruit of the labor of your hands;
>   you shall be blessed, and it shall be well with you.
> Your wife will be like a fruitful vine
>   within your house;
> your children will be like olive shoots
>   around your table.

Behold, thus shall the man be blessed
who fears the LORD. (Psalm 128:1–4 ESV)

As I grew to know and love this man, I discovered in Robert a man who truly fears the Lord. And by God's grace, what he had written in this book was not just theory but a sweet, established way of thinking and living. His humility and his strong desire to display the fruit of the Spirit—in public and within the four walls of his home— were clearly evident.

During that season I texted these words to Robert:

I have witnessed in you and in your family the blessings and fruit of a steadfast, long-term practice of what you have written. The heart, the values, and the habits you promote in this book are the way you live.

Robert's walk with Christ and his love for me poured a strong foundation for our relationship and eventually our marriage. How grateful and blessed I am to be married to this precious man whose character and heart point me daily to Christ.

When I learned Robert was planning to revise and update this book, I was encouraged and asked if I might write a foreword. I wanted families everywhere to experience the blessings of having a Christ-centered, God-honoring home.

Imagine what could happen—what a difference could be made in our world—if Christian homes were to be miniature outposts of the kingdom of God on earth. If our families would adorn the gospel of Christ and His Word, making it believable.

And so I commend this book to you. My prayer is that God will use it to build and enhance your home—your *most important place on earth*.

—NANCY DeMOSS WOLGEMUTH
July 2016

AUTHOR'S PREFACE

Ten short years after the original edition of this book was published, my wife of almost forty-five years stepped into heaven. Before Bobbie died—and she knew that doing battle with Stage IV ovarian cancer for over two years, her days were few—Bobbie told two close friends that she was eager for me to get married again and, specifically, whom she wanted me to marry.

She did not tell me about this. But two months after I began dating Nancy Leigh DeMoss, these two friends stepped forward to tell me that this was exactly what Bobbie wanted me to do.

Bobbie's love for Nancy was mutual. They had known each other for many years, and Bobbie knew that Nancy and I would be a perfect match. Bobbie was right.

When we were married in late 2015, Nancy and I had this printed in our wedding program:

Nancy and Robert are eager to acknowledge and honor the life of Bobbie Wolgemuth who, after a courageous and Christ-honoring journey with cancer, stepped into heaven in 2014. The impact of Bobbie's life and witness continues to resound in the hearts and memories of so many, especially her children and grandchildren. Her tenacious love for God and His Word was contagious. Her shameless and enthusiastic witness for the Gospel of Jesus ushered many into a saving knowledge of His grace and forgiveness. Bobbie's unwavering affection for so many, including those of us gathered here today, indelibly marked and shaped us. We are all grateful for the life and memory of this remarkable woman who has taken her rightful place among the mighty cloud of witnesses, cheering us on to lives of reverent worship and service to God.

At the close of Bobbie's funeral service in 2014, we played a short video of Bobbie walking and singing "Trust and Obey." As the large screens in the front of the church went dark, this Bible verse appeared in brilliant white letters. These words that our daughters knew by heart from the time they were very small became something of a prophecy:

> "Unless a kernel of wheat falls to the ground and dies, it remains only a single seed. But if it dies, it produces many seeds." (John 12:24 NIV)

I am deeply grateful to God for His faithfulness; the "seeds" of Bobbie's death continue to produce a sweet harvest in the lives of many people.

One of the first things Nancy read during our early dating months was *The Most Important Place on Earth*. She liked it, resonating with the way Bobbie and I had, by the grace of God, built our home. Even though she had never married, Nancy fully embraced these ideas, having hosted young families in her own home, some for years at a time. As she loved and mentored the families she hosted, many of the principles in this book reflect her heart as well.

So, like a runner in a relay race, Bobbie has passed the baton of matriarchy in the "most important place on earth" to Nancy. And welcoming Nancy in this role is something my entire family has done . . . with a great deal of joy.

Thanks be to God for his inexpressible gift!
—2 Corinthians 9:15 ESV

INTRODUCTION

For almost sixteen years I lived in Florida, where many of America's senior citizens come to live (or visit for long periods of time). During this time I grew accustomed to jokes about our state. Things like "Shuffleboard is a collegiate sport" and "It's a state for the newly wed and the nearly dead" and "Are automobiles shipped from their factories to Florida with their left turn signals permanently in the 'on' position?"

We used to say, go ahead, have your fun. You're just jealous.

Some of the other things that are often associated with senior citizens include eating dinner around 4:30 in the afternoon and enjoying cafeterias instead of sit-down-and-order-your-meal-from-a-server restaurants.

Because of this, Florida has its share of cafeterias and many of them are serving dinner quite early in the evening.[1]

If you've been to a cafeteria-style restaurant, you know how it works. Instead of looking at a menu with descriptions (or photos) of the food, you actually get to see all the fare, laid out orderly and colorfully behind Plexiglas shields. Nice people with their hair in shower caps hand you this food when you point to something that looks appetizing. And you put it on your tray and continue sliding it down the stainless steel rails toward another nice shower-capped person who will hand you another selection you point to, until you reach one final nice person at the cash register who's ready to take your money.

No one at these places expects you to point to everything you see. You get to pick and choose what fits your fancy at that moment. Don't you think that's a good idea?

Even though this is a book—and you know how a normal book works—I'd like for you to think of it as a cafeteria in printed form. Even though I believe that everything that's spread before you is good, there will only be a few things that you'll choose at a time. That's perfectly okay.

What's written here is an accumulation of over sixty years of family-living experience. Instead of being overwhelmed by the sheer volume of the ideas here, I encourage you to pick and choose those things that have special appeal. You can put them on your tray and slide along to the next thing.

"Hey, our family can do that today," you might say about something you read. Great. "We can do that one too." Great again. Or you may say, "That's a good idea, but we don't have time to put that into practice with our family for a while."

That's okay.

If you read something you think is off the wall or so idealistic or strange that it's unusable with your family, you may respond the same way I do when I see anything made with eggplant at the cafeteria.[2]

That's okay too.

What's important is that you take some of the ideas in this book and give them a try with your family.

DISTINCTLY CHRISTIAN

The subtitle of this book makes it clear what my worldview is. This is a book written from a Christian perspective. Because you're reading this, my supposition is you either have or want to have a Christian home—or at least you're not opposed to the concept.

If you're already convinced that having or wanting a Christian home is a complete waste of time, reading this book is going to be a pretty frustrating experience. Take it back to the store for a refund or tell the person who gave it to you that you'd rather have a book on gardening. The person will understand.

Since this is a book written from a Christian worldview, I've also made an assumption about the Bible. I believe it's true. And I think that it has a lot to say about important relationships, including ours with God and ours with each other. So I quote extensively from the Bible.

WHY ANOTHER BOOK ON THE CHRISTIAN HOME?

In case you don't already know it, there are already books on the subject of the Christian family. Lots of them. Entire sections in the bookstore are filled with them. In addition, some of the largest Christian ministries in America are dedicated to the growth and preservation of the family.

So what's unique about *The Most Important Place on Earth*?

The answer is mostly how it's organized. This isn't a book of lists—eighteen ways to have family devotions, thirteen keys to getting along with your kids, or six strategies to evangelize your neighborhood.

The approach here is on the desired *results* of those things—a home that makes you feel like a valued "customer" the moment you walk through the front door or a safe place where you can make mistakes.

The truth be known, I *am* eager for your family to find creative ways to pray together. I *am* convinced that a Christian home ought to be a place where everyone truly enjoys each other's presence (at least most of the time). And I strongly believe that your home *is* a kingdom outpost inside your neighborhood. It's just that the approach here will not be calculating or predictable.

I've also had some fun with this very serious subject of building a Christian home. Why? Because *balance* is the goal. A Christian family needs to know how to worship God with the sobriety of an Old Testament priest, and the home also needs to be a place where there's plenty of clowning around.

A WAKE-UP CALL

In 2003, just before I began writing the original manuscript for the first edition of this book, I read Alan Wolfe's *The Transformation of American Religion: How We Actually Live Our Faith*. Wolfe is a scholar who directs the Boisi Center for Religion and American Public Life at Boston College.

On the second page of the book, Dr. Wolfe writes: "American religion has never existed in practice the way it is supposed to exist in theory."[3]

I was stunned when I read this. I read it again, completely taken aback. Not, by the way, because I believe this is a false statement. I was dismayed because he's probably right. His contention was that the things that you and I believe often have little or no impact on our behavior. We claim that we have the right theology, but our lives—and our families—often bear no resemblance to what God may have had in mind for us in the first place.

So, in many ways, I've written this book in response to Alan Wolfe's simple assertion. My hope is that once you've read it and begun to place some of its ideas on your tray, your Christian home will begin, slowly but surely, to resemble your belief system. Then maybe another home in another town will do the same, and then another. In a while, Dr. Wolfe would be forced to rethink his premise. That would be a very good thing.

In the second chapter of *The Most Important Place on Earth*, I talk about having a home that smells like God. A fragrant place. The goal is to build a Christian home where, when people walk in—or even drive by—they take a deep breath and say, wow, God must be something else.

For them to identify your home as "Christian" simply because you have Bibles and Christian books on the shelf isn't good enough. That's why you'll find chapters about grace and humor and gratitude. These things are very important—in *addition* to having Bibles and Christian books on the shelves.

Please allow the following potentially distasteful analogy: As a kid, I made many visits to my grandparents' farm homes in Lancaster County, Pennsylvania. In almost every room of those homes, including the kitchen and the dining room, there were strips of flypaper hanging from a thumbtack in the ceiling. And unless my grandfathers had recently changed them, these sticky narrow strips of brown paper were covered with big, dead, black flies.

I'm sure my mother silently took issue with the cleanliness of these, but as kids, we never questioned them, even though some hung directly over the dining room tables where we ate our meals.[4]

Christian homes are their neighborhood's flypaper. They should be sticky places unsuspecting children who live next door or down the street are mysteriously drawn to and welcomed with open arms. Places that they know are filled with fun. Grown-ups should have no apprehensions about dropping in on one of these homes to borrow a cup of flour or eggs or to share good news . . . or tough news. They may have no idea what it *is* about these houses, but they *know* there's something different—wonderful—about them.

This book was written to help you build this kind of home. And my job, as you read along, will be to help you clarify the challenges and enjoy the experience.

PLEASE FORGIVE ANY PRESUMPTION

When your plane lands in Denver, the flight attendant welcomes you, "on behalf of the city of Denver." Has that ever hit you as strange? Who, for example, has given the employee of your favorite airline this authority?

And the other day, I heard—for the six-hundredth time—a "name your own star" radio ad. "What could be more meaningful than naming a star after someone you love?" the silken-voiced announcer pleads. Unfortunately, these stars already *have* names.

> He counts the number of the stars;
> He calls them all by name.
> Great is our Lord, and mighty in power;
> His understanding is infinite. (Psalm 147:4–5)

The presumptuousness of this radio spot is hilarious. What if your child's second-grade teacher would decide that your kid's name should be "Gillstrap" instead of "Melissa" and she applied for a birth certificate without your knowledge down at city hall to make it legal? As I said, a little presumptuous.

It may appear to you that I have employed the same kind of presumption in telling you to "step aside and let me tell you how to run your family." This is not my intention at all.

What I have done is to lay out some simple ideas that have worked for my family and for other families I know. And I've done my best to underscore what I believe the Bible says about the subject. The goal here isn't to help you create a home that looks like my parents' home. Or my grandparents' homes. Or mine.

But if you take these ideas and *literally* ask God to help you use them—or adjust them to your own taste buds—to make your home a wonderful place to live, then this book will have been enormously successful.

THE READING AUDIENCE

I know that, statistically, a growing percentage of homes—Christian homes—do not consist of one dad, one mom, and a couple of kids. Single-parent homes are everywhere. Maybe yours is one of them.

My hope is that something you read in this book will be helpful to you. But I've aimed it primarily at the dad-and-mom-and-kids paradigm. Of course, I mean no insult to single-parent families by taking this approach. But the decision I made—with the support of the publisher—was to make this "traditional" family the bull's-eye of the target. And, again, my hope is that even if you don't fall into this model, there will be plenty of good stuff to put on your cafeteria tray as you slide by.

Another assumption I've made is that even though, technically, you *are* a family before you have kids, this book assumes that one or more babies have arrived.

In 1971, when Bobbie and I brought our first newborn home from the hospital, we made a conscious decision. Driving east along Central Road in Glenview, Illinois, we prayed. We thanked God for our little girl and promised Him that we would do everything we could to raise her—and any other little ones that might follow—in a *Christian home*. We asked God for His special wisdom and grace.

Then we set out—flawed amateurs as we were—to build our own most important place on earth.

Three years later, after Julie was born, we prayed the same prayer driving along Central Road. Now these women are grown and gone. So this book gives you a looking-back newsreel into what happened with that prayer and what I did—right and wrong—as the dad in fulfilling that vision.

I'm honored to have you join me in working toward the building of your own dream home. Welcome.

—ROBERT WOLGEMUTH

1

WHY A CHRISTIAN HOME?

Different Is a Very Good Thing

Thunderstorms were standard fare in August. Like a huge charcoal-gray tarp being pulled across the sky from the plains to the west, you could see them approaching. A chill stung the air. Then the thunder. Deep rumblings that felt as if they were coming more from the ground than from the sky. And like flashlights clicking off and on under a blanket in the distance, lightning would illuminate the spaces inside the darkened canopy.

In 1974, television weathermen didn't spend as much time as they do now issuing "chances of rain" odds. But when we'd see the tarp and feel the chill and hear the rumblings and witness the lights, we knew that the chances were exactly 100 percent.

On this particular Friday afternoon in Chicago's western suburbs, there was something unusual about the August storm. It wasn't the wind or the thunder or the lightning that screeched across the late-afternoon sky that made it so dazzling. They were there, all right, but they weren't that peculiar. The singularity of this storm was the sheer volume of the unrelenting rain. Hour upon hour it came down. Cats and dogs. Buckets.

My family's homestead in Wheaton was at the vortex of the fury.

1

My late wife, Bobbie, and I were living in our first home in Glenview, Illinois, fifty miles northeast. Our piece of the same storm was real, but far less spectacular. Aside from the inconvenience of having to dash from our detached garage to the back door in time for dinner, I thought nothing of it. We received no reports about what was happening at the homestead.

After dinner and a little family-tumble playmaking with our babies in the living room, we tucked our daughters in for the night. By that time, the storm was finished. As Bobbie and I crawled into bed, I remarked how brilliant the full moon seemed to appear, casting distinct shadows from the trees onto our lawn.

Rrrringggg. Rrrringggg.

The telephone on our nightstand startled me fully awake. I looked at the clock. It was just past midnight.

"Hello," I said in my best you-didn't-wake-me-up voice.

"Robert?" I heard the man say.

"Dad?" I knew that voice very well. He was calling from Los Angeles.

My dad told me that he had been in meetings all day and had just returned to the hotel. A message was waiting for him at the front desk. "Call mother at home immediately," the note read. "The water is past the boys' bedroom floor." The desk clerk had written my brother Ken's name at the bottom of the note.

"Is it raining there?" my dad asked.

"Not anymore," I answered. "But we had a pretty good storm a few hours ago."

"I've tried to call home," he said, "but mother isn't answering. The message says the water is past the boys' bedroom floor! I cannot imagine that."

This was long before cell phones, so I found a piece of paper and a pencil, took his number at the hotel, and promised to drive to Wheaton first thing the following morning to check on mother . . . and the house.

I hung up the phone, glanced over at my wife, who had remained quite undisturbed in spite of the phone call, and went right back to sleep—something my mother was not doing.

The house where we spent most of our growing-up years—103 East Park—stood at the intersection of Park and Main Street. Although it wasn't a steep grade, Park Street elevated gradually as it snaked east for a few blocks. Having delivered newspapers as a boy to the homes on that street, I was very familiar with its sloping topography.

My brother and sister, Dan and Debbie, nineteen-year-old twins, had been home that afternoon. And like normal home-for-the-summer college students, they had Friday-night dinner plans with friends. Mother was alone.

As I said, August thunderstorms were common fare. But after several hours of the deluge, mother grew more and more concerned. From the upstairs corner bedroom, she looked out toward the street. A huge puddle filled the intersection from curb to curb. And the streets—especially Park Street from the east—were virtual white-water rivers carrying more of the wet stuff in their wake.

Trying her best to not sound too alarmed, mother called Ken, my brother, who, with his wife, Sharon, and two baby daughters, lived two miles from the homestead. True to form, Ken dropped everything.

By the time he got to our home, the water had risen toward the east and was halfway up our driveway. The rain continued without pause. He parked in front of the neighbor's house and ran, getting completely soaked by the time he reached the front door. Mother was reassured to have a man in the house and asked Ken to go to the basement family room to see if any water was seeping in. Ken obeyed, quickly looking for any unwelcome leaks.

"It looks okay," he hollered up two flights of stairs to our mother. "Everything's fine down . . ."

Ken stopped talking. At that moment water came bursting into our house, pouring down the basement steps like a waterfall. Struggling to climb through the virtual rapids, he made his way upstairs, soaked to the waist. "We have to call dad," he said as he reached my mother.

Under normal circumstances, mother resisted calling dad with bad news when he was out of town. These were anything but normal circumstances. Quickly dialing the West Coast hotel, Ken learned from an operator that my dad wasn't in his room. He left his panicked message at the front desk.

The rain did not subside. What had been our yard was gradually becoming a small lake. Then the lights went out.

Hearing someone at the front door, mother looked up to see a large and imposing man walk straight into the house without knocking. She did not recognize him, nor did she speak.

"Get out of this house," he ordered. "Get out of this house. This is a flood."

Not knowing that the phone lines were down as well as the power, mother told him that she couldn't leave because she was waiting for a call from her husband.

Lightning shocked the night sky with light once more, and a clap of thunder rumbled.

At that moment my mother lifted her face and her hands heavenward. "Precious Heavenly Father," she began to pray in a voice as strong and confident and resolute as if she knew exactly what she was doing. She did.

"Precious Heavenly Father, I love you very much," my mother continued. "Please stop this rain!"

The neighbor stood in startled amazement.

As if a giant spigot had been turned off, the rain stopped. Nothing was left of the raucous storm but stillness.

In the darkness my brother saw the man's eyes widen as though he had seen a vision. "You're an amazing woman," he said. He turned and was gone.

In just a few more minutes, mother and Ken stepped through the front door. The clouds gave way to the brilliant rays of a full moon.

They were both stunned at how dazzling the full moon seemed to appear through the purified air, reflecting perfectly onto the sea that covered what had been our lawn.

She began to pray in a voice as strong and confident and resolute as if she knew exactly what she was doing. She did.

The following morning, just as the sun was rising, I drove as quickly as I could to Wheaton. Along the interstate, as I got closer to our homestead, I saw places where water had gathered in open fields. Clearly the rain had been more severe there than at our home fifty miles away. But nothing could have prepared me for what I saw when I turned onto Park Street. The image is as clear in my mind today as it was in that moment.

Our home was standing quiet and alone in the middle of a huge lake. Water was tucked up under her all the way around her foundation. In the stillness, our home cast her exact likeness in the water that surrounded her.

I had never seen the home where I grew up from this beautiful yet precarious perspective. Ironically, today, as I look back on that place, I see it again . . . in yet another beautiful, precarious way.

This was my home. It was a *Christian* home. And this was the place where I learned exactly what "Christian home" meant. It was like no other.

Let me roll the clock back a few decades and tell you what I mean.

WHAT'S GOING ON IN THERE?

My three buddies impatiently paced back and forth across our yard. Between anxious glances into our kitchen window, John Strandquist, Bobby Shemanski, and Roger Morris halfheartedly tossed the football to each other. They were out of earshot, but the shrug of their shoulders and the shuffle of their feet let me know that their patience was wearing thin.

The three were waiting for me. But it was going to be a while, and they knew it. They'd done this many times before. When you're twelve years old, thirty minutes might as well be a month.

Looking back, I've often wondered what those boys were thinking. Oh, I know what they whined when I finally emerged from the house to finish the game, but what was *really* going through their minds? In fact, I'd love to take you with me and travel through time right now to visit my backyard during those minutes.

"What's taking Robert and his family so long?" we'd ask them. "What in the world are they doing in there? Why can't they just finish dinner like normal people? What is it about that family?"

The first few questions would have elicited spontaneous preteen speculation—big family, mother's painstakingly prepared meal, stern father—but this last question would have been the one to make them stop and think. *What* is *it about that family?*

Since time travel is still under development, I'll have to take a shot at telling you what was happening.

This was dinnertime . . . "supper time" back then. It was sacred. A time of enjoying my mother's healthy fare and catching up with each other on the day's activities and accomplishments. And it was a time for Bible reading and prayer—"family worship," my dad called it. Impatient friends pacing in the backyard, and my own restlessness, had no influence whatsoever on the proceedings.

From my first conscious thoughts as a little boy, I knew one thing about my family—one thing for sure. My family was *different*. We weren't like most others. Growing up, I vacillated between security in and embarrassment about this. At times the raw strength of my parents' love for me filled me with confidence. I felt safe there. This was almost palpable as I sat around the dinner table, interacting with my parents and my brothers and sisters—making John, Bobby, and Roger wait.

But as a youngster who wanted to be accepted by his friends outside those safe confines, I would have preferred a *normal* family, a *cool* family like the other kids'. I knew that my family was different . . . not normal and definitely *not* cool.

Today I'm very grateful for this.

DIFFERENT IS OKAY

For sixteen years, my late wife, Bobbie, and I lived in Orlando. Our home was exactly 8.5 miles from the entrance to a park that calls itself "The Happiest Place on Earth."[1] This place—known around the globe as Walt Disney World—was founded by a man who also grew up in a home known for its distinction in the neighborhood. Walt Disney was born in Chicago in 1901, the fourth son to Elias and Flora Disney. Two years later a little sister, Ruth, was born. And soon after that, Elias and Flora, "unsettled by the raucous, saloon-centered nature of their neighborhood," decided to leave the city for the quieter climes of rural Missouri.[2]

> I knew that my family was different . . . not normal and definitely not cool.

I wonder what Disney's buddies down the street would have said about that family. "Different" comes to mind—which is precisely why over sixty million people visit the Orlando area every year.[3] Disney World is like no other place, confidently fashioning itself as the "Happiest." Not simply "A Happy Place" or even "One of the Happiest Places," but "*The* Happiest." Walt Disney knew that different was okay. In fact, different was exactly what made his vision so very attractive to so many. Different became a prerequisite.

On July 17, 1955, when Disneyland in California was christened, Walt Disney said, "Disneyland is dedicated to the ideals, the dreams and the hard facts which have created America . . . with the hope that it will be a source of joy and inspiration to all the world. . . . I don't want the public to see the world they live in while they're in the Park (Disneyland). I want them to feel they're in another world."[4]

7

As the ideas in this book were taking form, several possible titles came to mind. I thought of calling it *So You Want to Have a Christian Home*, the name of a series I taught in Sunday school in the mid-nineties. *Building a Christian Home* also became a possibility, using my years in construction as a metaphor.

Then I thought about this place down the street from our home in Florida—dare I refer to it as an amusement park?—that has the brazen audacity to proclaim itself the happiest, the premier, *the* best in its class.

Why can't our homes be different in this wonderful way? Why can't they be places where our children feel as though they're "in another world," where "dreams and hard facts" are celebrated? Who wants to be normal? Everyone else is normal. This kind of different is good. So I'm taking a chance and tacking signs above the front door of my home and your home. They read, "The Most Important Place on Earth." The superlative works just fine here.

Ironically, *every* home, regardless of what's going on inside, might as well have this over its front door. For the children who live in these homes, it's a fact, good or bad: it *is* the most important place on earth. Sit down over a cup of coffee with any family therapist in the country and usually he or she will tell you that, for a kid, it's at home—whatever it looks like—where everything in life makes up its mind.

One of my earliest sports heroes was Bill Glass, number 80 all-pro defensive end for the Cleveland Browns. Following a successful career in football, Bill founded an organization that focuses primarily on ministry to prisoners. Bill tells of standing in front of inmates crowded into prison auditoriums to hear this former athlete speak. His delivery was spellbinding. Normally inmates pride themselves on being aloof and unaffected. But not when this gentle giant stood before them. Bill commanded their attention.

Nearly every time in his talks to prisoners, Bill Glass asked, "How many of your parents told you that this is where you'd wind up some-day?" He posed this question hundreds, perhaps thousands, of times, and the response was always the same. Almost every man or woman in his audience raised a hand. Sure enough, they didn't disappoint their parents. Their homes were the most important places on earth, and they had successfully walked the path set before them as children. They did exactly what they were told they would do.

THE METER IS RUNNING

You get one shot at this home-building thing. Only one. And time is not on your side.

Being a weekend-warrior-construction kind of guy over the years, I have made friends of the folks at the tool-rental centers close by every home we've owned. Tools ranging from jackhammers to heavy-duty pumps to trenchers to compressors to nail guns have been loaded into the trunk of my car in front of these establishments. But from the moment I pull out of the parking lots of these places until I return the tools, I carry a nagging sense of hurry deep inside. I know that the meter is running. Every hour costs me something, so there's a sense of urgency about the task. It's not recklessness—many of those tools are dangerous if not used properly—but it's certainly single-mindedness about the work I have to do so I can finish and return the borrowed tool.

> You get one shot at this home-building thing. Only one. And time is not on your side.

From the moment you tenderly unwrap the blanket around your first baby after the trip home from the hospital, the nagging sense in the pit of your stomach should be exactly the same. The hourglass has been upended. You have one chance at this.

I know that being a parent isn't all that's happening in your life. You've got your marriage to work on; your career is in need of your constant attention; there are errands to run and meetings to make. And you're exhausted.

Now I'm adding to your load by laying on a dose of guilt, telling you that you've only got one shot at this family-building thing.

But if you'll let me visit the rented tools one more time, the message here is not shame and blame. But it *is* urgency. Focus. Purposefulness. Intentionality. Care.

WHY A CHRISTIAN HOME?

Right here in the first chapter I'm going to tell you—in case you've not figured it out already—that this is a book about building a *Christian* home.

"Why a Christian home?" you might ask. "Why not a Cleveland Indians home or a Chicago Bears home?" Some people live in a University of Tennessee home. Because Bobbie and I lived in Nashville for sixteen years, on autumn Saturdays we'd see folks from UT homes drive up and down the street with orange flags sticking out of their windows. So why not a Vols home? Being a football fan is a good thing, isn't it?

Why a Christian home? How about . . . an American home? Would that be good enough? Or maybe a healthy home or a positive-thinking home or a musical home? I've visited friends who had laugh-a-minute homes. I went back to those as often as I could.

What is so great about a Christian home? It's rather simple. In a Christian home, there's something special. It's called *grace*. To be sure, there can be good stuff in these other kinds of homes. You can be a loyal fan, you can be a patriot, you can be a healthy eater and a positive thinker, but there's no power—no lasting redemption in any of these others.

So the answer to the question "Why would you want to live in a Christian home?" is pretty straightforward. In a grace-filled Christian home, there is salvation. There is forgiveness. There is hope. Genuine happiness. There is *purpose* there. *Power* there—for the parents as well as for the children. And as you'll discover in the chapters that follow, this kind of grace affects everything that goes on inside this home.

> In a Christian home, there's something special. It's called grace.

A few thousand years ago, King David described it this way:

> Unless the LORD builds the house,
> They labor in vain who build it;
> Unless the LORD guards the city,
> The watchman stays awake in vain. (Psalm 127:1)

ONE PERSON AT A TIME

The Bible tells us Jesus came to earth to redeem individuals. Salvation comes to men and women, boys and girls who put their faith in Him. He died for people—you and me—giving us access to a holy God as His dear children and releasing us from the power of sin. This is what it means to be a Christ follower, a Christian.

Jesus doesn't throw a blanket of salvation over homes. A relationship with Him happens one person at a time. In his classic book *Mere Christianity*, C. S. Lewis described it like this:

Imagine yourself as a living house. God comes in to rebuild that house. At first, perhaps, you can understand what He is doing. He is getting the drains right and stopping the leaks in the roof and so on: you knew that those jobs needed doing and so you are not surprised. But presently He starts knocking the house about in a way that hurts abominably and does not seem to make sense. What on earth is He up to?

The explanation is that He is building quite a different house from the one you thought of—throwing out a new wing here, putting on an extra floor there, running up towers, making courtyards. You thought you were going to be made into a decent little cottage; but He is building a palace. He intends to come and live in it Himself.[5]

When you gather a dad and a mother and children who have received this gift of salvation, something special happens. Your Christian home literally consists of multiple "palaces," and no less than the sovereign Creator of the universe lives inside each one. (Appendix A, page 241, is a description of how to lead your children to their own experience of God's saving grace through Jesus Christ.)

LITTLE HOUSE ON THE RUNWAY

My children were born in the seventies, Missy in 1971 and Julie in 1974. The same year Julie came into the world, Michael Landon's *Little House on the Prairie* series, based loosely on the classic books by Laura Ingalls Wilder, aired on NBC. Landon's father was a Jew and his mother an Irish Catholic. And although he held his personal faith close to the vest, Michael Landon created this series with an unapologetic Christian worldview front and center.

On Thursday nights at seven o'clock, our little family gathered around the television and watched *Little House*. We laughed at Mrs. Oleson's brashness and cried when Mary went blind. The series gave us family shorthand. When someone in our house was whining because of an "owie," we'd say, "Quick, go get Doc Baker."

The thing that Bobbie and I loved most about the series was that church attendance, prayer, and including God in the chatter of everyday life was completely normal. Mutual respect between Charles and Caroline was predictable. Tender affection between parents and children was open and genuine.

For the next nine years, our daughters trudged off to school early Friday mornings with the memory of those shows from the evening before. Grade-school conversations with their friends often led with "what happened last night on *Little House*."

Amazingly, it was possible in the seventies to catch a glimpse of what a Christian home looked like on network television. Families all over America saw one in a little wooden farmhouse on the plains of Minnesota. Without a companion instruction guide, they could have modeled a Christian home without even thinking about what they were doing.

I promise to stay away from my soapbox, but I know you and I can talk truth about what's happened to prime-time television since then. It's certainly not *Little House*. Coarse, rude, vulgar, disrespectful, and celebrations of immorality would be apt descriptions of almost everything during prime time.

Our "little house" today is no longer on the prairie. It's on the runway. Gentleness and tenderness and bedtime prayers and long walks to school have been replaced with unfortunate images coming and going at screaming speed.

Here's my point: for millions of American families, there is no model for a Christian home. In fact, for many, there is no memory of one. This may be true for you.

FIRST-CENTURY PARENTING

Between Christmas and New Year's Day 2003, Bobbie and I flew to Charlotte to spend the week with our children and grandchildren. We landed at Charlotte Douglas International Airport on Christmas morning and hustled to baggage claim to meet Christopher, our son-in-law, then it would be off to gather around the tree with our family.

Walking down Concourse D, we spotted a large poster advertising a new exhibit called "Raphael to Monet" at the Mint Museum of Art in downtown Charlotte. Bobbie didn't need any more encouragement. Nodding toward the poster, she immediately made her plan.

"Let's take the kids to see this," she said with predictable enthusiasm. "Yeah, let's," I agreed.

In a few days we were with our daughter Missy and her three kids, walking through the rooms of the museum, the muted lights showing off the unique beauty of each of the masterpieces.

One of the largest paintings was entitled *The Christian Martyrs* by the nineteenth-century French painter and sculptor, Jean-Léon Gérôme (1824–1904). It was a scene from the Coliseum of first-century Rome. I found our almost-eight-year-old granddaughter, Abby—her little brothers were being creative in the color-your-own-tunic children's area—and standing there in front of this masterpiece, looking at it together, I explained to her its historical significance.

Kneeling in the center of the Coliseum floor was a huddle of people, perhaps thirty of them, including children and grown-ups. In the center of the group, a peaceful lone figure stood. His white hair and beard made him look to be the oldest among them. His face was lifted toward heaven in prayer.

On the left side of the painting was a huge brown male lion entering the Coliseum through a large gate. His determined eyes were fixed on the group clustered in the center. Gérôme had flawlessly defined the animal with a massive mane and rippling muscles. His mouth was opened slightly, giving us a good look at his glistening teeth. Behind him we could see several other lions ready to follow.

Encircling the floor of the arena were crucifixion crosses—we could see twelve or so—each with a person hanging on it. Some were on fire.

"These people were all going to die," I said to Abby.

"What did they do?" she asked.

"They told the Roman emperor that they would not bow down to him . . . that they loved God and would worship only Him," I replied. "If these people had turned from their faith, their lives would have been spared. All they had to say was that they didn't love Jesus, and they would have been allowed to live."

Abby didn't say anything, her eyes and her heart gathering it all in.

"Can you imagine," I finally asked, "being killed because of what you believe?"

We stood there a moment longer; I took her hand, and we walked on.

In the van on our ride home, everyone talked about his or her favorite thing at the art museum. Of course, the boys were happy with the craft table, and Abby liked the early American dress exhibit. Bobbie and Missy's favorite was Rafael's *Madonna*. Mine was the painting I had described to Abby. I didn't say any more than that.

But as I drove through Charlotte's busy neighborhoods, enjoying the laughter and singing from the back of the van, I couldn't get the image out of my mind. *What would it have been like to be a Christian parent in Rome during the first century?* I thought. *What would mealtime have looked like there?*

CHRISTIAN HOMES IN ROME

In the year AD 64, a fire started in a small shop near the heart of Rome. The blaze grew until it had spread everywhere. For nine days the inferno destroyed most of the city. At the time, the emperor, Nero, was vacationing at his seaside villa. Because he refused to go back to comfort those who were suffering, rumors began to spread that Nero himself had ordered the fire so he could rebuild Rome according to his own self-aggrandizing plans.

> "Can you imagine," I finally asked, "being killed because of what you believe?"

In order to suppress the gossip, Nero created scapegoats. The historian Tacitus wrote, "Nero punished with every kind of cruelty the notoriously depraved group known as Christians. First, Nero had some of the members of this sect arrested. Then, on their information, large numbers were condemned—not so much for arson, but for their hatred of the human race. Their deaths were made a farce."[6]

Instead of killing Christians in the usual places of execution, Nero murdered them publicly in his gardens near his palace and in the Coliseum. "Mockery of every sort accompanied their deaths. Covered with the skins of beasts, they were torn apart by dogs and perished, or were nailed to crosses, or were doomed to the flames and burnt, to serve as a nightly illumination, when daylight had expired."[7]

What Abby and I had seen that day in the art museum depicted a real time in history when Christian homes were literally in the crosshairs of a raving savage. Imagine what it must have been like to sit down with your family and explain what being Christians in your neighborhood would mean.

The answer takes *different* to a whole new level, doesn't it? But the message has some similarities to your family and mine today. *Culture-friendly* can't be on our family's priority list. That builds nothing in our homes and takes us nowhere. *Different* should be on that list.

JUST LIKE NOAH

Noah's world was not unlike first-century Rome. He and his family had to face the challenge of standing out in their town. Wickedness was everywhere—so awful were the people that "the LORD was sorry that He had made man on the earth, and He was grieved in His heart" (Genesis 6:6).

> *Culture-friendly can't be on our family's priority list. . . . Different should be on that list.*

Amazingly, Noah wasn't affected by what was going on around him. Scripture describes him as "perfect in his generations," a man who "walked with God" (Genesis 6:9). Can you imagine that? Right there in the middle of all that nastiness was someone who dared . . . to be different.

The kids down Noah's street must have

noticed something about that house on the corner. The Bible doesn't fill in the details, but it's certainly likely that Noah, his wife, and their three sons were something unusual in their neighborhood.

When Noah had completed the great ship, the ark, and the pairs of animals were on board, God spoke to him. Listen to what He said: "Come into the ark, you and all your household, because I have seen that you are righteous before Me in this generation" (Genesis 7:1).

Did you catch it? Noah's faithfulness, his willingness to be marked as "different" in his community, saved the lives—literally—of his entire family. As their direct descendants, you and I have Mr. and Mrs. Noah to thank.

WHAT ABOUT THE CHURCH?

I suppose it's arguable that because we're Christians, the *church,* not our homes, is really the most important place on earth. Let's take a look.

Our culture is thoroughly spiritualized. Almost half of the United States population attends church; some only at Christmas and Easter, but more than half name a specific place when asked to identify a home church. Do these people believe in God, and is prayer an important part of their lives? The statistics are staggering. More than *90 percent* say yes to both.[8]

So we shouldn't need network television shows to model for us what a Christian home looks like, right? Our country is filled with religious people who should get it.

Sadly, the accounts of divorce, spousal and child molestation, infidelity, and substance abuse are almost indistinguishable between church-attending and non-church-attending people.[9] It's clear that our churches, by and large, *respond to* what families send them; they do very little to *change* their behavior.

In the mid-eighties, our good friends Mark and Susan DeVries joined the staff of our church in Nashville. Mark had graduated from both Baylor University and Princeton Seminary with honors. He and Susan had been vigorous leaders in Young Life for many years and were gifted in understanding teenagers.[10] If ever there was a man who was qualified to step into the role of youth pastor, it was Mark DeVries.

Because he and I had been close friends since his days as a college student, we frequently rendezvoused at a Nashville diner for breakfast to catch up on each other's lives. It didn't take long for the idealistic shine on Mark's hopes for successful youth ministry to begin to tarnish. We talked about this.

One morning, over cheddar cheese omelets, Mark resolutely told me what he had decided to do. I held my breath, fully expecting him to tell me that he was going to quit. But soon I detected a lift in his spirit. Mark had an idea that literally transformed his youth ministry. In fact, Mark eventually wrote a book about this discovery and has traveled around the world, teaching others to do the same.[11]

With all due respect to theologians and Bible scholars and ministers and church musicians everywhere, what Mark discovered was a very simple truth. All his expertise in youth ministry—his winsome spirit, his musical skills, his ability to deliver biblical truth to fidgety youngsters—was going to be a complete waste of time without also ministering to the *parents* of these teenagers. In other words, our church was *not* the most important place on earth for these kids. It was their *homes*.

A few weeks after Mark's discovery, I noticed a change in the church bulletin. Instead of "Youth Minister" next to the name of Rev. Mark DeVries on the staff roster, it read "Minister to Youth and their Families."

LET THE EXPERTS HANDLE IT

In his research, George Barna has discovered that instead of taking responsibility for the spiritual development of their children, most

Christian parents in America are satisfied by enrolling them in church programs.[12] "Let the experts handle this part of my kids' lives," they seem to be saying.

But as my friend Mark discovered, children's homes have more impact on what happens—or doesn't happen—at church than the other way around. The hope of busy parents is that church programs or classes at school on character development will bring them up to speed on moral and spiritual issues. Unfortunately, they've severely miscalculated. The *homes* have the most profound influence. *Parents* are the experts who must do the work.

You remember the story of David and Goliath, how the boy shepherd felled the giant Philistine with a single smooth stone rocketed from his slingshot. Coming face-to-face with Goliath and surrounded by two warring armies, David hollered to the monster: "You come to me with a sword, with a spear, and with a javelin. But I come to you in the name of the LORD of hosts, the God of the armies of Israel, whom you have defied" (1 Samuel 17:45).

David must have been some kind of very special young man, right?

Witnessing the spectacle from the sidelines of the battlefield, King Saul approached David's brother with a question. Listen to this: "'Abner,' Saul asked. 'What sort of family does this young fellow come from?'" (1 Samuel 17:55 TLB).

In the wake of one of history's most remarkable and courageous confrontations, the king of Israel wanted to know only one thing about the boy hero: "Tell me about his home."

Saul could have asked about David's occupation or experience in hunting or his availability for future conflicts. Instead he asked about his family.

So the breathtaking assignment of leading our homes comes back to you and me. Our children are counting on us. We are the proprietors of the most important place on earth. We are the specialists. No one can do this except us.

NO TIME FOR ORDINARY

In a book like this, I'll admit to you that it's tempting to be diplomatic. And why not? As a negotiator and salesman, I have learned the art of sneaking up on a possible customer with tact.

A few pages ago I said, "You get one shot at this home-building thing. Only one. And time is not on your side." My tendency might be to soften this a little by adding that you get points for honest effort and that, hey, you're only human. Your kids are resilient. They'll be fine. I prefer not being accused of being inflexible and dogmatic, so I'll spot us a few points. We're bound to make mistakes just as everyone else does. And speaking of everyone else, we're doing a lot better than a lot of parents we know, so *that* has to count for something.

Although that's my tendency, I'm going to push through it and warn you that even though I will be quick to tell you of my own failures in the process of Christian home-building, I'm not going to let us off the hook. This parenting thing is serious business, and there's no one on earth in a better position—or better qualified—than you and me to do it right.

Plus, my assumption is that you aren't about to follow advice that sets a low standard and admits that ordinary—mediocre—is good enough. You want to have an extraordinary home, and you're willing to do what's necessary to get there. Right?

Most of the time, you and I download new software onto our computers via the Internet. But back in the day when you wanted to buy a new software program, it usually came in a box with two instruction manuals. One is anywhere from three-quarters of an inch to two inches thick. The other is usually a couple of pages long and calls itself *The Quick-Start Manual*. Although you normally head for the quick start rather than the four-hundred-pager, these have something in common. They tell the truth about what you've just bought. They tell you exactly how to install the program and how to access the software's features. Why would you waste your time on anything else?

My point exactly.

This book is going to fall somewhere between the quick-start booklet and the four-hundred-page tome. But my promise is to speak as honestly as I know how, not letting either you or me out of this thing easily.

As you read, there might be times when you could accuse me of abject idealism—naïveté—in what I'm suggesting. Please stay with me. I have seen the principles in this book work again and again—and not just with my own family but with many others.

> We are the proprietors of the most important place on earth. We are the specialists. No one can do this except us.

"BE YE PERFECT"

One afternoon Jesus Christ sat down on a hillside in Judea. As with the presentation of an executive summary of a business plan, His goal was to clarify His message in crisp, bite-sized pieces. His topics ranged from relationships to spoken words to money to showing mercy.

Sometimes people accuse Jesus of being too gentle, flexible, and accommodating. But if ever there was a solid argument against this charge, this is it! In fact, right in the middle of His talk, Jesus looked straight into the faces of those who were listening. "Therefore you shall be perfect," Jesus said, "just as your Father in heaven is perfect" (Matthew 5:48).

So much for accommodation. ("Perfect" has a familiar ring to it, doesn't it? Remember Noah?)

I first learned of the Sermon on the Mount (Matthew 5–7) as a kid in Sunday school.[13] Because my Bible had Jesus' words printed in red, it was almost four consecutive crimson pages, the most in the whole New Testament. But not until I was a parent did I connect the final illustration with my family. This is for you too. Listen:

Therefore, whoever hears these sayings of Mine, and does them, I will liken him to a wise man who built his house on the rock: and the rain descended, the floods came, and the winds blew and beat on that house; and it did not fall, for it was founded on the rock.

But everyone who hears these sayings of Mine, and does not do them, will be like a foolish man who built his house on the sand: and the rain descended, the floods came, and the winds blew and beat on that house; and it fell. And great was its fall. (Matthew 7:24–27)

It's incredible when you think about it. Jesus' most important message to potential followers was one He summarized in an illustration about building a home, a Christian home. "If you take these things," He was saying, "and use them in your life, it will be just like building your home on a rock, not on the shifting sand."

So as you and I go through the chapters that follow, I'll include some other important truths from the Bible, things that are absolutely useful in your life and your home right now.

THAT SUCKING SOUND YOU HEAR

During our sixteen years of living in Nashville, I became friends with Mike Rose, a man who owned a salad-dressing factory. Even though public tours were not available, one day Mike invited me to walk through his plant. It was a remarkable experience, one I haven't forgotten. After hearing about my visit, you won't forget it either.

Mike's directions were exact, and I found the building without making any wrong turns. I parked next to a large silo, reminiscent of my uncles' farms in Lancaster County, Pennsylvania, and walked into the reception area where a woman sitting behind a desk greeted me with a friendly hello. In a few minutes, Mike came out to greet me. After a short conversation we were on the factory floor.

I was immediately taken by the fact that the place was immaculate.

Of course, these folks were making stuff for people to *eat*, but it's quite an experience to see a huge plant with giant pieces of equipment as pristine as a warm and shiny spoon you take from the dishwasher right after a wash cycle.

There were three most memorable moments during my tour. The first was when my friend told me that the silo I had parked next to was filled with tons of egg yolks. (I resisted asking Mike what it would be like to jump into the slimy stuff. Once a boy, always a boy.) The second was watching white, creamy mayonnaise belching from a two-inch chrome pipe at breakneck speed. And the third—which I'm going to describe in some detail—was seeing the plastic-jug-making machine.

My friend explained to me that he buys plastic pellets by the freight-car load. These are melted, then sent into an extruder that actually sucks the material into a mold shaped like a gallon jug. If you've visited a restaurant kitchen or if you shop at Sam's, Costco, or BJ's, you've seen these white jugs filled with mayonnaise. I stood and watched this process for quite some time: the softened plastic meeting the powerful force of the vacuum and being drawn into the form in a split second.

What a great word picture to help us understand what the apostle Paul wrote during the first century: "And do not be conformed to this world, but be transformed by the renewing of your mind, that you may prove what is that good and acceptable and perfect will of God" (Romans 12:2). One Bible paraphrase of this verse says, "Don't let the world around you squeeze you into its own mold" (PHILLIPS).

Visions of the plastic-jug-making machine should come to mind.

The same is true of our families. The pull of an immoral world outside our homes is as strong as the force that sucks the soft, white stuff into the form. Neutrality on our part as parents will result in failure. Without our intentional effort to defy it, our kids will have no chance but to be thoroughly drawn into those things that we fear most.

But transformation and intentionality—the willingness to claim unpopular territory even if it means focused resistance—on our part can create a home that stands out beautifully in our culture and our neighborhood: a Christian home.

When my late wife, Bobbie, was eight years old, her friend from across the street invited Bobbie into her home. Even at such a young age, Bobbie told me that the moment she walked into Homer and Libby Lay's house, she felt something she had never felt before. Something warm and wonderful and completely compelling. Homer and Libby routinely expressed their love for and belief in their children.

> Neutrality on our part as parents will result in failure.

Mutual respect was almost palpable. The Lays' home was a place where high expectations for behavior were clearly defined and discipline seemed fair. What Bobbie didn't know at the time was that this would be her introduction to Christ . . . inside a Christian home. It was the only such home in the neighborhood.

Because of the witness of this family across the street, Bobbie and her sisters were introduced to Jesus and committed their lives to Him in simple faith. Within a year their mom and dad were converted as well.

A family who graciously demonstrated the power of "different" became the model and the catalyst of the eventual transformation of Bobbie's home into a Christian home.

And, believe it or not, this can be the story of your home, the most important place on earth.

2

A GOD PLACE

God Lives in Your Home. What Does that Mean?

Your Christian home is a place where God has taken up residence. He actually lives in your house. And there's a way you can tell that He's around. There's a certain . . . smell.

MOTHBALLS

The walk from the family car, through the gate in the fence, to my grandparents' house is as familiar to me as if I had just made the trek yesterday. The gate latch wasn't very user-friendly for little kids—perhaps that was the point—but this was one of the reasons God gave me older brothers.

> And there's a way you can tell that He's around. There's a certain . . . smell.

A very narrow concrete sidewalk led us from the gate to the farmhouse where grandma and grandpa lived. For some reason, they didn't make sidewalks very wide back then. Perhaps it was a frugality thing, but there would never have been room for two of us to walk side by side. And the narrow walk was painted gray—slick as ice on rainy days.[1]

We rarely made the trip to my grandparents' house more than once a year—we lived in Chicago and they lived in Lancaster County, Pennsylvania. But we did make it every year. So there we landed, my whole family, walking single file from the car to the house, each carrying some form of luggage. Grandma was always the first to meet us. She wiped her hands on her apron, which, in my memory, she wore all day, every day except Sunday morning. And she was effusive about our arrival.

She'd kiss us, each one. The fuzz above her upper lip was always slightly damp from sweat, making this particular kiss something squeamish little boys hurried to finish. Presently grandpa made his appearance, often having emerged from the room of the house where his desk stood in the corner and books like little soldiers were lined up on the crowded shelves. That was his study. "Father Wolgemuth" was what everyone at the church he pastored for many years called him. Even though we knew that grandpa loved us, the heavy black caterpillar-like eyebrows and thick beard gave him an imposing and somber countenance. We hugged him, but the experience was more duty than passion. Still, we never would have considered *not* embracing the family patriarch.

With obligatory hugs out of the way, it was time to take our baggage inside. As familiar to me as the painted narrow sidewalks, the damp fuzz, and the caterpillars was what greeted us as we opened the screen door and headed inside. It was the smell, one like no other house I have ever visited. *Mothballs.* Except for the kitchen and bathroom, every single room in my grandparents' house smelled like mothballs. In fact, moths kept their distance from us for weeks after we returned home from Pennsylvania. Don't tell me that there's no credibility to the activists' assertions of the power of secondhand mothballs.

When I was in high school, we were studying the five senses—touch, taste, smell, sight, and hearing. Mr. Dusek, my high-school biology teacher, told us that the olfactory sense—the smelling sense—has the best memory. Thus, the connection between mothballs and my grandmother sixty years later.

You've probably noticed that most houses have their own distinct smells. Maybe your parents' or grandparents' home had a familiar aroma.² Perhaps you detect a customary scent when you visit a friend's house. Most likely, others smell something when they walk through your front door.

THE SMELL OF GOD

The importance of how a house smells has been around for a long time. In fact, for centuries people have been making churches smell like something very special.

If you grew up in a Roman Catholic, Episcopal, or Orthodox church, you know what a censer is. Even if you've seen a Mass or vespers only on television, you've probably seen a censer. It's the hollow, perforated silver or brass ball—about the size of a large softball—at the end of several thin three-foot-long chains that a priest swings back and forth as he processes down the aisle toward the altar. With each swing, a puff of fragrant white smoke escapes from the ball.

Inside is burning incense, and it doesn't take long for the whole church to be soaked with the sweet-smelling aroma. As you'd imagine, there's a good reason for this ritual.³ The primary purpose was to remind the people of the invisible presence of the Holy Spirit. But I love what happens the morning after. When you walk into the sanctuary long after the service has ended, you can still smell the residue from the smoke the day before. To be specific, the place smells like . . . God.

It's like Bobbie's visit to the neighbor's house: God is exactly what a Christian home *should* smell like. The moment folks walk through the front door, there should be something—although completely invisible—that reminds them of the God of the universe. And when you and your kids show up at work or school, there should be a trace of secondhand smell that others can quickly detect.

That sounds like a tall order, doesn't it?

Let's go back to the morning after church for a second. The sanctuary smells like incense because the priest followed the directions. As he's done for thousands of years, he put a piece of hot charcoal and a chunk of hardened frankincense sap on a little dish inside the censer and swung it back and forth. The result was that the whole place was filled with the smell.

Filling your house with the scent of the Almighty—God-cense—is really a matter of following simple directions. When you do, the smell is automatic.

A TIME WHEN NO ONE IS HOME

One of the most important ways for your home to have the aura of God is for you *not* to be home on a regular basis.

I'll never forget the conversation Bobbie and I had one Sunday right after our church service had ended. Along with our daughters, we were standing to leave when a woman who had been sitting behind us said hello. We exchanged some small talk, then she surprised us with a compliment, a question, and an incredible admission.

> Filling your house with the scent of the Almighty—God-cense—is really a matter of following simple directions.

"It seems like you and your children are here every Sunday," she said with a smile. "How on earth do you get your children to come with you?" And then with a resigned sigh she added, "My son and I argue every Sunday morning about coming to church, and he always wins."

On the drive home we talked about the lady's comment. Our daughters (about ten and thirteen at the time) acted genuinely surprised that a discussion about going—or not going—to church was even a possibility. I was amused, realizing that our children hadn't thought about *not* going to church, or if they had, they hadn't ever raised the question.

Bobbie and I talked about it later that afternoon. I wondered if our kids had felt brutalized by inflexible parents who forced them to get out of bed on Sunday mornings. "Well, they didn't before that dear lady told Missy and Julie about her defiant son," Bobbie joked. I laughed.

The conversation went on for some time, and our conclusion was unanimous: church is a nonnegotiable. It had been from the first Sunday after Bobbie and I were married, and it was going to be for the remainder of our lives. Our children had never heard us discuss any options or excuses. Sunday morning meant church. Period.[4]

Over the years we've been fascinated with how some families treat church attendance. Late Saturday night parties give them the solid excuse they need to stay home the next morning. Sometimes parents come without their children, unapologetically telling us that they had "rewarded" their kids with a nice quiet morning to sleep in because of busy schedules—soccer, homework, sleepovers with friends, late-night activities, or whatever.

This is a problem.

It probably wouldn't surprise you to know that the Bible has something to say about going to church: "Think of ways to motivate one another to acts of love and good works. And let us not neglect our meeting together, as some people do, but encourage one another" (Hebrews 10:24–25 NLT).

This may sound legalistic to you. It's not. Going to church as a family isn't about hard-and-fast rules designed to get you a nice pat on the head from God. It ought simply to be standard operating procedure—as standard as eating and sleeping and getting dressed. "Assembling together" is God's idea. That should be enough.

Several years ago I took a flight from Los Angeles to our home when we lived in Nashville. I had found a terrific fare on a Northwest Airlines direct flight that had only one stop in Memphis. Since I didn't have to change planes, I stayed in my seat while we unloaded the Memphis-bound passengers. Leaning forward, I watched the buzz of activity on the tarmac outside the window. Like busy ants, the little tugs pulling baggage trailers scurried about. Food and fuel trucks hustled back and forth. I stared at the plane next to us, amazed that the huge thing could actually leave the ground and fly.

> "Assembling together" is God's idea. That should be enough.

And then I saw something I had never seen before, at least not from that perspective. Although the wheels under airplanes are huge by automotive standards, they look tiny when compared to the size of the aircraft above them. I looked out toward the runway and watched several planes taxiing by.

There were those gigantic planes tentatively lumbering about on what looked like tiny skateboard wheels. The longer I stared at the oddity, the more comical the sight of these baby wheels under the belly of the lumbering giant above them became.

Why did they look funny? Because airplanes are built to *fly*. Of course. They zoom down the runway at full power, streaking into the air with a window-shaking roar. Then the tiny wheels are tucked into their aluminum bellies until it's time to land and refuel.

Taking precious time to go to church every week—off-line from your busy and productive schedule—may seem like a complete waste. It's not. It's *the* place where you and all the other harried and hungry "aircraft" in your community need to stop to rest and refuel.

In a Christian home, going to church is not optional. It's essential. Being committed church people creates a distinct and noticeable aura around the place.

BIBLES FOR EVERYONE

Like the priest following simple directions to make the church smell like God, you can do other things to fill your house with this special aroma, such as buying everyone a flashlight.

Even though the folks at our electric utility company do a good job of keeping the power on, every once in a while the lightning from one of our summer thunderstorms hits a transformer in the area, temporarily shutting everything down.[5]

Because I've learned about the difficulty of walking through my house in total darkness the hard way—why didn't we get more padding on our shins?—I know exactly where two flashlights are. I could close my eyes and walk straight to them any time of the night or day.

> Your word is a lamp to my feet
> And a light to my path. (Psalm 119:105)

You could refer to it as your personal owner's manual or guidebook, but the Bible describes itself as a flashlight for your life. In life's total darkness, it is light.

Question: Which member of your family should be without his or her own light?

Many churches give third-graders a Bible. Sometimes the kids' names are inscribed on the front. Maybe your church does this. It is a terrific tradition. However, if you have a third-grader and this is the first time they've owned a Bible, you have missed a huge opportunity. At what time in a child's life does this Book become a lamp and a light? At what point does this Book become the antidote for sin?

A long time before third grade.

My parents believed that their children should have their own Bibles. So I received one when I was a little boy and kept it in my room and carried it with me to church. Even though I was unable to

At what time in a child's life does this Book become a lamp and a light?

read most of the words or understand the doctrine, this Bible was my very own, and somehow that gave me a sense of delight. Today, if you visit the Christian bookstore in your area, you'll find a wonderful array of Bibles for children of all ages. You can even find Bibles with little plastic handles, perfect for toddler hands to carry. Little kids carry things that are important to them. Shouldn't they begin to know at a year and a half that God's Word is a lamp to their feet and a light to their path?

When you read bedtime Scriptures with your kids, read from *their* personal Bibles. If the children are small, show them the picture of Noah's ark and tell them about the rainbow and God's promises. Or show them the picture of the children gathered around Jesus and remind them of His love. Doing this will be a visual reminder of the life-transforming power of God's Word in your life too.

As your kids get older, you'll find many excellent choices of Bibles for young students, filled with helpful insights into the truth of God's Word that meet the unique needs of an adolescent.

THE GIFT THAT KEEPS ON GIVING

If you want to fortify their minds, you'll need to go further than just reading the Bible. You also need to help your children to memorize important verses. Their brains are like wet cement, and the verses they learn will be pressed on their hearts forever. My parents helped me memorize Psalm 1, Psalm 23, and Psalm 100 by the time I was six. I haven't spent a moment since then trying to remember what I had tucked away in my memory bank. But today I can recall every verse, word for word.

An easy way to do this is to write a verse out on an index card and then look for chances to repeat the verse, phrase by phrase, to your kids. You can also have it available on your smartphone so with a quick tap of your finger, it's there. Riding in the car on the way to school or sitting around the breakfast table are perfect chances for you to work on your verse together.

Here's a great one to get you started: "I can do all things through Christ who strengthens me" (Philippians 4:13).

One day Bobbie took a neighbor boy named Ben on a walk. "Let's do a Bible-verse game," she said playfully. "I'll say this verse and emphasize the *first* word. Then you say it and emphasize the *second* word. Then I'll do the third word, and we'll keep going until we finish it."

Bobbie started: "*I* can do all things through Christ who strengthens me."

Ben couldn't wait for his turn: "I *can* do all things through Christ who strengthens me."

"I can *do* all things through Christ who strengthens me," Bobbie responded.

Turning up the volume and really getting into it, Ben almost shouted, "I can do *all* things through Christ who strengthens me."

Back and forth they went until they finished. One time around our block, and young Ben had memorized Philippians 4:13.

One September in the mid-seventies, Bobbie and I left our younger daughter, Julie, with my parents for a week. I don't recall where we left our older daughter, but since she was only five, I'm confident that we didn't leave her home alone.

When we returned to pick up Julie, my mother announced that our daughter had a surprise for us. Of course, we were expecting some gift made with Popsicle sticks or paper plates. But that's not what we received. Standing in the center of the kitchen floor in her yellow sunsuit and sandals, Julie began to recite, "A—All we like sheep have gone astray. B—Be ye kind, one to another. C—Children obey your parents, this is the right thing to do.

"D . . . E . . . F . . ." Her recitation ended with "Z—Zacchaeus, come down. I must stay at your house today." (A list of all twenty-six Bible verses can be found in appendix B, page 251.)

We were stunned and asked mother how she had done it. She showed us a multicolor construction paper booklet with twenty-six pages, pasted with magazine cutouts showing pictures of sheep, children, and anything that could have represented a word in each verse. As Julie did the pasting, mother repeated the verses over and over again until Julie knew each one by heart.

The next month Julie turned two. I'm sure this sounds like an outrageous exaggeration. It's not.

You probably already know this, but the reason we need to give our children their own Bibles and help them to memorize portions of Scripture is because they—along with you and me—have a serious problem. From the moment they drew in their first gasp of air, they were poisoned by sin. And the Bible provides the perfect antidote:

> Your Word I have hidden in my heart,
> That I might not sin against You. (Psalm 119:11)

When your children have a sinus infection or the flu, you don't consider it a sacrifice to drive to the drugstore to find something to help them. If they get really sick, taking them to the emergency room takes no forethought at all.

That's why you give them their own Bibles, something that for thousands of years has been the only remedy for sin . . . the greatest problem they'll ever face. And a house with well-worn Bibles scattered around throws off a lovely fragrance.

And a house with well-worn Bibles scattered around throws off a lovely fragrance.

GOD TALK

When I was a senior in high school, I became a part of a student exchange program. In the fall of 1964, about twenty of us from

Wheaton Community High School traveled east to Fair Lawn High School in northern New Jersey, where we stayed with students' families for a week. Then in the spring they came west and spent a week with us in Illinois.

In preparation for the trip, each of us filled out a short biographic summary that we shared with our interstate partners. I sent mine to Peter Schulman, the guy our school had assigned to me.

One of the questions on the form dealt with religious affiliation. I wrote a few sentences about my Christian faith and mailed it to Peter. He and his family were Orthodox Jews. When our exchange group met our New Jersey friends at the Newark airport, I shook hands with my new friend and his family for the first time. They were extremely warm, and I experienced a week of a special kind of hospitality. On my visit to Peter's home, I was introduced to lox for breakfast as well as smoked gefilte fish. I would have rather licked an ashtray, but I did my best to be a good sport.

Not having any Christian buddies, Peter had no idea what to expect. About halfway into my visit, Peter confessed to me that, given what I had written about my Christian faith in the profile, he had fully expected me to greet him at the airport with a "Verily, verily, and how art thou?"

This is not what I mean by "God talk." Here *is* what I mean: if I'm with someone who's married and that person, after a day or so, doesn't mention his family to me, that's a problem. Now I could say to him, "You know, you ought to talk about your family; make me think that you love them."

But what's the real problem here? You know, don't you?

If my friend is not thinking about his family or talking about them, the problem is in the relationship. It's the same with God. We talk about Him in our Christian homes because of the way we feel about Him. We talk about Him with our mates. We talk about Him with our kids. We just talk about Him. We include Him.

In other words, we speak two languages in our Christian homes.

Spanish is America's second language. In fact, like many

communities in Central Florida where I lived for sixteen years, my neighborhood was filled with bilingual families, and it's not only Spanish they spoke. Families from Syria, Lebanon, Iran, India, along with those from the Spanish-speaking countries of Spain and Puerto Rico, lived within earshot of our house.

Standing on the sidewalk during our annual ice-cream social, I often asked my neighbors which language they spoke at home. Some said they used the language of their birth; others stuck to English.

A Christian home is also bilingual. Your family has a street address so your mail can find you, but you're only a visitor. Your home is a heavenly one. It's a place where God lives. Those neighbors of mine who fall back to their native tongue are reminding their children that their homeland is somewhere else. They live in America, but their roots aren't here. You get the picture, don't you?

You speak the language you are familiar with, and you also communicate with a special "language" that represents your faith—your rebirth—when you speak God talk. And it should be as natural as your native tongue.

Here are a few vocabulary words to get you started with your new language.

Isn't God Amazing?

From the time children are small, they need to hear you say something like, "Wow, would you look at that sunset? God is such a great artist!" Or you can stop to watch ants following each other in a continuous single-file parade along the sidewalk: "Can you believe that God gave these little critters the ability to follow each other to the food? Isn't He amazing?"

In our home, we didn't belabor the point and try to draw some three-point conclusion or recite a Bible verse; we just left it at that.

> You also communicate with a special "language" that represents your faith—your rebirth—when you speak God talk.

Our children and yours can get the idea that God is a part of our lives when we mention Him in everyday conversation.

Thank You for This Food

When it's time for a meal to begin, at home or in a restaurant, lead your family to bow their heads and thank Him for the food. Ask Him to use it to make you strong. When you stop to think about it, praying before meals shouldn't be up for argument.

When you thank Him for the meal, you're recognizing that He has blessed you and your family. It isn't everyone in the world who has the luxury of doing this three times a day. Yours is a life of rare privilege, and saying a prayer before a meal reminds everyone around the table that this is true.

It's also a miracle that those things you put in your mouth are transformed into the complex nutrients that make your body work. It isn't simply natural law that does these things. It's a spectacular miracle of God that all that dead stuff on your plate becomes the fuel that keeps your body's engine going. Thanking Him before diving in makes everyone mindful of this.

A prayer before a home-cooked meal also gives the prayer a chance to thank God for "the hands that prepared this food." If you've taken the time to cook dinner, and you hear this from someone in your family during their prayer, it says that you're a lot more than minimum-wage kitchen help.

The Lord Willing

Like almost everyone on the planet, I carry a cell phone. The electronic calendars on these devices can go into the future for centuries. Now, *there's* a useful feature.

When you think about it, booking a commitment on your schedule a year or so ahead of today is quite a striking presumption. Someone calls to see if you're going to be available for a meeting next November, you check your electronic calendar, and sure enough, you're available. So you book it. But who says you'll even be around when that date comes? Where's your guarantee?

A friend told me that there's nothing quite as sobering as sitting down at the desk of a person who has just died unexpectedly. Notes, to-do lists, follow-ups, calendars that include commitments: these things are waiting for someone whose "Sure, I'm available on that day" took on a whole new meaning.

> A man's heart plans his way,
>   but the LORD directs his steps. (Proverbs 16:9)

Years ago some friends encouraged me to preface statements about future activity with "the Lord willing" or just "Lord willing." I don't do it every time, and when I don't, no penalties are assessed. But it's not uncommon to hear me say, "My plane lands, the Lord willing, in Los Angeles at 4:25 tomorrow afternoon." Or "Lord willing, the grandkids will be here next Tuesday."

Saying these words is a simple reminder that every day, every activity, every safe flight, every new year is a gift from God. And when He decides to change the future, we'll make the adjustments.

> Come now, you who say, "Today or tomorrow we will go to such
> and such a city, spend a year there, buy and sell, and make a profit";
> whereas you do not know what will happen tomorrow. For what is
> your life? It is even a vapor that appears for a little time and then
> vanishes away. Instead you ought to say, "If the Lord wills, we shall
> live and do this or that." (James 4:13–15)

"The Lord willing" may feel awkward at first, but try it, and soon you'll find yourself using it automatically. Language like this becomes second nature.

What Did God Say to You Today?

When my kids were young, we had a dinnertime ritual, asking about each other's day. This usually came in the form of two questions: "What was your happiest thing today?" and "What was your saddest thing today?"

These questions seemed adequate and always evoked good conversation, giving us a small window into each other's day and activities. Doing this helped to teach the children how to share their feelings. This was a good idea.

I wish I had known Marilynn and Henry Blackaby and their family when our children were very young.[6] Our friendship goes back only a couple years, but here's one of the reasons why I wish I had met them a long time ago.

The Blackabys did something at mealtime that takes conversation in an exceptional direction.

When Henry and Marilynn's children were small, the question around the table was this: "What did God say to you today?"

Because of the question they knew they'd be asked over dinner, each day the Blackaby children—four sons and one daughter—had their ears tuned to God's voice, listening carefully. Each of the day's events was cast in the light of *God's* activities and purposes. This is a *great* idea.

Dinnertime reports became an encouragement to the whole Blackaby family that God was doing something in each of their lives, even the youngest among them.[7]

FAMILY DEVOTIONS

Some families have no trouble establishing a regular time of Bible reading and prayer—family devotions—together. Others find it almost impossible.

> The question around the table was this: "What did God say to you today?"

Bobbie and I discovered a direct relationship between the growing up of our children and the difficulty of doing this as a whole family. When they were sitting—trapped—in high chairs, we could do whatever we wanted. But when they had outgrown the high chairs and had places to go and outside people to play with, the tug-of-war began. Maybe you can relate to this challenge.

We decided to work on something manageable. We chose a specific book of the Bible—vacation was a terrific place to do this—and worked through it together.[8] When we finished that, we waited for a while before diving into another study. This kept our family devotions feeling like an adventure to our children rather than a life sentence.

Memorizing scriptures was a regular part of our family devotions routine too. Over breakfast we'd rehearse these together: Psalm 1, Ephesians 2:8–9, Psalm 139, 1 Corinthians 13.

Sometimes on long car trips we'd memorize a hymn together such as "A Mighty Fortress Is Our God," "Like a River Glorious," or "Holy, Holy, Holy."

And even though Bobbie and I knew that what we were doing in family devotions was serious business, we never let on that this was anything but great fun.

PRAYER

Almost five hundred years ago, Martin Luther wrote, "To be a Christian without prayer is no more possible than to be alive without breathing."[9]

Let's start with you, the mom or the dad. You probably agree that prayer needs to be a predictable habit in your own life. One of my close friends says this prayer nearly every morning before his feet hit the floor: "Good morning, Jesus. Thank You for loving me with such incredible love. What do You have going today? I want to be a part of it. Amen."

Whether it's your regular time of day to pray, such as early in the morning, or spontaneous "prayer on the fly," as I call it, you can be a person who prays intentionally. Over the years I have had the amazing joy of finishing conversations with people I know or who are total strangers with, "How can I pray for you?" So far no one has said no to this request.

"Be anxious for nothing, but in everything by prayer and supplication, with thanksgiving, let your requests be made known to God" (Philippians 4:6). Just as conversation is the bridge that connects you with those whom you love, prayer is the glue that affixes your heart to your heavenly Father.

When you pray, start with your children. *But what should I pray?* you might wonder. *Exactly what should I ask God to do for them?*

These are good questions, and it probably won't surprise you that the answer is in God's Word.

> For this reason we also, since the day we heard it, do not cease to pray for you, and to ask that you may be filled with the knowledge of His will in all wisdom and spiritual understanding; that you may walk worthy of the Lord, fully pleasing Him, being fruitful in every good work and increasing in the knowledge of God; strengthened with all might, according to His glorious power, for all patience and longsuffering with joy; giving thanks to the Father who has qualified us to be partakers of the inheritance of the saints in the light. (Colossians 1:9–12)

> Prayer is the glue that affixes your heart to your heavenly Father.

Here's the list of things you can pray for the children God has entrusted to you: knowledge, wisdom, spiritual understanding, a walk pleasing to God. You are praying for them to be patient, joyful, and grateful.

This is a great prayer for you to pray for your kids.

At Bedtime

If your house is even close to typical, *calm* is usually not the word that would most often describe its daily ambiance. *Active*, maybe even *frenzied* may come closer to what it's really like.

But all of that changes when the kids crawl into bed at the end of the day. There's something hallowed about those pajama-clad, pre-bed moments—that brief time when your children have had a story read to them, they've pottied and brushed their teeth, and they are lying faceup in their beds, the covers pulled up to their chins. You sit on the edge of the bed or kneel down on the floor next to them, clasp their hands in yours, and pray.

"Dear Jesus," I begin, "I love You. Thank You for this precious girl. Thank You for Your presence during this day that we just finished. Thank You for loving us. Thank You for forgiving our sins. Thank You for protecting us. Thank You for all Your blessings. I ask You to give Missy a good sleep tonight. Please help her to be a girl who loves Jesus. Help her to know how much her daddy loves her and wants the very best for her as she loves and follows Jesus, her Good Shepherd. Please bless grandma and grandpa in Washington and Aunt Lois in the hospital . . ."

By the time you say amen, you'll discover a distilled air of quiet hovering over the moment. This is a perfect time to remind your child how much you love her and how thankful you are that she's yours. It's a moment as close to sacred as you'll get with your kid all day. Take your time. Drink it in.

Pull the covers up, and give a tender forehead kiss and a final "I love you."

The Prayer Road

Over the past decades, wherever I have lived, I have designated common streets as "prayer roads." Don't worry; this isn't as strange as it might sound.

Years ago, when Bobbie and I lived in Orlando, on Sunday mornings we would drive northeast on Interstate 4 toward church. When we got to the Anderson Street exit, we prayed. Sometimes we were busily talking about something else when we saw the exit sign, but the moment it was in view, one of us took the other's hand and we would stop what we were discussing and pray. We asked God's blessing on our worship service, on our ministers, and on our Sunday school class. We asked our heavenly Father to prepare our hearts to meet with Him. Anderson Street, the approach to the exit ramp, and a couple of blocks east of I-4 was one of our prayer roads.

The same was true when we'd head to the airport. The airport exit that goes south off the eastbound 528 was another prayer road. When I'd take Bobbie to fly to Charlotte to be with the kids and grandkids, I'd reach across the console and hold her hand. Out loud I prayed for her safety and for a wonderful time with the children. When I'd fly out on business, she prayed for me. The airport exit became the place for holding hands and holding audience with the One who kept our hearts bound while we were apart.

This all started when our children were very young. Northbound Franklin Road between Brentwood and Nashville was our church-bound prayer road. Granny White Pike was our on-the-way-to-school prayer road every day. The first few miles of Murray Lane was our prayer road when we were headed out for a suitcases-packed-and-in-the-trunk family trip.

These times of family prayer gave us a chance to thank God for His blessings. They also gave us an opportunity to ask Him to give us hearts to worship at church, for wisdom at school, and for His guidance and protection.

The prayer roads are places to celebrate. We usually keep our eyes open—especially the person who's driving—and it's not as if we suddenly get to the prayer road and become somber or morose.

In fact, one morning as we were driving to church, our eighteen-year-old was praying. She spotted a used white Honda Accord in the hardware-store parking lot next to the highway with a For Sale sign propped in the front window. Without missing a beat, she prayed, "And Lord, thank You for that Honda over there, *which is exactly the car I'm looking for!*"

I hit the brakes and did a U-turn right in the middle of Franklin Road. We pulled up next to the Honda and wrote down the phone number listed on the sign. After church, I made the call and negotiated a fair price with the owner. The next afternoon the car was in our driveway, Missy's answer to prayer and her school transportation.

Perpetual prayer roads are runways and landing strips wherever my family travels by air. Once the captain tells the flight attendants to "prepare for takeoff" and presses the throttle, we close our eyes and pray. The G-force of being squeezed back into our seats is a reminder to pray silently for safety and for the members of our immediate family. When we fly together, we always hold hands in prayer.

I still smile over one of these takeoff family prayers. When Missy and Julie were in their teens, the four of us were headed for a vacation. As our airplane was hustling down the runway, gathering takeoff speed, we all took each other's hands and closed our eyes. We were flying on an airplane that had three seats on one side of the aisle and two on the other. On the three-side, I was on the window, Bobbie was in the middle, and Missy was on the aisle. Julie was on the two-side aisle seat, so as we hurried down the runway, she and Missy reached across the aisle to hold hands.

I guess I finished praying first, because when I opened my eyes and looked down the row at my family, I laughed out loud. There was a young man we had never met, about Julie's age, sitting next to her in the window seat of the two side. She was holding his hand.

When she finished praying and opened her eyes, she told him about our family prayer road ritual. He didn't seem to mind at all.

Prayer Hooks

Pray without ceasing.

—1 THESSALONIANS 5:17

The whole idea of praying nonstop presents quite a dilemma to most Christians. What did the apostle Paul mean? How is it possible to get anything done if you're spending your whole day praying? That's a fair question.

For us, "prayer hooks" get us closer to obeying this directive. Like prayer roads, prayer hooks are ordinary events or things in the day that remind us of someone. When we do or see those ordinary things, we breathe a prayer for that person. My two sons-in-law, Jon and Christopher, are very important men in my life. Not only are they the husbands of my daughters, they're also daddies to my five grandkids.

> How is it possible to get anything done if you're spending your whole day praying?

Several years ago, while we were visiting Jon and Missy, I noticed that Jon kept extra trash bags at the bottom of the kitchen trash can, so when he emptied the full one, there was a new one, ready to unfold. A good idea, I thought. Now we do the same thing, so every time I change the trash bags, I pray for Jon. "Dear Lord, thank You for Jon. Please bless him right now, wherever he is and whatever he's doing. Protect him and give him wisdom. Thank You. Amen."

Christopher is a ChapStick man. Like me, he keeps one in his pocket at all times. Don't be grossed out by this, but when one of us doesn't have access to our ChapStick, we borrow the other's. So because ChapStick reminds me of Christopher, every time I pull mine out of my pocket, I pray for him. "Dear Lord, thank You for Christopher. Please bless him right now, wherever he is . . ."

The laundry room provides a vast assortment of prayer hooks for moms or dads who wish to transform the space into a virtual sanctuary for intercession. My daughters tell me that there are unlimited prayer hooks in every unfolded basket of clothes. That's when a mom can fold a shirt and pray for the heart that will soon be inside it. With each pair of socks (if you can ever find the mate), you have a chance to ask God to direct the steps of the feet they will cover.

We know one mother of young children, Emily, who framed and hung this Scripture over her washing machine: "Whatever you do, work heartily, as for the Lord and not for men" (Colossians 3:23 ESV). This reminds her that her laundry room is a place where she does the work of laundry and of prayer.

Another creative mother painted a border around her laundry room with these words:

> Wash me, and I shall be whiter than snow.
> Make me hear joy and gladness . . .
> Create in me a clean heart, O God,
> And renew a steadfast spirit within me. (Psalm 51:7–8, 10)

It's better than wallpaper to remind this young mother that as she manages load after load of dirty laundry, she can be praying for her own heart and the heart of each member of her family.

> These little habits—prayer hooks—are a way to include the heavenly Father in your daily routine.

You get the idea. These little habits—prayer hooks—are a way to include the heavenly Father in your daily routine. Maybe these will give you some good ideas. As you begin to "pray without ceasing," you will find your own creative ways to remember the people you love.

A house where prayer happens is a house with a distinct scent. And people you meet for the first time can catch it right away.

PHIL THE APPRAISER

In the early two thousands, because interest rates were nice and low, Bobbie and I decided to refinance our home. We shopped around for the best deal and settled on a Florida-based company.

The first order of business was to have an appraiser come to be certain that the amount we were financing wasn't more than the value of the property. (As you know, banks will not lend you any money unless you can prove to them you don't need it.)

A week before he came to the house, a man named Phil called to see when we were available. He showed up right on time. It was early on a Saturday afternoon, and Phil walked slowly through the house, measuring and photographing. When he was finished, he came to my home office to give me an invoice for the appraisal.

"You have a nice home, Mr. Wolgemuth," Phil said. He didn't look to be much younger than I, but since he was waiting for a check, he decided against being too casual.

"Mr. Wolgemuth was my dad," I joked. "I'm Robert."

Phil laughed.

Then he added something I'll never forget. "I've appraised a lot of homes." He paused for just a moment. "But there's something different about yours. I can't tell you exactly what it is, but I felt it the minute I walked in the front door." He took one more run at putting it into words. "There's just a kind of warmth here. I can't quite explain it."

I didn't walk Phil through the mothball story—it would have taken too long and I would have had to tell him about my grandmother's fuzzy upper lip—but I did tell him that it was a Christian home. That was probably the reason.

"I knew it," Phil replied with a broad smile. "I'm a new Christian myself." We had a few minutes of encouraging conversation before he left. I gave him a book about being a man of the Bible, I asked how I could pray for him, and we prayed a short prayer together.

Remember that filling your house with the scent of the Almighty—God-cense—is just a matter of creating simple but intentional habits. There's no magic to it at all. If you do these things—commit yourselves to a church, use God talk, and "pray without ceasing"—He'll take care of the smell.

Okay, I have a question. What *does* your house smell like? What's the aura that greets people when your door closes behind them? "Now thanks be to God who always leads us in triumph in Christ, and through us diffuses the fragrance of His knowledge in every place. For we are to God the fragrance of Christ" (2 Corinthians 2:14–15).

SECONDHAND SMELL . . . A REPRISE

Keeping a clean car was twisty-tied to my DNA the moment I was conceived. My grandpa Wolgemuth—the one with the eyebrows—was a hopeless eccentric about this. He kept his car in one of the barns on the farm, probably fifty yards from the back door of the house. I can see him walking briskly from the house to the barn with a bucket of water in his right hand and a chamois in his left. The resolve on his face and the staccato of his step let everyone know that he was on a mission.

Local folklore was that grandpa could wash his car with a single bucket of water without getting the floor of the barn wet. I believe it. Only on rare occasions would the man have been seen in a dirty car. His son, my dad, inherited this convention and I got the full load as well.

When I move to a new city, I make a practice of scoping out the good car washes. Although no one cleans my car as well as I do myself, I have, over the years, found some pretty good runners-up.

Not more than two weeks after we moved to Orlando in February of 2000, I found a car wash less than ten minutes from our home. It was a Simonize franchise (I've used their wax since I owned my first car), they do a terrific job, and my average is about one visit every two weeks. At least.

I made friends among the folks there. I met Richard, Eric, Brian, and Marquesh outside, and Beverly and Tina at the cash register inside. It was fun to chat with these folks as my car was wending its way through the suds.

Many years ago, Eric and I were talking about the Christmas holidays. He became unusually animated as he told me about his sons and their delight with the celebration. Several guys were vacuuming the car and saw my Bible on the front seat.

"Is this your Bible?" Eric asked loud enough to make other customers look in our direction.

I nodded.

"You're a Christian!" he said with a surprising sense of authority. It wasn't a question.

"Yes, I sure am," I said with a smile.

"I knew it!" Eric said, a huge grin crossing his face as well. "I knew it."

There is nothing special about me. I promise. I simply try to practice the things that I've told you about here . . . things I learned from my parents and Bobbie and from some wonderful mentors I've watched for a lifetime. Do you remember the censer and the incense? Filling your house with the scent of the Almighty—God-cense—is about following simple directions.

If you do these things, the smoke takes care of the smell. Even your car and your clothes can't help but pick up the fragrance.

3

THE MOST IMPORTANT
PEOPLE IN THE MOST
IMPORTANT PLACE

What Is It Like to Walk into Your Home?

How does it feel to walk through the door into your home? A Christian home is a place where every person is honored. What does that look like?

HELLO . . . I'M HOME. IS ANYBODY HERE?

Delivering the *Daily Journal*, Wheaton's local afternoon newspaper, was my first paying job. I landed this when I was in the fourth grade. Two years later I graduated to the *Chicago Tribune*, which I delivered early in the morning. My dad wouldn't have considered letting me quit paper-routing, but he did let me make the change so my afternoons wouldn't be encumbered with deliveries. Plus a morning route was somehow cooler among my peers than an afternoon route. Don't ask me to explain this because I don't know why. It just was.

The summer after my freshman year in high school, I approached my dad with a proposal to let me find a more "grown-up job." My older brothers, Sam and Ken, worked in retail stores, and as far as I was concerned, they were *very* cool. Dad agreed to let me look for a *real* job. The following Saturday, I rode my bicycle into downtown Wheaton and went door-to-door, looking for employment in one of our town's retail stores.

Before the afternoon was gone, I had secured a job at DuPage Photo and Hobby Shop, having boldly walked into the store, asking Phil Jones, the man who was standing behind the counter, if there might be an opening. "Yes," he said without a moment's hesitation. After six years of delivering newspapers, I was finally going to have a job that I thought people would respect. Monday morning I called the *Tribune* and told them that the next week would be my last week. This was a very happy phone call to make.

It didn't take more than an hour at the photo shop Monday after school for me to realize what fun it was going to be. I loved the people there: Phil, Dick Payne, and Mrs. McVay in the greeting-card department. And it was great fun to wait on customers.

An electric eye that chirped when a patron walked in had been installed at the front door. We all loved hearing that little high-pitched squeal. It meant business. The people who walked into our store were the most important people in our town, and everyone in the store knew it.

"May I help you?" I eagerly asked when customers walked in. I knew that without those folks spending their money we'd be out of luck, so I wanted to make them feel good that they had walked into *my* store.

Like what we tried to do when people walked into the photo shop, a Christian home is a place that should make people feel special too. The most important people in the world walk through your doors. And they need to discover this as they step across the threshold.

> A Christian home is a place that should make people feel special.

MAN'S BEST FRIEND

In 1994, when our house was about to become an empty nest because Julie was going off to college, Bobbie announced that she was going to buy a little dog that could jump up on her lap. I say "announced" because I could tell by the set of her jaw and the timbre of her voice that this particular statement was not an invitation to discussion. I gingerly took a run at it anyway.

"But we already *have* a dog," I said, trying not to sound too whiney. (The rule in our house has always been that if you whine, you automatically lose whatever you're lobbying for or against.)

My suspicions that Bobbie had already made up her mind and this was an announcement were confirmed when she ignored my complaint as if I hadn't said anything at all.

Several weeks later, when I came home from work, I noticed a laundry basket in the corner of the kitchen with a blanket bunched up inside. Bobbie was smiling one of those wistful, I'm-sooooo-happy smiles. She took me by the hand and walked me over to the basket. Inside was a black-and-brown fur mitten. At least that's what it looked like. Upon closer examination, I discovered that our family had just grown by one—a baby Yorkshire terrier named Bear.[1]

At that moment my heart became a Popsicle in the direct sun on a July afternoon. Bobbie had been right. We *did* need a little dog.

For more than a dozen years, that Yorkie brought our family a lot of joy. For one thing, Bear taught me where the "man's best friend" expression came from, and she did this just inside the front door.

Whether I was gone for a four-day business trip or a forty-five-second journey to the mailbox, she greeted me the same way. She stood on her hind legs, bouncing up and down. And she'd smile at me. Don't sneer, or I'll tell you other cute things she'd do.

Bear made the entrance into my home a thoroughly enjoyable experience, albeit not an unfamiliar one. Assuming that she'd forgive the comparison to my dog, my mother did the very same thing when I was a little boy. When she heard the door open, she stopped what she was doing, hurried to greet her son, and knelt down to hug me at eye level. She asked about my day, and she listened carefully to my childish gibber. If I had done a craft (one more crinkly underwater seascape in finger paints), she carefully lifted it from my outstretched hand as if it were a crystal vase. At that moment I was the most important person in the world to her. The memory of this still overwhelms me.

I grew up in a Christian home, not only because my dad held court during family worship but because my mother treated me as if I was a star.

And I wasn't the only one she treated this way. My five siblings got the same treatment. And during the years that she was a part-time eyeglass wearer, mother kept her glasses on a cord that hung around her neck like a necklace. She was a frequent visitor to her optometrist to repair her bent and twisted glasses, crushed because she hugged everyone who walked into our home. Growing up, I carried the constant suspicion that many of my friends hung out with me only so they could walk into my house and have my mother hug them.

> I grew up in a Christian home, not only because my dad held court during family worship but because my mother treated me as if I was a star.

Lucky for me, in 1970, I married a woman who did the very same thing. As newlyweds, we both worked outside our house— apartment—but when she first saw me at the end of the day, Bobbie's greeting was absolutely predictable. I couldn't wait to pick her up from work or walk through the apartment door because I knew what was waiting for me on the other side. Her smile, her hug, and her verbal greeting expressed sheer delight that I was there. Who in his right mind *wouldn't* feel great with a greeting like that?

Exactly.

HOMECOMING

You already know this, but not every home is this way. In some homes—even Christian homes—kids don't even look up from their electronics or the TV when someone walks in the door. They may grunt a hello when dad calls out his greeting, but it's hardly audible. Some wives barely speak to their husbands when they cross the threshold into their palaces, and some husbands barely mumble a sound when they see their wives the first thing in the morning.

Something is seriously wrong here.

Imagine you walked through the door into your garage and there, right where your nine-year-old minivan normally sat, was the sports car of your dreams. Would you burble something and walk past it? Not on your life. You'd holler and dance a jig like a wide receiver in the end zone. This is the car you've always wanted. You're not sure where it came from, but now it's all yours—finders, keepers.

What if you walked into your living room and discovered that someone had magically replaced all your scratched, sagging, and threadbare furniture with spectacular pieces from a decorator's showroom, in all your favorite color schemes? On the coffee table sits a bouquet of fresh tulips. Every lamp is new. Would you shuffle past it and sigh something about how tired you are from your busy day? Never. You'd squeal with delight and hug everyone in sight.

Walking into your house means seeing people you love: your children, parents, and spouse. You'd give your life for these folks, something you'd never consider doing for the new car in your garage or the beautifully furnished living room. Greeting the most important people in the world should always be a celebration.

> Greeting the most important people in the world should always be a celebration.

Years ago Bobbie's walking buddy, Peg, invited her over for dinner while I was on a business trip. Peg was in the kitchen, stirring one of her orange-peel-and-cranberry sauces, when the opening garage door sounded the arrival of Peg's husband of twenty-six years, Grant. Already a big fan of their great marriage, Bobbie later told me the highlight of her day was what happened next. Grant entered the back door, peeked out from behind the door frame at his aproned wife, and like a kid on his birthday, sucked in a gasp of air. "Uhhh," pretending to see her for the first time. Ever. Peg stopped her stirring, laid down the sauce spoon, and said "Uhhh" back as she smiled and bear-hugged her groom.

I received similar walking-into-the-house treatment during my more than forty-four years of marriage to Bobbie. One of Bobbie's favorite lines to sing was from the 1964 Broadway musical *Funny Girl*. It goes like this: "Oh, my man I love him so, he'll never know."[2]

I know this because she sang it—just this one line—to me literally hundreds of times. She made me believe that my walking into the house was the best moment in her day. At that second, I was the most important person in that most important place.

When people walk into your house, this is exactly the way you want them to feel. It's Christmas morning, and they're Santa Claus. It's the championship game, and they're the home team. It's a state dinner, and they're the president.

Don't worry, you don't need to install one of those beeping electric eyes on your front door, but those who walk through it are no less important than the customers who entered the photo shop. The most important people in your world come through that door, and when they're inside your home, it's your job to surround them with love. People will have every reason to celebrate just because they walked into your home.

THE SAFE HAVEN OF RESPECT, LOVE, AND NURTURE

In the first chapter, I mentioned how God told Noah to build a boat in order to save his wife and kids from the Flood. The ark rescued this family by providing refuge from the chaos of the storm that surrounded them.

In your family, here's what shelter looks like: A Christian home is a place where dad is respected and mom is really loved. It's a place where children are nurtured.

Respect Dad

Most men don't mind the battle. Every man *does* mind disrespect.

You can take on a man nose to nose. You can challenge him on the tennis court or baseball diamond and not smile. You can go for it. But don't roll your eyes or look askance at him. Don't talk carelessly about him with your friends. Don't disrespect him. When a man falls into an affair, it's rarely about sex. He's found someone who respects him.

In your refuge, family members may not always agree with dad, but they always respect him. "I think you're wrong" works. "You're stupid" does not.

Love Mom

Like every new husband, I entered marriage with no experience. Yes, I had sound models in my father and other men I looked up to, but there were certain quiet nuances for which I was completely unprepared. Thankfully, I married a woman who alerted me to these necessary refinements . . . with respect.

"I know that you love me," she began. "But during the day when we're apart, I just want to know that you're thinking about me." She was not whining. In love, she was telling me how to love her—how to make our home a refuge in the middle of our chaotic lives.

So way back then, every once in a while, I'd pick up the phone at the office and call her. "Hi, honey, it's me," I said. "Look, I'm on my way to a meeting and just have a second, but I want you to know how crazy I am about you. You're the best. I've got to run. I'll see you tonight." That was then, but now a text message with the same words is such a good idea.

Remember what it was like when you first noticed each other and your heart did one of those skip-a-beat things? Reaching out to express your affection was something that you did a lot. This was not obligatory. It was something you wanted to do. You loved each other so much that you literally couldn't help yourself. Thinking about each other throughout the day was common fare. The Bible calls this returning to your "first love" (Revelation 2:4).

"So husbands ought to love their own wives as their own bodies; he who loves his wife loves himself. For no one ever hated his own flesh, but nourishes and cherishes it, just as the Lord does the church" (Ephesians 5:28–29). In these verses, Paul gave us two other powerful clues to loving mom: nourish and cherish.

Nourish literally means "to feed"—something that has to happen multiple times every day. What if the last meal a woman ate was on her wedding day? Of course, she wouldn't live very long. In the same way you must eat to live, the verses say that a husband's love for his wife literally nourishes her. He can't get away with saying, "I love you . . . until further notice." Expressions of his love must be as regular as the sustenance that comes from daily meals.

Cherish is what a mother bird does as she broods over her nest. She guards her eggs, protects them from danger, and keeps them warm. Yes, I know that this is a very feminine-sounding concept, but there are very few woman alive who wouldn't say, "I wish I had more of *that* in my home."

These first two qualities speak to husbands and wives. There's something important to note: one of the most important qualities of a Christian home is a great relationship between dad and mom. The foundation of a good home is a good marriage. It's simply not possible to have a good home without a good marriage. A strong marriage is the engine that moves your home forward. It's what gives it strength. And power. And delight.

If your "first love" is a distant memory, go ahead and start treating your wife like you did when you were first winning her heart. Just see what happens. Make a conscious decision to woo her once more. She'll respond like she did the first time. You'll see.

Nurture the Kids

> And, ye fathers, provoke not your children to wrath: but bring them
> up in the nurture and admonition of the Lord.
> —Ephesians 6:4 KJV

If you've ever had a vegetable garden, you understand the idea of *nurture*. You do the hard work of preparing the soil; you plant the seeds; you water, fertilize, and hoe the weeds . . . then you water, fertilize, and hoe the weeds some more. This nurturing thing is a lot of hard work, but if you want a plentiful harvest, it's what you must do.

Raising children in your home takes this kind of nurturing work: love, discipline, affirmation, correction, tenderness. This makes them feel whole and secure.

And notice the verb Paul used is "bring"—"bring them up." It doesn't say "send" them up or "tell them" to grow up. It says "bring." Like a pace car in a race, parents go first. Like a kid hollering to his parents from a high dive, parents are saying to their children, "Watch this." When it comes to attitudes, conduct, or instruction of every kind, you go first.

And remember that your goal as a parent isn't perfection. It's transparency.

A home where dad is respected, mom is loved, and the kids are nurtured is one very safe place. As with Noah's construction project in his backyard, you're building something very special. When he, his wife, their sons and daughters-in-law crossed the threshold and the door to the great boat was closed behind them, they were out of harm's way. Can you imagine the relief those people must have felt? Can you see them embrace each other in gratitude as the thunder clapped and the rain began? Their tangible experience of God's grace and protection must have been overwhelming.

Your house is this kind of sanctuary for your family. When

people walk through your door, the celebration with words ("I'm so glad you're here"), affection (a bear hug), and focused attention (look into their eyes) will assure them that they are . . . home. For the time being, the rest of the world is outside where it belongs.

You, your spouse, and your kids (and their friends) are safe. You've found refuge in a place called a Christian home.

They're the most important people in this most important place.

TELEPHONE MANNERS

When I wrote the first edition of this book in 2004, the telephone was the most commonly used electronic entry into our homes. It was a "land line," and when people wanted to reach you or someone at your house, they'd dial a number, and this phone would ring. Now everyone has his or her own phone.

So even though most people step into your home by way of technology rather than through the front door, there is still a right way to make them feel welcome.

For years television ads ran for Publisher's Clearing House. I'm pretty sure that this was a magazine distribution outfit and somehow they were able to give away millions of dollars. They did this by showing up unannounced on people's front porches with a huge cardboard check tucked under their arms. Even though I don't think this check was legal tender, the point was that the person whose name was next to "Pay to the Order of:" was instantly rich.

Can you imagine the fun of having this job?

"And what do you do for a living?"

"Well, I knock on people's doors and hand them millions of dollars, and they go crazy."

> You, your spouse, and your kids (and their friends) are safe. You've found refuge in a place called a Christian home.

Here's the point: when you or your kids answer the phone, you should pretend that the guy from Publisher's Clearing House is on the other end. And you can't wait to hear his voice.

I had parents who modeled this kind of telephonic enthusiasm. "Much better, now that I'm speaking to you," my dad said when I called and asked how he was doing—something he did until just a few months before his death. When my mother, now also in heaven, heard my voice on the phone, she acted as if this phone call was the best thing that happened to her all day.

After she was out of the house and married, my daughter thanked Bobbie after she answered the phone one day.

"You're welcome," Bobbie replied, surprised. "For what?"

"Thank you for answering the phone like you've been waiting all day for me to call," Julie said.

Teaching your kids to treat a beeping telephone like it's the electronic threshold for someone you love is a terrific idea.[3]

Rrrring (or whatever ring tone you've set).

"Hello, this is Luke answering my dad's phone."

"Hi, Luke, this is Ron Perry."

"Oh, hi, Mr. Perry, how are you?"

"Fine, thanks. May I speak to your dad?"

"Sure, just a minute."

"Thank you for answering the phone like you've been waiting all day for me to call."

Luke lays the phone down and goes to find his dad. He does not holler "Daaaaaad" at the top of his lungs—the redneck intercom—while he still has the phone in his hand. The telephone exchange happens with consideration and calm. "Love one another with brotherly affection; outdo one another in showing honor" (Romans 12:10 ESV).

Question: How does Ron Perry feel about this conversation? Does he feel he was treated like a valued person—customer—as he crossed the electronic threshold to your home? Does he feel like the most important person in the world?

Go ahead and ask him. You'll see.

THE TWO BLUE CHAIRS

You may have figured this out already, but in order for the crossing-the-threshold-at-your-house celebration to work, someone needs to be home.

Our first house was on a quiet cul-de-sac in Glenview, Illinois. It was a one-story ranch house, forty feet wide and twenty-four feet deep. These dimensions are still firmly imprinted on my brain because for Christmas in 1974, I built a to-scale dollhouse for the girls.

Bobbie was pregnant with our first baby when we moved into that little house during the spring of 1971. She finished that semester at Trinity College and eventually left her part-time job as a dental assistant. In September, our baby, Missy, was born.

Because I was in youth ministry with a salary to match, Bobbie decided to see what she could do to create a little additional income. Making some phone calls to the folks in our neighborhood, she found a working mother looking for a day-care solution for a six-year-old boy named Scotty.

That was perfect for Bobbie. She could stay home with her baby and earn a few dollars. So every weekday, the school bus stopped at the end of our short street—Garden Court—and little freckle-faced Scotty stepped down and walked to Miss Bobbie's house until his mother got home from work.

As you'd expect, when Scotty opened the front door and stepped inside our house, he received a happy welcome and arms-all-the-way-around hug. A snack at the kitchen table and a complete rendition of "My Day, by Scotty" followed. The first-grader's dark brown eyes sparkled as he gave Miss Bobbie his detailed and animated report. This happened every day.

One evening a few weeks into Bobbie's day-care experience, she came to me with a look of serious concern on her face. "What's the matter?" I asked, hoping I hadn't been the culprit.

"It's Scotty," Bobbie responded.

"What did he do?"

"Oh, it's nothing he did wrong," she said.

"It's just that . . ." She stopped speaking, her eyes welling with tears. Once she had gathered her composure, Bobbie told me about her conversation earlier that day with Scotty's mother. Bobbie's time with the energetic and expressive first-grader had become very special. In fact, as it turned out, *that* was the problem. Because Bobbie was there when Scotty got home from school, she's the one who received his I'm-home hugs, catching all the good stuff about his day over milk and a cookie. By the time Scotty's mother got home from work and picked up her youngster, there was really nothing left for him to say. He and his mother always were happy to see each other, but it was too little, too late. This made Bobbie feel guilty.

"Scotty's mother should get what I'm getting every day from Scotty," Bobbie concluded with plenty of emotion. "He's such a treasure, and she's missing these moments of pure delight."

So that day, when Scotty's mother came to pick him up, Bobbie invited her in for a few minutes "to catch up." Over a cup of tea, Bobbie gently poured her heart out. She talked about how animated Scotty was every day when he got home from school, how his eyes widened when he told her about his teacher and his friends but how subdued he was a few hours later. Scotty had given his report and was on to the next thing. His own mother was missing something that could not be repeated.

"*You* need to be the one to greet him after school," Bobbie finally asserted, knowing that she was putting her own day-care income at risk. "I'm getting all the good stuff from your son. It's a reward that shouldn't be lavished on me. It's priceless time, and it belongs to you."

Scotty's mother sat quietly stirring her tea. Then she told Bobbie that she was working because her husband had told her that *she* was responsible to pick up the tab for the family's decorating expenses.

"All we need is two new blue chairs for the living room," she finally concluded. "Just as soon as I have enough to buy them, I'm going to quit my job, and *then* I'll be home for Scotty . . . *then* I'll catch the moments you're talking about."

Bobbie did her best to challenge Scotty's mother without insulting her. But soon it became clear that her heart was set on those blue chairs, and nothing Bobbie said was going to change her mind.

Months later the furniture truck unloaded the upholstered chairs at Scotty's house. Unfortunately, once the new chairs were in place, the couch across the room started looking quite ratty by comparison.

NO CHOICE?

Please hear me on this. You and your spouse may have no choice. Your blue chairs may be the mortgage payment or food for the table.

This is not to heap guilt on your head, but please hear me on this as well. You get only one shot at creating something special just inside your front door.

Many years ago Bobbie and I got to know Larry and Beth, an attractive young couple in our town. He had grown up in a Christian home, but there were times when we detected some unresolved anger when he spoke of his parents, especially his father. One day we found out why.

> You get only one shot at creating something special just inside your front door.

Larry had grown up with plenty of nice things. His dad, although not wealthy, made a substantial salary. Larry's mother had been a career person before her pregnancy, and just as soon as Larry was born, she dove back into the corporate world. With tears welling up in his eyes, Larry told us about the awful day in grade school when he went to the nurse's office. "I was so sick I couldn't stand up. I had to lie down on the cot," he told us.

The school nurse phoned Larry's dad, who promised, "I'll be right there. I'll come right away." Larry waited for his father to arrive. And he waited. "Something must have come up," Larry told us. "My mother's office was all the way across town, but my dad's office was just around the corner from my school."

"Someone's here for you," the school nurse finally announced to the sleepy Larry curled up on the cot.

Larry looked up, longing to see his dad. "But it *wasn't* my dad. He sent his *administrative assistant* to pick me up." Larry's face let us know the twenty-year-old wound was still plenty fresh.

"My dad's assistant took me to our house and dropped me off. I spent the rest of the day at home by myself." Larry told us that when his dad came home later that afternoon, he didn't say anything to his boy about what had happened.

Again, you may have no choice. You and your spouse just *can't* be available. Your jobs won't allow it. But if you can try to think what a day—or an hour—feels like from your kid's perspective, it may change yours.

May I take one more run at this? Can I ask you one more time? Are you sure? Is there some creative way you can be there?

Another of Bobbie's experiences was a deep e-mail conversation with an extremely bright and accomplished young mother named Jennifer, who was contemplating leaving her Washington, DC, professional job to stay home with her baby. "This time will pass very quickly," Bobbie told her. "You don't get any do-overs."

> If you can try to think what a day—or an hour—feels like from your kid's perspective, it may change yours.

Jennifer was struggling with how to balance her career and motherhood. "When I'm at work [and the baby is in day care]," she wrote, "there's a lot of time that I miss my little girl. I will drive across town to get her organic yogurt or pasta with beet powder because I think it's the best thing for her to eat. Yet I believe that I'm her best caregiver and am not doing that. That doesn't seem right to me."

The young mother followed her heart. She decided to leave her job and set up a consulting business from her home. A few weeks later we received an e-mail from her. "I quit my job yesterday! Thank you so much for your prayers, e-mails, and support. We know this is the right thing. God has been so faithful. We have been committed to moving forward regardless, but even yesterday as I was preparing to go in to talk to my boss, I got word of another client that is ready to hire me, and I can work from home!"

My daughter Julie is hopelessly entrepreneurial. From the time she was in grade school, she's had her own business, one way or another. During her final two years in college, she set up her own corporation from her sorority room and sold almost fifty thousand dollars' worth of T-shirts, sweatshirts, and other customized apparel. Soon after she and Christopher were married, she started her own stationery business, specializing in wedding invitations.

Two and a half years later, little Harper was born, and fifteen months later, baby Ella arrived. Julie couldn't imagine cutting back on her business. Selling had been in her blood since she sold her first candy bars, riding her bicycle door-to-door in the neighborhood.

But in spite of plenty of available horsepower under the hood, Julie followed her heart too. She cut back so she could spend more time with her baby girls. Not long after she had made her decision, she sent a few digital photos to Bobbie and me with the following note: "Just in case you wonder why I love my job, it's because I get to spend my days with these two precious babies! This is a little documentary on Harper's first cake-baking adventure. The first one is her helping me make the cake, and then she loved sharing it with Ella, as well as eating it herself."

Or she could have sold a few more wedding invitations that month.

Back in the first chapter I confessed my natural propensity for diplomacy—my tendency to soften things a little by adding that you get points for honest effort and that, hey, you're only human. Your kids are resilient. They'll be fine. I prefer not being accused of being inflexible and dogmatic so I'll spot us a few points.

But I concluded by saying that I don't care if I am accused of being inflexible. I'm not going to let us off the hook. This parenting thing is serious business, and there's *no one* on earth in a better position—or better qualified—than *you* to do it right.

This is a place for the kind of straight talk I was referring to. What good is it if the most important person in the world walks into an empty house?

> This parenting thing is serious business.

Again, you may truly have no choice in the matter. Both you and your spouse may have to work outside your home. Of course, I trust your judgment on this. But if there *is* a way for either one of you to be there with your children when they're small—to be home when your kids' feet cross the threshold—then do it. Bobbie was right. You do not get a do-over.[4]

When our Missy was in the third grade, her teacher asked the students what their favorite thing was about their mothers. Missy could have mentioned a number of wonderful things that my wife had done for her. But when it was her turn, she told her class that the best thing about her mother was "When I come home from school, my mom says 'Hi, Missy.'"

That was it!

The daunting list of sacrifices, favorite toys bought, school room-mother activities, and homemade Halloween costumes didn't make it to the number-one spot. It was just "Hi, Missy."

See what counts to your child? It's your presence.

That doesn't sound too complicated, does it?

"IN YOUR DREAMS" STREET

In 2003, Bobbie and a few of her friends went to the annual new home showcase. Some communities call this the Parade of Homes; our area called it the Street of Dreams. It's when five to ten builders and decorators show what they can do in a handful of new homes on the same street. People pay admission and walk through these unbelievable houses . . . ooohing and ahhhing . . . trying not to begrudge the fact that they live in tar-paper and cardboard shacks by comparison.

When she returned from her excursion into home-building dreamland, Bobbie insisted that I go back with her and see these incredible dwellings myself. In a few days we were there. The most striking thing to me about these houses was the way new innovations had transformed kitchens and bathrooms. Computerized appliances, televisions *behind* mirrors, and very cool plumbing fixtures were my favorite things.

As we were driving home, excitedly talking about our stroll through "tomorrowland," something dawned on both of us. Every bedroom in every Street of Dreams home was complete with its own spacious closet, full bathroom, and media center, including the latest in high-definition everything. A sophisticated intercom system connected these bedrooms to the command center in the kitchen.

"Coming home these days is like checking into a fine hotel," I quipped.

"Yeah, you get everything but valet parking and room service," Bobbie joked.

But as we talked about what this kind of autonomy meant to the families living in these homes, it stopped being so funny. "What is happening to our homes?" Bobbie asked.

Although she expressed her comment in the form of a question, she didn't need an answer. We had just experienced a whole street of homes that, on purpose, sent family members to their own self-contained, isolated worlds of comfort.

Given what you and I can personally afford in decorating and appliances, our homes may never qualify for the Street of Dreams. But we may be closer than we think to looking more like a hotel than a home.

And with the advent of cell phones for everyone, autonomy is sacramental. It's everyone for themselves. Like a spoked wheel without a hub, our homes may be failing because they're losing their centers.

KUDOS TO OUR KITCHENS

My parents were either remarkably brilliant and very frugal, or they just lucked out by making a great decision, but the last appliance they bought for our house—and they didn't get it until I was in college—was a dishwasher. So in addition to the intentional family suppers and apologies to my buddies waiting for me to come out to play, we did the dishes as a family.

I remember serious conversations about life as we took part in the assembly line that led to a clean kitchen. I remember times of levity and adventure as we pretended we were swashbuckling pirates when we dried a knife. I still have a self-inflicted scar on my left index finger to prove this one.

But mostly I remember standing next to my mother with her hands in the sudsy sink. She'd wash something, rinse it from the scalding spigot, and put it in the Rubbermaid rack on the counter. We took what she had just rinsed and dried it off. When she wasn't looking, we snapped each other with the dish towel.

We thought we were doing the dishes. But we were doing what families have been doing for centuries: working together, laughing together, and learning to love each other in the process. And this was all happening in the kitchen—the most important place inside the most important place!

In the winter of 2004, I flew to Charlotte to help Jon and Missy with the construction of an addition to their home. The plan was to expand the size of their kitchen. A few months earlier Missy, who loves to entertain, told us that when they have friends over, "they all cram into the kitchen." Several summers before, Jon and Missy had built out their unfinished basement with a large family room. But when they invited lots of people to their home, did these folks go to that nice, big room? No.

Like sardines, their friends all packed into the kitchen, the hub of almost every home. Missy demonstrated how fifteen to twenty people wedged themselves within ten feet of the kitchen sink while the rest of the house sat empty! We laughed at her dramatic presentation, but we all knew the truth of what she had just said.

> We thought we were doing the dishes. But we were doing what families have been doing for centuries: working together, laughing together, and learning to love each other in the process.

Like Charles and Caroline Ingallses' little house on the prairie, your kitchen—the place where the family sits together to eat—is the center of your home. As terrific as it might be for your household to have more than its share of extra rooms and technological niceties, you cannot afford to let your children check in and out like hotel patrons. On a regular basis, you must draw them back to the kitchen.

"But," you might argue, "our family's schedule is crazy. Soccer practices, gymnastics, and piano lessons on top of school and church activities make sitting together for dinner almost impossible."

I understand. I really do.

So why not be intentional and set a reasonable goal, such as three no-interruptions family dinners together per week? Or four? Or two? Write them down and protect them as an armed guard would protect priceless treasure inside the vault at your local bank. That's exactly what you're doing.

If you had grown up in Italy, this would not be a radical suggestion at all. *Sacro desco* is what they call it—"sacred table"—and the goal is

Your kitchen—
the place where
the family
sits together
to eat—is
the center of
your home.

to sit down for a family meal once a day. World-renowned Italian cookbook author Marcella Hazan says it this way: "I'm saddened because there isn't much that brings families together these days. But we all have to eat to stay alive, so why not enjoy [meals] as a family? It worries me that in America family mealtime is falling by the wayside because people believe they are too busy."[5]

You and I know she's right, don't we? Even though our schedules are filled with activities, we're *not* too busy for this.

Oh, and one more thing. *No TV or any other electronics allowed during the meal.* If you want to have a sweet evening with your mate over dinner, do not go to a sports bar with televisions mounted on every wall. Focused conversation will be impossible. It won't happen.

Family dinners *that count* cannot include electronics. It's not a welcome guest. Turn it off. The people in your family won't feel important at all unless they have your undivided attention.

WHAT DO WE DO NOW?

Okay, now that you're welcoming one another when you walk through the door, speaking enthusiastically to each other on the telephone, and sitting around the table a few times a week, what do you do now? How do you treat one another in this Christian home?

I'm glad you asked.

"Let all bitterness, wrath, anger, clamor, and evil speaking be put away from you, with all malice. And be kind to one another, tender-hearted, forgiving one another, even as God in Christ forgave you" (Ephesians 4:31–32).

We're going to talk more about forgiveness and tenderness in chapter 4 and about the importance of the words we speak in chapter

5, but the heart of this challenge from Paul the apostle is wonderfully simple. He admonished us to be kind to one another.[6]

Several years ago I was doing an interview in a television studio. We were talking about the special relationship dads have with their daughters. One of the things I mentioned was the need for kindness in our homes.

> The heart of this challenge from Paul the apostle is wonderfully simple. He admonished us to be kind to one another.

After the interview I was gathering my personal effects in the back of the studio when the floor director came over to me. "Can I tell you something?" she asked.

"Sure," I responded.

Even though we were standing in the shadows of the studio lights, I could tell that she was on the brink of deep emotion.

"Everyone in this town knows my husband," she said. "And everyone admires and respects him."

She paused. I didn't fill the empty space because I suspected that she wasn't finished.

"I just wish one thing about my husband." She leaned in and whispered, "I just wish he'd be nice to me . . . and to our children." She looked straight into my eyes like a frightened animal, as if she had unwittingly disclosed her personal prison. When she realized what she had done, she turned and walked away.

As I drove to the airport that afternoon in my rental car, her words kept turning over and over in my head. I pictured the woman's husband, warmly greeting people at church. Glad-handing folks down at the club. Bumping into acquaintances at the mall. "Such a nice guy," people probably said to each other after one of those chance meetings.

In spite of all this public decorum, he was not nice to his family. Perhaps we've just given definition to the word *hypocrite*.

But before you and I consign this guy to a life sentence of hard labor in Siberia, let's take a quick look inside ourselves. We may be just as guilty.

I can remember a time when Bobbie and I were standing in our kitchen, embroiled in a heated argument. Neither one of us had ever been accused of being passive and withdrawn. Driven and strong-willed (bullheaded, if we were in one of these arguments) best described both of our constitutions.

Anyway, we were really into it. As I recall, we were both tired, frustrated, and very angry. A lethal combination.

In that moment of doing verbal battle, I would have told you that my emotions were uncontrollable. Yet right in the middle of the fire, the telephone rang. I checked the caller ID, and it was a business associate. I picked up the phone. "Hello, this is Robert," I said in a voice as undramatic as if I had been ordering a Big Mac at a drive-thru. Bobbie stood silently in amazement as I spoke.

When I finished the call with a "Good to talk with you too. Thanks for calling," the look on Bobbie's face said it all. In a flash the tone of my voice had gone from fevered pitch to gentle and calm.

Truth be known, my emotions were completely under control. I had *chosen* to speak unkindly to my wife in a vicious tone of voice. And the phone call proved it. Bobbie had caught me, and I was embarrassed.

Has this ever happened to you?

Try as we might to rationalize our thoughtlessness at home and set it aside with lots of legitimate-sounding excuses, this encounter reminded me of an absolute truth: kindness is not an emotion. It's a conscious decision. It's a choice. In fact, given what the apostle Paul said in the previous verses, kindness is a command.

> Kindness is not an emotion. It's a conscious decision. It's a choice.

You have more control than you think. Make a decision to be kind to each other. Period.

To everyone, including—no, *especially*—those you live with at home. It's a great way for them to feel like the most important people in the world.

CYNICS NEED NOT APPLY

Perhaps you saw the Tom Hanks movie *Castaway*. Hanks played an executive with Federal Express whose plane—a cargo plane on which he was bumming a ride—crashed into the Pacific Ocean. The only survivor, Hanks washed onto a deserted beach where he remained for four years. Next to the events leading to his rescue (sorry if I just spoiled this movie for you), the most exciting moment in the film was when he was able to start a fire.

The fire brought him heat, light, and hope.

What if, the moment Hanks had finally gotten his fire going, someone had sneaked out of the jungle and poured a gourd full of water on the tiny and very precious flame? I've just described the destructive power of cynical words.

As you have read this chapter, something may have sparked an idea. *Yeah, I'd like to start doing this in our home,* you may have silently resolved. *I'm going to start treating folks like prized customers when they walk through our door. I'm going to take my cell phone out of my own hands when we sit down to dinner as a family. And I'm going to invite my family to do the same. These are some things we can do better around here.* But before trying to enact your plan, you take it to your mate. Using your best in diplomacy, you explain your idea. Your spouse turns to you with a look of disdain. The eyes roll—your most unfavorite thing.

"What a silly idea," the cynic says with a sarcastic grin.

Whoosh! So much for the fire.

I have a suggestion. Before presenting your strategy to your spouse, verbally put yourself on the deserted beach. Mention the fire. Talk about how important the fire is to you and that you need someone to protect the little flame from the wind. Maybe that'll help.

Okay, let's try this one more time.

"Hello! I'm home. Is anybody here?"

4

AMAZING GRACE

It's What Sets Your Home Apart

Although the morning sun had yet to peek over the eastern hori-zon, its effect had already turned the predawn sky to a deep azure, framing the brightest stars that remained. It was August. Harvest. The farmer rose early and drove into town to collect laborers for the day. That was the way it had always been in that part of the country during the late summer. Those looking for work—the most eager ones—rose early and gathered in the town square. Those who needed work done that day drove to town and made their offers—auction-like—to the waiting workforce.

On this morning, the farmer estimated the number of workers he needed, described his offer to a group of strong-looking men, and quickly closed the deal. Satisfied with the terms, the farmer and his laborers headed off to work.

But by midmorning, despite the diligence of his workers, the farmer realized that he hadn't hired enough men. He would never be able to finish what he had planned by day's end unless he had more help.

So the farmer drove to town to find more workers. He spotted a group of men standing on the street corner, sipping coffee. They had slept in that morning and missed the first call. But the farmer was able to strike a deal, and soon they were off to spend the rest of the day alongside those who had already spent half of the morning toiling in the fields.

By noon, as the workers were eating lunch, the farmer took inventory again. *I'm still short of help*, he concluded. *I won't get all the work done with these few men.* So he jumped back into his pickup and drove into town. He found a group of men, lazily chatting under the shade of a leafy tree in the town square. He approached them with an offer, then they looked at each other as if to collectively bargain the proposal and nodded their agreement in unison.

Soon these men were working alongside the other hires in the farmer's field.

By mid-afternoon, the farmer took inventory once again. *I'm still short of help*, he said to himself. *This work must be finished by sunset.* So off he went to find more workers. And a few hours later, still concerned that all the work wouldn't be completed, he did the same and found a handful of men to work for him.

A single hour before quitting time, the farmer took one final look at the workers and the work that remained. *If I had just a few more men*, he thought to himself, *the work would be finished for sure.* So he drove to town and found a few more men—calling them "workers" would be a stretch, since they had spent their entire day playing checkers and sipping tea at an outdoor café adjacent to the town square.

"Why not?" they joked to each other after the farmer had made his proposal for an hour's work.

The sun was slowly pulling down the shade on the horizon as the workers lined up to receive their wages. Casting a willowy shadow, the farmer stood to address them, thanking them for their hard work and congratulating them on finishing the project on time.

The men who had been working since sunrise glared at the others who had not put in a full day's labor, because these undeserving ones were nodding their heads, receiving the farmer's compliments as though they had.

And then the farmer asked all the men to file past the bookkeeper's table to receive their wages. Some on the early morning crew called out to him, asking if they should organize by groups so the clerk would be able to identify those who had worked all day.

The farmer didn't look their way. Perhaps he hadn't heard their request.

By the time all the men had been paid, it became apparent to everyone that each worker had received exactly the same pay. The all-day workers were the first to notice since the bookkeeper hadn't asked the men how many hours they had worked as they passed his table.

But when the other workers—those who had come to work late, *especially* the handful of men who had only worked one hour—realized that they had been paid the same as the men who had worked all day, they were shocked and overjoyed. Slapping each other's hands in celebration, the laggards began making plans to return to town and party all night with the money they had "stolen" from the farmer.

The all-day workers seethed with rage. "How could the farmer treat us like this?" they muttered to each other. "It's just not fair," one bawled loudly enough for the farmer to hear.

Soon the angry workers were surrounding the farmer, demanding reparation. "You hired us before the sun was up," they challenged. "But those bums over there who only worked an hour got paid the same." By then they were shouting. A few hollered obscenities.

The uproar didn't faze the farmer. He lifted his hands, quieting the clatter. Once order had been restored, he looked into the faces of the men who had worked since early morning. His countenance was an extraordinary blend of understanding and pity.

"How much did I promise to pay you this morning?" he asked one of the more vocal of the all-day workers.

Without missing a beat, one man toward the back of the group called out the dollar amount of the promise.

"That's right," said the farmer, his voice calm and unshaken. "And how much did you receive?"

The workers looked into their hands. Of course, they had received exactly what the farmer had committed to them twelve hours before.

"But that's not the problem!" another worker shouted. "Those men over there didn't work all day like we did, and you paid them the same amount!"

The farmer's eyes scanned the angry group. "Whose farm is this?" he finally asked.

There was no answer. *Everyone* knew whose farm it was.

"And who should be able to make the choices of who gets paid what?"

Again, no answer.

"It's *my* decision to pay everyone the same, regardless of how long he worked," he said, his voice brimming with confidence. "If I want to pay you the same as the ones who worked only an hour, that's up to me. You really don't have a say in it."

At that the farmer turned and walked away.

I'M IN TROUBLE

I cannot stand this story. I can barely stomach its message. The thought of such a thing actually happening is scandalous to every one of my sensibilities. And it probably angers you too. But it's in the Bible. And it's there for a reason.

This story is in the Bible for people like me.

For the first eighteen years of my business career, I worked for someone else. But in the spring of 1987, my friend Mike Hyatt and I took the plunge. We raised some capital and started our own business.

Until that time I would have described myself as "careful" when it came to spending my boss's money.

> This story is in the Bible for people like me.

But once my name was on the letterhead, my spending really tightened down. Why? Because I was spending my *own* money. Every nickel I could save was a nickel I could keep. Such is the peril of every business owner . . . and farmer.

During those years when I owned the business, I was teaching a Sunday school class on the life and ministry of Jesus. One week I bumped into the story that I had heard as a youngster. It's the one you just read about the farmer and the workers from Matthew 20. Given my entrepreneurial life stage, this parable hit me like a wrecking ball. As the co-owner of a company, I would have found it inconceivable to do such a thing.

All my life, hard work was a requirement, perfectionism a sacrament. I mowed the yard more frequently and with lines straighter than the neighbors', washed the family car better than the dealer, cleaned the garage better than my brothers could, and scrubbed the basement floor in record time. I learned diligence and perseverance as a construction worker. I remember silently playing mind games on the job, furiously swinging a pickax against the reluctant clay or hand-spreading a huge pile of gravel, trying to show the boss that I could work harder than anyone.

The end of such a day of working like this left me feeling proud, and, frankly, superior to the rest. And I thought my feelings were thoroughly justified.

I grew up in a religious tradition where superior performance meant superior recognition. In fact, on Sunday mornings at my grandparents' churches, you could even spot the most pious among the congregation by how they dressed, how they fixed their hair, or how they grew their beards—even the color of the cars they drove. This system of dividing humanity into "worthy" and "not worthy" was stapled to my birth certificate.

And being a hopeless competitor, I quickly found myself making a game out of nearly every conceivable thing. If you can stand straight, I can stand straighter. If you can be nice, I will be nicer. If you dress well, I will dress impeccably. If you eat fat-soaked french fries, I will eat healthy wheat crackers (even if they taste like cardboard). If you use foul language, I will abstain—at least in public.

Winning these "games" made me a good—a worthy—man. No actually, that's not right. Winning these games didn't always make me feel like a good person, but it *did* make me feel like a better person than you.

"Anything you can do, I can do better. I can do anything better than you."[1]

And that was enough.

GRACE STEPS IN

Now you understand why I take umbrage at the story of the farmer and the workers. Why it makes my heart pound with indignation. But it was precisely for pull-yourself-up-by-your-bootstraps, self-righteous people like me that Jesus told this story in the first place.

In the first chapter I asked this question: What is so great about a Christian home? My answer is, in a Christian home there is something special. It's called grace.

Grace is the one thing that sets your home apart from all the rest.

In the providence of God, on August 30, 1916, the day she was born, her parents, Monroe and Susie Dourte, had the presence of mind to name my mother Grace. So from the first time I heard the word in a spiritual context, it was very easy to put an actual face on what could have been an abstract concept. In 2010, my mother stepped into heaven. For her eulogy I included this: "Her parents named her Grace. How did they know?"

> Winning these games didn't always make me feel like a good person, but it did make me feel like a better person than you.

> Grace is the one thing that sets your home apart from all the rest.

You remember the way my mother greeted my friends when they walked through the front door of our house? Remember how she'd ruin her eyeglasses because she kept crushing them inside her embraces?

What I didn't mention was that this was true if I had brought home the captain of the football team or a geek who wasn't cool enough to be elected the chairman of the cleanup crew at the chess club. She hugged every one of my friends. She didn't seem to notice how straight their teeth were or what their reputations might have been or how well they were dressed. As with the farmer on payday, these things didn't matter to my mother.

A Christian home is a place adorned by people of grace. It's a place where grace is conspicuous, a place where the "scoreboard" that compares a stellar performance to a substandard one is unplugged.

THE MANY FACES OF GRACE

It was six men of Indostan
To learning much inclined,
Who went to see the Elephant
(Though all of them were blind),
That each by observation
Might satisfy his mind.
The First approached the Elephant,
And happening to fall
Against his broad and sturdy side,
At once began to bawl:
"God bless me! But the Elephant
Is very like a wall!"[2]

This clever poem was printed in our high school literature text.

I recall being fascinated and amused by the image of six blind men trying to define an elephant by what they felt: a wall (its side), a spear (tusk), a snake (trunk), a tree (leg), a fan (ear), and a rope (tail).

In a Christian home the inhabitants are like the blind men, and grace is like the elephant. They catch a sense of her in varied and fantastic—yet often incomplete—ways, but she's the same powerful creature.

"For by grace you have been saved" (Ephesians 2:8).

The apostle Paul summed up God's love for us—His relentless mercy and kindness—with the word *grace*. Throughout the Scripture, men and women's responses to this gift have taken many forms, and these are some of the things you and I can do in our Christian homes in response to God's grace.

REPENTANCE AND FORGIVENESS

Although the words *repentance* and *forgiveness* sound religious and clean, the practice of these two grace-based words takes sleeves-rolled-up hard work. They're tough, and they're sweaty.

I'm a sinful man. This fact—and my willingness to confess it—releases the effects of God's grace in my home. And because I am a sinful man, I am in desperate need of a Savior. Try as I might, including showing up for work before everyone else and working harder than the guy next to me, I cannot save myself.

One of the traditions to which my dad held very tightly was a family game of Battleship on Thanksgiving Day. Commercially created copies of this game are now available, even in electronic editions, inside those everything-under-one-roof toy megastores. You can even download the game from the Internet.

But when I was a boy, we played this game using sheets of graph paper. After turkey, stuffing, and pumpkin pie, we marked out the "ocean," twenty-six squares high and twenty-six squares wide. We numbered the rows one through twenty-six and the columns A through Z.

Then, each with his own sheet, we secretly laid out fleets of ships. With our pencils, we concealed two submarines, a few battleships, cruisers, destroyers, and aircraft carriers. Then, one by one, we went around the room and tried to locate—and sink—each other's hidden ships by calling out letter and number coordinates. The game often lasted two or three hours.

Because there were so many of us playing Battleship, we inadvertently chose the same squares as other players did to place our ships. That meant that as we got deep into the game, we began to get a sense of where our opponents' (enemies') fleets were located. We could tell because they avoided shooting ships in those areas themselves. Inevitably some of their ships were in the same locations as ours. So when it came time to sink a competitor's fleet, we deftly circumvented those places so as not to reveal the location of our ships in the same locations. *I won't sink you, if you won't sink me* was the silent armistice.

Comparing ourselves to others will never work. And avoiding the truth of our own sinfulness because someone else—even our children—has the same problem doesn't get us off the hook either.

Jesus understood the tension we faced as we studied our graph-paper game boards.

Comparing ourselves to others will never work.	"Why do you see the speck that is in your brother's eye, but do not notice the log that is in your own eye? Or how can you say to your brother, 'Let me take the speck out of your eye,' when there is the log in your own eye? You hypocrite, first take the log out of your own eye, and then you will see clearly to take the speck out of your brother's eye." (Matthew 7:3–5 ESV)

One of the conundrums of being a mom or dad is that if we accuse our children of sin that we ourselves are guilty of—foul language, rudeness, gossiping, lack of discipline—we're afraid that they'll challenge our hypocrisy. So we avoid correcting their wrongdoing—memories of tiptoeing around my brother's battleship on Thanksgiving Day.

When it comes to you and me, parents in our Christian homes, we cannot sidestep the admission of our guilt. In selecting dads and moms to manage families, God had no choice but to pick sinful people. We were on that list. Sinfulness comes as standard equipment.

Before we rebuke our children when they are dishonest, we must be quick to repent when *we* get caught shading the truth. When they are rude to their siblings and we call them to account, memories of our *own* confessions of our own thoughtless remarks must be ringing in their ears. "I'm sorry. I was wrong. Will you please forgive me?" needs to be a familiar refrain on our own lips, one our children frequently hear.

As I said, this is hard work. In every home located on Planet Earth, pride and dishonesty are relentless taskmasters. We accuse others while smugly hiding behind our own façade, acting as though we would never do such a thing.

Several years ago creative Christian actress and author Nicole Johnson wrote a dramatic sketch called *The Ledger People*. In it a husband and wife carry ledger books wherever they go. When someone in the house—usually a spouse—does something wrong, the offended spouse whips out the ledger and makes a notation. "That'll cost you five points," he or she snaps. The sketch, both outrageous and hilarious, was filled with sobering truth.

Our natural tendency is to keep score—to overlook good things but use indelible ink when logging offenses, grading other's misdeeds more harshly than we wish to be graded ourselves.

> For as high as the heavens are above the earth,
> so great is his love for those who fear him;
> as far as the east is from the west,
> so far has he removed our transgressions from us.

As a father has compassion on his children,

so the LORD has compassion on those who fear him. (Psalm 103:11–13 NIV)

God's grace in your home means no more ledger books. As difficult as this is to comprehend, the Creator of the universe hears our confession and forgives our sins, placing them in a landfill that no one can find. He carries no record. No ledger. In fact, He *forgets* them.

When there's genuine repentance, forgiveness follows like a healing salve on a scraped knee.

There may be no more stunning picture of forgiveness in the Bible than that of the prodigal's father lovingly embracing his once-defiant son. The boy had asked for his inheritance, which his father reluctantly gave him. Then he took the money and wasted it on wine, women, and song. Soon, however, he ran out of money and friends. He found a job feeding pigs. In his despair, the son began longing for home. So he returned to his father, well-rehearsed speech in hand.

The son said, "Father, I have sinned against heaven and in your sight, and am no longer worthy to be called your son" (Luke 15:21).

These words revealed the heart of the runaway boy. The father—who in the story represents Jesus Himself—had forgiven the son even before the kid asked for it. The runaway's repentance and utter contrition was met with his father's full embrace, and a celebration followed: "'Bring out the best robe and put it on him, and put a ring on his hand and sandals on his feet. And bring the fatted calf here and kill it, and let us eat and be merry; for this my son was dead and is alive again; he was lost and is found.' And they began to be merry" (Luke 15:22–24).

> When there's genuine repentance, forgiveness follows like a healing salve on a scraped knee.

The story of the prodigal son also includes the account of his older brother. Because he hadn't taken his father's inheritance and wasted it all, this model son felt that the family patriarch should have treated him with more favor. Of course.

Hey, I took piano lessons. I remember how we learned the notes on the lines of the treble clef: Every Good Boy Deserves Fudge.

Hard work. Big rewards. I'm for that.

Alas, we're back to the farmer, aren't we? The older brother was a faithful all-day worker. His little brother came to work much later. But the love of the father was equal for both. That's grace.

Intellectually you and I understand this concept fully. We read it in a book and may even nod as we read along. But when we're embroiled in a situation where others seem to have been given a prize that, frankly, we think we deserved, we point our self-righteous finger and declare the situation, "not fair." Or when we've been wronged, forgiveness seems impossible to give. Or when *we've* been caught red-handed, repentance requires unbelievable courage. When we confess—"Honey, I did a foolish thing. I let you down on this one"—and ask forgiveness—"I know you may not feel like it, but will you forgive me for being late again?"—we're throwing ourselves on the mercy of the one we've wronged. Our pride is going to be completely trashed in the process. This is not a pretty sight, but that's okay.

> Applying repentance and forgiveness in our homes is tough and sweaty work.

Applying repentance and forgiveness in our homes is tough and sweaty work. But the grace party that follows promises to be more fun than you've ever had.

GRATITUDE

Since time began, parents have tried to get their little kids to say "Thank you." It's an important response to grace.

As cave-dwelling parents handed their toddlers pieces of

tyrannosaurus-rex hide to gnaw on, they asked, "Mwrofun du bleem swarphut?" ("What do you say?")

To which the children dutifully replied, "Blarchenkine twim." ("Thank you.")

The cave parents then gently patted their teething children on the head and turned the rex hide loose.

And every parent has done the same thing since then.

Why? Teaching our children to be thankful is on the top of every parent's stuff-my-kids-absolutely-must-learn list. We have no interest in raising unpleasant little miscreants who think the world owes them something.

Your parents probably held to the same list. Mine certainly did, but being thankful is still a huge challenge for me.

When I opened my eyes this morning and looked at the clock on the nightstand, I wasn't immediately thankful for a good night's sleep and the chance to live another day—but I should have been.

I'm alive. I have plenty to do. These are two good reasons to be thankful.

Then there was the warmth of our home. Compared to the cool outside, it was a toasty seventy degrees inside. Did I even think about that? No. But it was something I could have been thankful for today.

There was the English muffin I put in the toaster and cool jelly from the refrigerator—hmm, let's see, food and electricity every time I need them. When I brushed my teeth, there was running water.

In a little while, I heard my wife's footsteps. I had a wife (a reason to be thankful) who also made it through another night safely (another reason).

"Hi, sweetheart," she called to me.

"Hi, honey," I called back. She loves me. And she has a husband who loves her back. *Thank You. Thank You.* Two more reasons to be grateful.

Only thirty minutes into my privileged day, it hadn't really dawned on me that I had so much to be thankful for. Tomorrow morning, I'll do better.

A Christian home where grace lives is a home where people are grateful—a place where no simple abundance goes unnoticed. An attitude of thank you is pure magic at your house. Here are some ideas of how you can start sprinkling some of this magic around.

> An attitude of thank you is pure magic at your house.

Just Say It

We're going to talk more about the power of spoken words in chapter 5, but let me at least mention the importance of saying the words *thank you.*

And here's the big "little" idea: don't catch yourself thinking only, *what a great day* or *I love my family.* Leave no doubt that you're grateful. *Say the words.*

Random Symbols of Gratitude

You can turn ordinary things and events into opportunities to express thankfulness. That's what my mother (the person named Grace) modeled.

One day many years ago, this person named Grace found a teaspoon at an antique store.

My siblings and I called it the "new spoon," even though it was probably forged during the Hoover administration. The spoon didn't match our everyday flatware design, but that was the point. Sometimes when we sat down to our family supper, one of us noticed that the setting at his or her place had that unmatched spoon lying next to the knife. "I've got the new spoon," the person announced, holding it aloft as if it were the Stanley Cup.

This gave Grace a chance to explain to the rest of the family why she was especially thankful for the recipient of the spoon. For example, Ken, my next older brother, may have offered to set the table or do his homework without being asked or perform one of his legendary good deeds.[3]

That silly new spoon was a symbol of our mother's gratitude for something we had done in the ordinary of our days. And it was extremely motivating. Thankfulness does that.

Thank-You Notes

I've written about this in other places, but it deserves a quick mention. Dropping someone a thank-you note after he has done something for you—big or small—can be an amazingly significant gesture.

And even though I've done my best to keep up with doing this, I've still missed plenty of chances to put my gratitude in writing. Of course, e-mail gives us a thirty-second chance and text messaging offers a ten-second opportunity to say thank you. Although this is better than completely ignoring the good deed, I will always be a bigger fan of handwritten thank-you notes.

Primarily because of Bobbie's influence, our family has tucked thank-you notes on tops of pillows, in school lunches, amongst the underwear in a traveler's suitcase, or on a Post-it note on the steering wheel. This has become a fantastic tradition. When I began dating Nancy DeMoss in 2015, it quickly became clear that she was also a tireless handwritten note sender. Perhaps the Lord is eager that I not forget this sweet habit.

No, we don't officially keep track of who writes thank-you notes and who doesn't (remember the ledger conversation), but I've heard that friends can be divided into two groups: those who send thank-you notes and those who don't. I want to be in the "do" group. You can help yourself and your kids be "doers." Take a few minutes to put it in writing.

A Sense of Wonder

This one is more difficult to define, but let me take a run at it because it may be the most important of all. Living with gratitude in your home means something about the way you identify website favorites on your computer or tune your spirit like a radio preset on your favorite station. It's a mind-set of humility in which, as the Bible says, you "value others above yourselves" (Philippians 2:3 NIV).

I've mentioned the poisonous effects of cynicism and sarcasm; a sense of wonder is the polar opposite of these.

When I presented my mother with a craft I had made in grade school and she handled it as if it were a masterpiece, *that's* the sense of wonder I'm talking about. When one of your children tries to please you with an independent act of service, praise him or her for honest effort; don't point out how he could have done a better job, at least not right away.

This reminds me of the time Julie, who was probably thirteen at the time, tried to surprise me by mowing the lawn when I was out of town on a business trip. As I pulled my car into the driveway, the crooked lines and clumps of mown grass told me that a teenager had wreaked havoc on my lawn's usually perfect appearance.

I stepped into the house and called for Julie. She wasn't home. So I put on my work clothes and went outside to "fix" my lawn. What I didn't know was that Julie was directly across the street, babysitting for the neighbor kids. When she heard the mower, she looked out and saw me remowing our yard. She walked across the street with tears streaming down her face.

> I've mentioned the poisonous effects of cynicism and sarcasm; a sense of wonder is the polar opposite of these.

In a moment when my heart should have been filled first with sheer gratitude, my critical spirit—and the perfectionist living deep inside—leaked through. Shame on me for missing a chance to celebrate. No sense of wonder there.

No doubt you've been invited to fund-raising dinners under the cloak of a "free meal with a table of friends." Bobbie and I were invited to one of those: an "all-expenses-paid" weekend ministry fund-raiser with four hundred of our closest friends. It could have been hosted at an inexpensive hotel since, after all, the folks in the ministry were picking up the tab. But the invitation was to the Ritz-Carlton in Puerto Rico. And from Friday afternoon, when the airplane's wheels screeched our welcome to San Juan, until we lifted off on Sunday afternoon, we were treated to pure luxury at someone else's expense.

Even though we knew that Saturday night was going to bring an official appeal for funds, we didn't mind at all. The whole weekend was filled with a sense of awe. And when we bumped into our host— the late D. D. Davis—I knew he could see our genuine gratitude for his generosity. And his humble spirit filled us with even more joy.

God is the gracious host in your Christian home. Just as promised, He has provided for your every need. Beginning with you, the parents who live in your house, your attitude should be one of wonder and gratitude.

Gratitude Is Serious Business

Some people—certainly not you or me—might consider a conversation about gratitude in our homes to be like talking about decorating with throw pillows or the preferred wattage of the lightbulbs in our lamps: nice, but not all that critical to our well-being.

Perhaps you should brace yourself for this one, but when the apostle Paul was identifying ungodly and unrighteous people as the targets of God's indignation and punishment, he included the following on the list identifying their heinous sinfulness: "Nor were [they] thankful" (Romans 1:21).

You and I may not consider *not* being thankful as *sin*. Apparently God doesn't see it that way.

And when he was writing a letter to the folks in Thessalonica, Paul summarized what it takes to live in concert with God's will. Listen to this: "Rejoice always, pray without ceasing, *in everything give thanks; for this is the will of God in Christ Jesus for you*" (1 Thessalonians 5:16–18).

There will be times when you're not certain where God wants you to go and times when you're not sure about what He wants you to do. But being thankful cannot be included on the list of uncertainties.

Test tracks in Detroit give auto manufacturers a chance to see what their new cars can do under safe conditions. Tasting kitchens at food-processing plants do the same under careful supervision. Christian homes—places of grace—are proving grounds for thankfulness.

> You and I may not consider not being thankful as sin. Apparently God doesn't see it that way.

TENDERNESS

Another expression of grace in your home includes tenderness.

You'll remember in the last chapter, we read the passage from Ephesians: "And be kind to one another, tenderhearted, forgiving one another, even as God in Christ forgave you" (Ephesians 4:32).

We've talked about repentance and forgiveness as examples of grace, but Paul also encouraged us to be "tenderhearted." Literally, the word means "to smear with inward affection." Isn't that a great word picture?

If you've been in your car at a stoplight directly behind two lovebird teenagers, you certainly know what outward affection looks like. Tenderness may include gentle touches, but instead of necking and kissing, we are to inwardly plaster each other with gentleness just as we might do with grape jelly on that morning English muffin.

Because I frequently travel by air, I'm often sitting next to strangers. "Tell me about your family" is one of my favorite conversation starters. Once my three-hour friend answers my question, he or she usually turns it around. "And how about *your* family?" I reach for my cell phone—on airplane mode, of course—and slide the photos inside my album of my wife, children, and grandchildren. As I describe each family member to my seatmate, I feel myself inexorably drawn to these people I love. Even though we're miles apart, my heart literally speeds up a little as I look at the images of their faces and realize how truly blessed I am with each one.

Tenderness is not a spontaneous emotion; it's premeditated . . . *that's* what I'm talking about. Loving thoughts about your family when you're apart puts you into a mind-set to be tender with them when you come home.

The prodigal father's attitude toward his returning son wasn't made up the moment he saw him in the distance trudging down the lane leading to his home. The father's love and longing for the way-ward boy were firmly in place even while the kid was blowing his inheritance. He had dreamed of the moment that he would wrap his arms around the youngster. Then when his chance came, there was something wonderfully familiar about the experience.

Not surprisingly, our heavenly Father's tenderness toward us, His children, is exactly like that: preplanned and deliberate. "But God demonstrates His own love toward us, in that while we were still sinners, Christ died for us" (Romans 5:8). There, do you see it? No matter how messy our lives are, God's love for us is complete and in place before we come to Him in faith. He doesn't wait to see if our activity is clean enough to warrant His love. He has already made up His mind.

> Remember, O LORD, Your tender mercies and Your
> lovingkindnesses,
> For they are from of old. (Psalm 25:6)

There it is again. God's tenderness is better than a priceless antique. It's been there since time began.

Back in the mid-eighties, Dr. Denis Waitley authored the idea of "instant preplay." Of course, because you and I watch sports on television, we are familiar with instant *replay*. Once something spectacular happens on the field, we are able to see it again, often from different angles and in slow motion. This gives us a chance to get a really close look.

A consultant to Olympic athletes and Super Bowl champions, Denis had the big idea that we can prepare for what's to come by setting ourselves mentally and emotionally. Many years ago I loved watching Dwight Stones, the great high jumper, prepare to leap over the bar.[4] As he was standing at the end of the runway, the television camera zoomed in on the jumper's face. Before actually taking a single step, Dwight nodded as he "saw" himself taking each loping stride, then successfully leaping over the bar. Before actually taking a single step, he took his practice run in his mind.

Denis Waitley and Dwight Stones knew how to premeditate what they were about to do so that when the time came for them to actually *do* what they were planning, they had some experience under their belts.

Tenderness is a quality you prepare *before* you're with your spouse and your children. Ahead of time, affirm the things you love about the people in your home. Preplay a gentle embrace and tender words for each one. *How could I be so lucky?* you think. Then when you're actually with your family, the presentation matches what you've prepared. Even when circumstances call for toughness, your spirit is one of loving discipline—which we'll talk more about in chapter 8—and not one of anger or revenge.

GENEROSITY

Another picture of grace in your home is the spirit of generosity. Call it *an abundance mentality*. If you're about to pay your check in a restaurant, it's the *gratuity*—an excellent grace word, especially if you're a big tipper.

Whatever you call it, your home is the best place to practice generosity. But this expression of grace does not come naturally.

Put a few toddlers in the same room with a bunch of alluring toys strewn about. In minutes you'll hear a couple of the little ones screaming. And you already know what they're screaming about, don't you? "That's mine!" "No, it's mine!" *"It's mine! Waaaaa!"*

You hustle over and try to calm the frantic children. And in the middle of the noise, you try to teach something. "That's Mary's dinosaur." You use your best diplomacy. "Let's find something else to play with." Then you summarize with a statement that's profound beyond your immediate understanding: "There are plenty of toys for everyone."

Without knowing it, you've summarized the reason for generosity in your home. There *are* plenty of toys for everyone. And regardless of where you place yourself on the economic scale, this is true in your life, isn't it? *Plenty* of toys.

Growing up in my parents' home, I don't recall a single speech on generosity. Dad never called a town hall meeting to espouse the virtues of giving. All he and my mother did was live it. My siblings and I knew this because, as all children do, we paid attention to what they did with *their* things.

In church I never saw an offering plate pass my father without his drawing something out of his wallet. Even when we were on vacation, visiting a place other than our home church, dad always put something in. He could have lectured us on the importance of stewardship, but all he did was show us. The message came through.

I've already mentioned how she was generous with her affection, but our mother fed more guests than some of the diners in our town. She scoured the newspaper for new recipes she could make on a budget. Occasionally, she had to let her family know that there wasn't enough of a certain entrée, so she'd whisper to one of us, "FHB on the green beans." We'd quietly pass her message on to our siblings, knowing that meant "Family hold back." Just take a couple of beans so the guests could have plenty. The important thing was that the abundance of our dinner table made people feel welcome in our home.

Jesus said it best: "It is more blessed to give than to receive" (Acts 20:35).[5] My dad and mother would have amended this slightly: "It's more fun to give than to have."

As an adult, you know this is true. Your happiest Christmas memories since growing up are probably those marked by what you gave, not by what you received.

And don't we love to see our kids "get it" when it comes to generosity? Many Christmases ago, a young mom told her prayer group that one of her happiest moments was when her toddler walked over to the manger scene displayed in the living room and handed her favorite pacifier to baby Jesus.

> "It's more fun to give than to have."

"I didn't think she had understood when I was telling her that we need to give Jesus our gifts of love," she said. "I was amazed that our little girl took the idea and translated it into giving away her most prized possession."

A Christian home is a place where the door is open to guests, where at least 10 percent of your income is invested in your church or other worthy ministries, and where people inside are willing to share their toys.

Fill your Christian home—the most important place on earth—with repentance and forgiveness, gratitude, tenderness, and generosity.

Amazing grace.

5

THE POWER OF WORDS

Real Bullets at Home

I'm not sure who told us about it, but in the late eighties our family bumped into the movie *The Three Amigos*. If you want an intellectually stimulating experience, this isn't it. But if you're looking for a laugh, this will work. The story centers on three men: Dusty Bottoms (Chevy Chase), Lucky Day (Steve Martin), and Ned Nederlander (Martin Short), who are members of a Mexican-Western-style acting and singing troupe called the Three Amigos. In their movies these three perform great acts of bravery, singing their way into the sunset after yet another heroic deed.

But fantasy and reality have a head-on collision when a little town in the Southwest calls on these men to save their town from the ruthless, dreaded, and extremely ugly El Guapo. The townspeople think they're getting brave men to save them. The Three Amigos think they're landing a singing and dancing gig.

Eventually the Three Amigos are face-to-face with El Guapo and his band of ruthless, dreaded, and equally ugly (where do they *get* these actors?) thugs. One of El Guapo's men pulls out his revolver and shoots Dusty, knocking him off his horse. Fortunately the bullet only grazes his shoulder, but as Dusty stands to his feet and discovers what has happened, he utters the immortal words that our family has co-opted as our own:

"Oh great. Real bullets!"

In the world of the Three Amigos, everything was fake. Outfits were costumes. The scenery was a façade. Life was fully orchestrated, and bad guys were only actors. But when they encountered the real thing—an authentic criminal—they discovered that his gun wasn't loaded with blanks.

What I mean by "co-opted" is that, since we first saw the movie, we have used this expression to describe the power of words.

When words are spoken, they're always real. Words are never blanks. They're actual bullets, and their impact is absolute. Every time.

> Words are never blanks. They're actual bullets, and their impact is absolute. Every time.

HAPHAZARD WORDS

I was in our neighborhood grocery store scanning my list to be sure I hadn't forgotten something when I heard the commotion. A frustrated mother in the checkout line was doing her very best to keep her composure. Sitting in the grocery cart, her young son was reaching for the gum and candy and magazines and batteries, all well within his reach. She pleaded with him to stop. "No, Michael, we're not going to buy any candy; we don't need batteries; mommy has plenty of magazines. Please, obey me. Please."

And then she said something that made everyone within earshot of the pathetic scene smile. "Why don't you grow up?" she whined. "Just *when* are you going to grow up?" she added.

Ah, the power of words, haphazardly spoken. (Michael *will* grow up, mom. It'll take a few years, but eventually, it will happen.)

And speaking of haphazard words, here are a few you may recognize:

"Not guilty, your Honor."
"The check is in the mail."
"There are no hidden charges."
"I'll be home by six o'clock."

You and I may smile at some of these statements and promises, but there's nothing funny about them. Why? Because these are real words with real meanings. They may have been spoken hypocritically or as a delay tactic, but they carry promises. They have meaning. Even if they were uttered as blanks, they are received as real.

When words are spoken, we want the truth. When precision plays second fiddle to expedience or convenience or silly outbursts, you and I are the losers.

Your home—your Christian home—must be different from this. It must be a place of true words. Accurate words. Your home has to be a place where people treat words as valuable and precious . . . and they must speak them precisely.

Jesus summarized what I'm saying like this: "Let what you say be simply 'Yes' or 'No'; anything more than this comes from evil" (Matthew 5:37 ESV). Think of living in a home where "I'll do that for you" and "I'll be home soon" mean exactly that. Every time.

Of course, the influence of words goes the whole way back to your childhood. Your attitude toward and habits with words in your home start with the family you grew up in. People in professional circles refer to this as the effect of your "family of origin." For example, if your parents often broke verbal promises, thinking they were shooting blanks, or said things they really didn't mean, then it was only natural for you to pick up that pattern.

It's no fun living in a place where words are carelessly tossed about like foam-rubber Nerf balls. No intended impact. No truthful meaning. But for the recipients of these words, they're always real.

So let's say that you marry a person whose family of origin taught him or her to wink at the accuracy of words. And let's say that, in contrast, your parents treated words the way Jesus admonished. Everyone's word was everyone's bond. There's trouble brewing in your house!

We're going to talk about the need for laughter in your home in chapter 7, but broken promises and treating words as worthless are no laughing matter. Mouths are loaded guns, and the words they speak can be lethal.

> Mouths are loaded guns, and the words they speak can be lethal.

As you and I know all too well, failure to use words to speak truth has brought people plenty of anguish. Take for instance, Bobbie's dad.

SOMETHING TERRIBLE HAS HAPPENED

When Dr. Raymond Gardner, my late father-in-law, was in his teens, he learned a painful lesson about words. Both Raymond's dad and mother, like most in their generation, were no-nonsense when it came to the importance of truthful words. One evening while his father was out of town, Raymond's mother told him that he couldn't go out with his friends. With unfinished homework, there would be no socializing. The young man told his mother he would obey, then went to his room and straightaway climbed out of the window to rendezvous with his friends at the community roller-skating rink.

Because Raymond's father was out and his mother didn't have a driver's license, he concluded that he could get away with the caper. This was a serious miscalculation. Suspicious about the quiet coming from his room, Raymond's mother checked it out, only to find the bedroom empty. She promptly gathered her coat and hat, called a neighbor, and asked for a ride to town to find her son. She guessed that he had escaped to the roller rink.

The organ music played loudly as Raymond glided around the turn. To his complete dismay, there in the visitor's gallery he spotted a woman who looked just like his mother. Sure enough, it *was* his mother. What made it worse, she had a panicked—not angry—look on her face. As Raymond hurried over to his mother, a combination of embarrassment and fear filled his heart. When he reached her, Velzetta May Gardner said to her boy in a voice that spoke of terror, "Come home quickly. Something terrible has happened."

That wasn't what he had expected. Her countenance was so severe that he was certain some calamity had befallen his family—perhaps his father had been killed. Or one of his brothers.

Raymond took no time to say good-bye to his friends. His heart pounded as he loosened the laces on his skates. *What could have happened? What could have happened?* the frightened youngster reviewed over and over.

No one spoke on the way home. The neighbor dropped Raymond and his mother in front of their house, and the two of them hurried inside. Raymond slumped onto a kitchen chair while his mother removed her hat and her coat. Then she sat down on a chair facing her worried boy.

"Something terrible has happened," she finally said again. She paused and looked into her son's eyes, making certain that her next words would sear themselves into his memory forever. "My son has just lied to his mother," she said, each word piercing Raymond's heart. "My son has lied," she repeated.

Forty years later I heard this story from my father-in-law. His voice cracked with emotion as he recalled the details of the account, grateful that his mother had created a moment that would survive for the remainder of his life: a profound lesson in the worth of words and the critical importance of those words being truthful.

I have participated in dozens of weddings. I've officiated, stood in as the best man, and been an usher. And twice I've had a chance to be the groom. But I've never been the ring-bearer. At my age, I've given up on the possibility of being asked.

Because you've been to a lot of weddings, too, I have a word picture for you, thanks to the little boy with the pillow.

Words spoken in your home are as valuable as the wedding rings gently placed in the center of the pillow, secured with satin ribbons. These words need to be carried about with utmost care. They are precious. And they are formidable.

> Words need to be carried about with utmost care. They are precious. And they are formidable.

THANKS, MRS. HALLEEN

I don't think I was any more than twelve years old. My family and I were hanging around our church narthex right after the service had ended. We—mostly my dad and mother—were greeting friends. My siblings and I were eager to go home.

In the midst of my impatience, I heard something I'll never forget. My mother was chatting with her friend, Romaine Halleen. The wife of Mr. Harold Halleen, the bank president and a prominent leader in the community, Mrs. Halleen was one of our town's most elegant ladies. Her home was often the venue for the fancy crystal, silver, and linen women's luncheons local reporters covered in the "Living" section of the newspaper.

"Your Robert is one very special young man," Romaine Halleen said to my mother. Neither woman had a clue that I was listening. "Why, if I were a young woman," Mrs. Halleen added, "I'd certainly keep an eye on him."

Until that moment I didn't know that this important woman even knew my name. She was telling my mother that I was a sparkler. I can promise you that as an awkward preteen, I would never have included the words "very special" on my own list of personal qualities. They were just a few simple spoken words by a woman who didn't even know I was listening, but that moment will be forever soldered to my memory.

You may have a story like this. If you do, you know exactly what I'm talking about.

My own mother remembers Mrs. Katherine Rettew, her second-grade teacher. Because Mrs. Rettew went to the same church as my mother and her family, she was also able to watch little Grace grow up. When she was sixteen years old, Grace was feeling quite inferior to her older sister, Mary, who was all-world in everything from academics to boy-catching. That was the year mother's best friend, Elizabeth Engle, said something she never forgot. "Mrs. Rettew told me," Elizabeth reported to my mother, "that she thinks Grace Dourte is a nice girl."

That was all: "Grace is a nice girl."

In a conversation with her a few years before she died, this mother of six, grandmother of twenty, great-grandmother of dozens of children, told me again that this was one of the most important character-shaping moments of her life.

Can you imagine that something so simple could be this profound? Of course you can. It's another example of the indelible impact of words.

The apostle James also had something to say about the power of spoken words.

If anyone does not stumble *in word*, he is a perfect man, able also to bridle the whole body. Indeed, we put bits in horses' mouths that they may obey us, and we turn their whole body. Look also at ships: although they are so large and are driven by fierce winds, they are turned by a very small rudder wherever the pilot desires. *Even so the tongue is a little member and boasts great things.* (James 3:2–5)

Just so we wouldn't miss the point, James compared the tongue, the seedbed of words, to the bit in a horse's mouth or the rudder of a great ship. A little yank here, a slight turn there, and everything changes.

A GOLF TIP FROM PAPA

Although he really enjoyed playing golf, my dad was not one to give anyone instructions on his game. *Unorthodox* would certainly describe the way he hit the ball. But one day, several years ago, he gave a terrific lesson to his grandson . . . and his son.

Dad and mother were visiting Kansas City, where my brother Dan and his wife, Mary, lived. It was summer, and, of course, dad packed his golf clubs.

One warm afternoon, Dan, along with his two teenage sons, Andrew and Erik, took dad—"Papa" to the grandsons—out for a round of golf. As Dan described it to me, Erik was in a groove. His drives were straight and true, his approach shots accurate, and his putting precise.

But Andrew was struggling. One shot was fine, but the next shanked into the tall grass. One putt came close to the pin, but the next recklessly skittered several yards past the hole. Focused on his son's poor performance, Dan provided lots of uninvited coaching. Andrew was not amused.

"Slower on the backswing," he reminded Andrew. "Keep your head down, son," he said. Hole after hole, the frustration between father and son built. Papa was quiet but not disengaged. Dan could tell that he was paying close attention. Like a squirrel looking for an opening to cross a busy highway, my dad waited to make his move.

The men were on the tenth green. Because Andrew's ball was the farthest from the hole, he was the first to putt. Dan's instruction had not brought any desired result, so he stood quietly, tending the pin. He'd run out of things to say to his frustrated son.

Andrew carefully lined up his putt, then stood over it, ready to strike it toward the pin. He braced himself for another piece of advice from his dad.

"Come on, Andrew," Papa encouraged in a voice loud enough to be heard but gentle enough to go straight to the teenager's heart. "You can do it," he added with a hopeful lift.

Andrew hesitated for a moment, then confidently struck the ball. It caught the slope of the green and bent to his left, exactly as he had planned. Plunk! The ball dropped straight into the hole—"center cut," as the guys say on TV.

The teenager threw his arms in the air, celebrating his best putt of the day. He ran straight toward his grandfather for a high five. Even his younger brother joined the dance. But his dad stood speechless a few steps from the revelry.

"I had given him every piece of instruction I knew to give," Dan told me. "But I had forgotten to speak any words of encouragement."

My brother told me this story on the second anniversary of our dad's death. His eyes were moist with tears of gratitude as he recalled the unforgettable lesson our dad had taught him about the power of words.

> Pleasant words are like a honeycomb,
> Sweetness to the soul and health to the bones. (Proverbs 16:24)

THE DARK SIDE OF WORDS

"Sticks and stones may break my bones, but words will never hurt me!"

"I had given him every piece of instruction I knew to give. But I had forgotten to speak any words of encouragement."

I can still hear kids in my childhood neighborhood shouting this to each other in order to neutralize an unkind thing they had just heard slung in their direction. But you and I know that no greater lie has ever been repeated. Words can—and do—hurt.

Remember the little rudder and the great ship? Katherine Rettew and Romaine Halleen impacted my mother and me with their encouraging words. But simple words also have the power to destroy. In the first chapter, I mentioned Bill Glass and his ministry to prisoners—how most of them had parents who told them they would "wind up in a place like this."

I have a friend who has spent years in therapy desperately trying to overcome a first-grade teacher's biting indictment: "You're never going to make anything of yourself." Like a deep rut on a muddy lane or the screen saver on his laptop, these are the words he defaults to when faced with uncertainty or failure.

You and I, of course, would never tell our children that they will grow up as failures. Our "prophecies" come in more subtle forms.

YOU ARE . . .

We had a rule in our home that no one could finish "You are" with a derogatory word. For example, when someone interrupted a conversation, we tried not to say, "You are so rude." Rather we said, "I'm sorry, it's not polite to interrupt. Please wait until I'm finished talking, and then I'll answer your question." It's the difference between an indictment and a correction.

"C'mon," you might say. "I don't have the time for that. I'm accustomed to getting to the point. We cut to the chase in our house."

Okay, but remember that words, even small ones, have incredible power, and you have just told your child that he *is* rude. You've used a word that has the potential of unconsciously sentencing your child to wearing a mantle of rudeness. It's not a blank. It's a real bullet.

If your child listens to what you've said—and listening to you is what you *want* him to do—he now has a legitimate excuse to continue to be thoughtless. The most important person in the world—you— just told him he *is* rude. *Unkind words come from rude people*, your child reasons. *So what else should I expect from myself?*

Here are some other examples:

Situation	Improper Indictment	Proper Correction
An unkempt room	You're such a mess.	Your room looks messy.
Inappropriately loud voices	You're always screaming.	That's not the way to speak.
Unwillingness to look at people when they're speaking	Why are you so shy?	Please look at the person you're speaking to. It makes him feel special.
Wearing sloppy clothing	You're so sloppy.	That's not an appropriate outfit. Please change your clothes.
Catching your child in a lie	You're a liar.	That wasn't the truth.

You may have already thought about this, but when you look at this list it becomes clear *why* we use indictments. They are so much stronger than corrections. We want impact when we correct our kids, so we choose to drop "You are" bombs.

When we were first married, Bobbie and I discovered the awful power of "You are" words. So we established our own Geneva Convention agreement for the words we speak to each other.[1] For example, because of our deal, I could not say, "You are lazy" or "You are just like your mother." These words were damaging, often escalating a common argument into a full-scale war. And she couldn't call me an insensitive, perfectionistic, hard-driving, Germanic, uh . . . you get the idea.

I encourage you to consider the same kind of moratorium of incriminating "You are" statements in your home.

You'll see what I mean.

ENDORSEMENTS

It's fascinating to me that the simple phrases Romaine Halleen and Katherine Rettew spoke were not actually spoken *to* me or to my mother. They were, in fact, spoken *about* me and my mother.

I have spent most of my career in the book publishing business. One of the things I learned early on was the power of a third-party endorsement. The author of the book can prance around to the talk shows and tell everyone how terrific his book is, but when someone else says, "Hey, this really *is* a terrific book," there's more credibility.

Romaine Halleen told my mother that she thought I was special. Ironically, this probably had more of an impact on me than if Mrs. Halleen had told me directly. For some reason, it was more authentic. The same thing happened with Mrs. Rettew's words about young Grace.

Imagine yourself as an eight-year-old Charlie, lying in bed late one night. Your dad and mother are in the next room and you can hear them talking.

"You know," your dad says, "I've been thinking about Charlie."

Your ears perk up. You can feel your heart begin to pound. *What's dad going to say about me?* you wonder.

He continues, "I couldn't be prouder of our son. What a special kid he is. Just today he . . ."

For the next few minutes you hear your dad say good things about you. And although he's not actually speaking to you, his "endorsement" has a profound impact. Lying there in the darkness, you bubble over with inspiration. There is no way to describe how good this moment feels.

When my children were small, we always tried to say good things about them to others—even when the kids were not around. And we encouraged them to do the same with each other. Can you imagine the impact of hearing that your sibling was bragging on you?

In fact, one of the ways we encouraged our children toward good attitudes and conduct was to endorse other children to our kids. "Did you notice how Jennifer set the table without her mother asking?" you say to your child. "She is such a nice helper."

You have just given your child a specific thing that he can do to please you. And you've done it without endlessly bleating about the need for good manners.

There's one critical thing to remember about these kinds of endorsements: never talk about another child's good qualities in areas where your kid could never achieve. "That boy standing over there is so tall. He is so handsome." "Doesn't that girl in the front row have beautiful blonde hair?"

Even though they may never verbalize it to you, your short son and brown-haired daughter can be crushed by these unachievable endorsements.

HE AND SHE

Many years ago Bobbie and I were out to dinner with a married couple several years our senior. Although we'd known these folks for many years, we didn't see each other very often. During our time together, something caught my ear. I didn't say anything to Bobbie about it until later that evening when we were alone.

"Did you notice that when Harold and Anne spoke about each other," I remarked, "they never used each other's name? I can't think of a single time that Anne referred to her husband as Harold or he referred to his wife as Anne. All night it was 'He did this' and 'She said that.'"

Bobbie thought for a moment and then agreed that this was what they had done. She also noted how unattached this sounded. Then we reminded each other that one of our encouragements about words in our home when our kids were young was this very thing. At the dinner table, when one girl had a grievance against her sister, "She said this" or "She did that" was not acceptable.

The unspoken condescension of avoiding a person's name was undeniable. Someone who has been relegated to a pronoun has lost something. When there was a discussion about a sibling, it had to be "Missy said this" or "Julie did that."

This gave the defendant a chance to explain without losing face. After all, what kind of rights does a generic *he* or *she* have?

Once again, I could be charged with making a big deal out of nothing. *Come on—pronouns? someone* might wonder. *Aren't you going a little too far with this words thing?* Maybe. Maybe not. Try it for yourself and see.

> Someone who has been relegated to a pronoun has lost something.

Thousands of years ago, King Solomon weighed in on the value of words:

> A word fitly spoken is like apples of gold
> In settings of silver. (Proverbs 25:11)

As brilliant as he was with words, it was almost as though Solomon was completely taken with the priceless value of each one, using the images of *both* silver and gold in pounding home their worth.

A HABIT OF GOOD WORDS

Before leaving the subject of words in your home, let me add another idea. Placing a high value on the power of words and using this power wisely is only part of the picture. You may want to begin to proactively create some spoken-word traditions—some words that you speak each time the same situations arise.

Happy Epithets

It's easy to use the simplest words to attach to your children's names, giving them a picture of what they are . . . or could be. For example, I've always wondered how the boy named Alexander became the world's most powerful man three centuries before Christ. What I *really* wonder is who gave him the nickname—epithet—"the Great" and what kind of impact this had on him. I suppose that no conjecture is needed.

Every morning when your children pad down to the kitchen for breakfast, you have a chance to give them happy epithets. You have the same chance when you pick them up from school or speak to them on your phone.

One summer our granddaughter Abby came to visit Bobbie and me in Florida. Bobbie wanted to teach her one of the old hymns of our faith that week. They made quite a game out of it as they learned verses while they ate, played, and swam. Every morning, when Abby came down the stairs for breakfast, I heard Bobbie say, "Good morning, Abby. How's my happy hymn-singer?"

Our daughter Missy has been doing this for years. "Good morning, Luke," we hear her say when we're visiting. "How's my slugger?" When Isaac comes into the kitchen, we've heard, "Good morning, sunshine."

Abby loves to sing hymns, Luke is quite the baseball player, and Isaac smiles day and night. All their mother does is speak the words. Because they're so powerful, the words do the rest.

Don't Forget; You're a Tassy

Christopher Tassy is married to my daughter Julie. With his Caribbean ancestry, "The lad will play soccer" may as well have been added to the doctor's announcement, "It's a boy." Jean-Arnaud—he goes by "Tass"—his Haitian-born father, was a college Division I All-American for his skill on the soccer field and is a highly decorated varsity soccer coach at the University of Buffalo.

Both Christopher and his older brother, Jake, followed suit as all-American soccer players. From the time they played in their first game, Tass said the same thing to his boys as they trotted out to play: "Don't forget; you're a Tassy." These are words they heard again and again.

This was not a prideful statement. There was no arrogance in it at all. That admonition repeated hundreds of times was Christopher and Jake's perpetual reminder to be worthy ambassadors of their family: to do their best, to play hard and honorably, and to remember that because they were Christians, people were watching them on the field as followers of Jesus Christ. Not surprisingly, both of these men grew up to live their lives exactly as they had played the game. These words their father spoke carried incredible power.

Aren't You Sam's Boy?

Very similar to Christopher and Jake's reminder when they ran onto the soccer field was the identity question my brothers and I used to get every summer. Because our dad was a minister, more often than not, our family church camp experiences included having dad as one of the week's speakers.

Because of what some people considered "a strong family resemblance" (as in *cloned facsimiles*) between my dad and his sons, we often (constantly) heard these words: "Aren't you Sam's boy?"

During our self-image-exploring years, this wasn't always an enjoyable question for us to hear. But most of the time, because we really *were* proud of our dad, we'd smile and say, "Yes I am."

Of course, we knew that this association with our dad included some serious responsibility. People saw misbehavior not as "Robert Wolgemuth's misdeed" but as "the foolish behavior of Dr. Samuel Wolgemuth's son."

I don't remember our dad ever telling us to be careful because we represented him wherever we went—it would have sounded too brash for him to say this. But because we were asked this question constantly, we somehow *knew* that we were miniature replicas of our father. These words were powerful reminders of that fact.[2]

The Lord Be with You

Although we grew up in very informal churches and were unaccustomed to the liturgy that many ceremonial churches use in their worship services, Bobbie and I learned and adopted a saying from our more liturgical friends as one of our family rituals. We began repeating to each other "The Lord be with you" when saying good-bye on the telephone or dropping the kids off at school.

This habit began and has stuck with our family through our children's college years until now. I know it won't surprise you to learn that this is a blessing that has been around for thousands of years.

And the Lord spoke to Moses, saying: "Speak to Aaron and his sons, saying, 'This is the way you shall bless the children of Israel. Say to them:

> "The LORD bless you and keep you;
> The LORD make His face shine upon you,
> And be gracious to you;
> The LORD lift up His countenance upon you,
> And give you peace.'" (Numbers 6:22–26)

Then God added a poignant postscript to the blessing. Listen to this: "So they shall put My name on the children of Israel, and I will bless them" (Numbers 6:27).

Verbally bless your children with these words, God told Moses. Use My name when you do . . . and I *will* bless them.

Sometimes we return "the Lord be with you" with "and also with you." These simple words pronounce a profound blessing.

Happy Birthday Gifts

Here's an idea for the next time someone in your family has a birthday. While you're seated at the dinner table, go around, one at a time, and tell the birthday person "what I love about you." Give your family notice before the party so they can be prepared, and give everyone a chance to talk, even the youngest at the table.

Doing this might not work as a substitute for real presents, but it's a fantastic experience. And the recipient is lavished with priceless word gifts, many of which he or she will remember for a lifetime:

"I love you and like how you give me hugs and call me 'buddy.'"
"I really am amazed at how hard you work every day for our family."
"I love you and like that you're such a good listener."

Some might say that this really doesn't make sense. "All you're giving is words." Of course, those people haven't considered what you and I know to be true. Words are powerful and priceless.

Several summers ago I was wakened in the middle of the night by an excruciating case of appendicitis. I'm not a doctor, but I do know where my appendix is (was), and it felt as if someone had stuck a blunt ice pick into mine.

> At the dinner table, go around, one at a time, and tell the birthday person "what I love about you."

In a few hours I was lying on a hospital gurney, just a few minutes from giving my inflated appendix the rest of the day off. Chill bumps completely covered my body, not because I was scared but because, for some reason, hospitals keep the areas around operating rooms very cold. I guess germs don't multiply well in refrigerators.

Bobbie asked the pre-op nurse if she could bring me a blanket. In a moment the nurse returned with an armful of them.

Even though this was years ago, I can still feel exactly what it was like when she began wrapping me with the blankets. How can I remember? Because these blankets had been stored in an oven. They were as warm as toast. Having them tucked around me was an incredible sensation. Immediately, my chills were gone.

Words we give as gifts are exactly like those warm blankets. There is no way to adequately describe what they do for the birthday boy or girl or mom or dad, but words do their own warming work quite beautifully.

The next time someone in your family has a birthday, try giving him or her words before passing them the wrapped presents. You'll see.

Good Night, Sweet Dreams

When our nephews, Erik and Andrew, were little boys, their parents lived less than twenty minutes away. Every once in a while we had the fun of having them stay overnight at our house. One night, as Bobbie was tucking Erik into bed, she noticed that he was looking quite sad. In moments like these, we tried to remember not to make comments about dad and mom, such as "Oh, I bet you really miss your parents." Even novice babysitters know not to do this.

Sitting on the edge of the bed, Bobbie saw the gloomy look on Erik's face and said in the most reassuring tone of voice she could muster, "I'm glad you came, today, Erik. Aunt Bobbie loves you so much." She looked into Erik's eyes. Her words had scored something, but it wasn't the zinger she had hoped for.

A few moments of silence followed. "Aunt Bobbie," Erik whispered, unsuccessfully trying to keep his voice from quivering.

"Yes, Erik."

"Would you please give me a *happy thought*? My mom always gives me a happy thought before I go to sleep."

Isn't that brilliant? Right then, his mother, Mary, shot to the top of our "smart mother" list. Erik's mom knew that all a little boy needed was a small handful of words that could lie down right next to him and comfort him until he fell asleep.

Happy-thought good-night words can be "You fed Snoopy a treat today, and he licked your face because he likes you," or "Remember that Jesus promises to stay right here next to you all night—you're never alone," or "If I could have picked out any girl in the whole world to be mine, I would have picked you."

> All a little boy needed was a small handful of words that could lie down right next to him and comfort him until he fell asleep.

Our friend Jessica's eight-year-old used to have bad dreams and learned to ask her mom at bedtime, "Would you say two good things for me to dream about?" On the day they had been to a strawberry farm to pick berries, Jessica simply said, "How about strawberries for your dreams tonight?" and that seemed to do the trick, along with a reminder of a friend's upcoming birthday party.

The apostle Paul had the same idea: truth, nobility, justice, purity, lovely things—those worth repeating—think about these good and strong words (Philippians 4:8). Go to bed with words like this spinning in your head.

Words like these will give your child a peaceful night's sleep and confidence to take on tomorrow.

WARNING: FOLLOW PROPER DOSAGE

What I'm about to say is going to put me in a pigeonhole with *old fogy* printed over the top. I may never be able to crawl out, but I'm willing to go in there anyway.

One of the secrets to using words effectively with your family is giving yourself a chance to use them. Please follow me here.

Going back for a moment to Charles and Caroline Ingalls's little house, those folks did a lot of talking with each other. Walking to school, riding on the seat of the buckboard to pick up supplies in downtown Walnut Grove, or sitting around their tiny home, there was constant conversation. The reason they did a lot of talking is pretty easy to figure out: there was absolutely nothing else to do.

Okay, now let's beam ourselves ahead a century and a half to now. We *don't* do a lot of talking in our homes because . . . go ahead, finish the sentence.

That's right. We don't pass words around as much as families used to because there are scads of other things to do.

At home we have smartphones and televisions and computers and DVDs and CDs and video games. As I described in chapter 3 about visiting the Street of Dreams, many of these electronic goodies are located in bedrooms where members of our family can enjoy them in complete isolation.

Now, here's the old fogy part.

These electronic appliances can be wonderful. Really they can. But like the warning labels on most of the medicines in your home, they can also be extremely dangerous if not taken in proper doses. By this I mean they can be *extremely dangerous to the health of your family*.

The reason should be apparent. These wonderful things must be used in moderation. Because when they're in use, we're *not talking* to each other. And when we're not talking to each other, we're *not connecting*. And when we're not connecting, we're not acting like a family. And when we're not acting like a family, we're going to be dangerously unbalanced.

Before she celebrated her second birthday, our granddaughter Harper acted up almost every time her mother was talking on her cell phone. She whined. She did naughty things. She tormented her baby sister and made her cry. What frustrated her parents was that this behavior was quite out of character for her. One day, Julie, Harper's mother, figured it out. When Julie was on the phone, it meant that she wasn't available to her little girl. Even if Harper had been playing quietly on her own, the moment she knew that her mother wasn't available—just in case she *was* needed—it made her anxious. So she *acted* anxious.

> Electronic appliances . . . can be *extremely dangerous to the health of your family*. . . . And when we're not connecting, we're not acting like a family.

Of course, I'm not saying that Harper's conduct was acceptable. After all, every little kid's mother has no choice but to spend time on the phone. What I *am* saying is that even toddlers understand the isolating effect of these electronic gizmos in our homes. And if they're not used in moderation, the members of our family will slowly move away from each other, passing, as they used to say, like ships in the night.

CAR TRIPS

When I was a kid, at least the car was sacred.[3] Sure, we had a radio, but it was only AM, and the programming back then could be best described as painfully boring. And on long trips, the AM stations faded out every time we hit the next county. So car trips were great times for family talk, games, singing, and such. Okay, you're right. They were *also* times for a little harmless conflict—"He's on *my* side!"—but at least we were connecting.

Just think back to your own childhood and riding in the car. As parents, we may find it hard to remember that we are creating memories, not just getting there (in record time). Joni Eareckson Tada's family made memories with melodies—spoken words put to music.

> I remember long car trips with my parents and three sisters marking miles by making music. It really did make time go faster. And from my little perch on the ledge beneath the back window (long before child safety seats were required), I was filled with awe when I spied the majestic Rocky Mountains rising up over the horizon. That's when my daddy began to sing "Rock of Ages, cleft for me," and we girls chimed in from the back seat. I can relive those moments of pleasure every time I tote along one of those old family favorites.[4]

But no more.

Bobbie was talking once to an old Tennessee friend by telephone. This young mother was filling Bobbie in on how her children were doing, especially the ones now going to school. The mother reported that because her kids were in a private school, they had to be carpooled.[5]

Then she told Bobbie that they had just bought a new van with a factory-installed DVD player. "I get a little peace and quiet," she preened, "because the kids are absorbed with their favorite cartoons on the way to school."

Bobbie was stunned.

No happy chatter among the children about school? No chance for prayer or encouraging words from parents to get the kids' day started right, or a listening ear when it's time to download the news of a busy school day? No. Instead it's the sound effects and chatter of some animation filling the airspace. The sounds of frying pans bonking people on the head and characters talking with voices that resemble your dog's squeak toys. Blathering noise in exchange for this priceless time with your children? This is a poor substitute for something very precious.

DVDs in your new van might be a good idea if you're driving nonstop from Miami to Anchorage—or another really long trip—but otherwise, this is a disaster.

Warning: use extreme caution when operating electronic equipment.

CELL . . . AS IN HELL . . . PHONES

I know, I know. Everyone has a cell phone. I have one. You have one. Our daughters and their husbands and children each have one. And they can be terrific. But sometimes we get a little carried away, don't we?

One weekday afternoon Bobbie and I were driving to our good friends' home on the other side of Orlando. During certain times of the day, our city boasts the world's largest parking lot. Some also refer to it as Interstate 4. We were almost to town, doing three miles an hour, when we looked to our right. There in the next lane was a woman driving a convertible. In the backseat was a child in a car seat, which meant he wasn't quite five years old. The mother was talking on her cell phone. Of course, that's not worth reporting (unless you live in one of those states where this is illegal), but the little kid—I'm not making this up—was *also* on a cell phone.

I know what you're thinking. *Chill out, Robert; it was a toy cell phone.* No it wasn't. Bobbie saw it too. We know fake cell phones. When they were babies, our grandkids had them. This was a *real* cell phone. The kid was on a *cell phone.* His *own* cell phone. So much for car talk—precious words—with your child.

We've all seen this in restaurants: people sitting with their friends but talking on their cell phones or tapping out text messages. We've seen it in checkout lines at the neighborhood drugstore: people standing in front of the clerk while he totals up their order. No chance for "Isn't it a beautiful day, Mr. Beezley?" Instead, it's "And can you believe that Seymore and Blanche have split up? . . . Yes, I know. . . . Uh-huh. . . . He's a slime bag, bless his heart.[6] And their kids are already such brats. . . . Uh-huh. . . . But that's not the half of it . . ."

One day we're going to see Mr. Beezley step around to the front of the counter, gently take the phone from his customer, and smash it to the floor, stamping on it until the largest piece is the size of a Rice Krispie. If I saw this, I would personally testify on his behalf when he's sued.

Warning: use extreme caution when operating electronic equipment.

THE RING-BEARER'S PILLOW: A REPRISE

Remember the little boy carrying the wedding rings down the aisle? This is the picture we must keep in our minds regarding the value of words. First, they must be spoken. The wedding ceremony isn't complete without them. Then treat these words as what they are: treasures. Each one spoken must be true. Thoughtful. Precise.

The children in your Christian home need to experience the great gift of learning how to use—and treasure—words this way. They need to understand, from your example, that words are not blanks. They're not simply noise. Spoken words are powerful. They penetrate hearts. They have consequences. Their impact is mighty.

6

THE POWER OF WORDS PART II

The Family Vitamins

This chapter is also about spoken words. But rather than including the material in chapter 5, making it way too long (publishers don't like that), we decided to make it a chapter of its own.

There's one more thing you need to know about words. Actually, there are *five* more things.

In the early years, as we were trying to fit the pieces together in our Christian home and make it a happy place to live, Bobbie and I came up with an idea, a way to keep our family healthy.

We call them our Family Vitamins.

AND THEY WORK

In 1978, I received a call from a good friend. A year or so before, Diane had lost her husband. A year later she met a single man named Bob—also a good friend of ours—in our Sunday school class. After a brief courtship, they were getting married and wanted me to help officiate the ceremony.[1]

Although I had assisted in weddings before, this was a first for me, standing in front of a bride and groom but joining *two families*—Diane had one son; Bob had three—into one blended family.

What could I say that would be an encouragement to Diane and Bob, understandable by their boys, and actually helpful in their new lives together?

In my study I reviewed my life as a father and tried to pull together something that the whole family could use. And then it came to me. "The Family Vitamins!" I whispered out loud. "They'll be perfect."

Seventeen years later Bob and Diane came to Florida for a corporate meeting of Bob's software company.[2] They came by and visited with Bobbie and me. As we sat on our back deck, reminiscing through the years, Diane told us that even though the boys are all grown, "we still use the Family Vitamins." I admitted to her that after almost thirty-five years of marriage, "We do too."

I believe that these vitamins are as important for your family as they are for ours. These are *not* pills that you take. They are vitamins you *speak:* potent phrases for you and your family. And they come with the following guarantee: if you and your family begin using these on a regular basis, the results will be profound. Measurable. That's a promise.

> They are vitamins you speak: potent phrases for you and your family.

Oh, and two final reminders: (1) these vitamins must be spoken *in full*. Half-vitamins are powerless and won't do the trick, and (2) these vitamins must be spoken with the recipient's full attention.

VITAMIN #1: "I LOVE YOU"

During my high school years, when I worked at DuPage Photo and Hobby Shop, I became quite the connoisseur of greeting cards. Hallmark had just released its hilarious Contemporary card line (only twenty-five cents each back then), and our store had a terrific selection of them. One of my favorites had a really forlorn-looking guy on the front with the headline: "Since you've been gone, I've gotten a little melancholy." On the inside was a guy holding a cute little mutt, and the inscription: "They're as smart as dogs and not quite as messy."

I liked that one.

Another had a classic illustration of a woman reclining on a chaise lounge. She had this passionate look on her face, and the card read: "Please tell me those magic three words I've been longing to hear from you." Inside, the card read: "Scratch my back."

That one also still makes me smile because, as you know, those *aren't* the magic three words at all. The *real* ones are *I love you*.

The impact of these words is clear to everyone. You can flip on your TV and hear a guy going on and on about how much he *loves* his Toyota. Or you can go to a sporting event and hear the fans yell and scream about how much they *love* the Dodgers.[3]

You may hear a woman exclaim to her friend how much she *loves* those new shoes.

But there's nothing to compare with the power when two people are romantically gazing into each other's eyes, and one of them says, "I love you." Or when a telephone conversation with someone special ends with "I love you." Or when you say to your spouse over dinner or to your child at bedtime, with all the tenderness and sincerity you can muster, "I love you."

This was our first daily-for-life vitamin, and we learned from each other how wonderful the sound of these magic three words could be.

After bedtime prayers were said and we were tucking our children in for the night, a kiss and an "I love you" guaranteed comfort and sweet dreams. In fact, we learned a powerful ending to add to this vitamin that made it even sweeter: it was putting the child's name at the tag end. "I love you, *Missy*." "I love you, *Julie*." These words connected us to our children's souls.

Remember that "I love you" must be spoken in its entirety and does not count if delivered on the run. A breathless "love ya" shouted over your shoulder as you dash out of the house with a toasted bagel in one hand and your computer case in the other doesn't count. Sure, it *is* better than "Clean your room" or "Stay out of trouble," but when this vitamin is spoken in part or in a hurry, it doesn't qualify as a Family Vitamin.

> "I love you . . ." These words connected us to our children's souls.

Some Extra Dosage

Many years ago the Austrian-born writer and marriage expert Walter Trobisch wrote a book called *Love Is a Feeling to Be Learned.* The title says it all, doesn't it? Years later, a book was published with the same big idea tucked into its title: *Love Is a Decision.*[4]

If we said "I love you" only when you and I had chills running up and down our spines, as we did the first time we held hands, we would rarely say them at all. Why? Because getting through a day—and much less a life—means a lot of hard work, daily interruptions, and drudgery: "Clean out the garage." "You're late." "What's for dinner?" "Are we there yet?" "Oh no, I think I'm going to be sick."

Add to that: sometimes the people in our family act in such a way—whining, arguing, disobedient, silent, distant—that makes them quite *un*lovable.

The titles of these books remind us that love is something we *decide* on and *learn* about and *work* on. Love is not something we hold out for until everything is in perfect order and the feeling hits us.

"I love you" means that regardless of the circumstances, regardless of what has happened, you can count on me.

Let's pretend that you and I are sitting

> Love is not something we hold out for until everything is in perfect order and the feeling hits us.

across the desk from the most popular marriage counselor in your town. We ask him about this. "How many couples tell you that their marriage is in trouble because 'we never loved each other in the first place'?"

The counselor gives us a knowing smile and tells us that many—most—of his clients say exactly that.

Are his clients lying? No. This is really how they *feel*. But what they're actually saying is, "I don't have that same tingle I had when we first met . . . [or] when we announced our engagement . . . [or] when we got married. It's been so long that I don't remember the last time I had that feeling."

After many years of marriage to Bobbie, we understood this. But "I love you" is really "I love you *anyway*." "I love you *regardless*." "I love you, *and that's final*." This is something that comes from our minds as well as our hearts. It's a feeling to be learned, a conscious decision that we make.

One more thing. Sometimes "I love you" is tough. For example, "I love you too much to let you do that to yourself . . . or to us . . . or to our family." And so you tell your spouse the truth or you discipline your children *because* you love them.

"I love you" is Vitamin #1.

VITAMIN #2: "I NEED YOUR LOVE"

—————————————
"I love you"
is Vitamin #1.
—————————————

It's one thing to tell someone in your family that you love him or her, but what if you want that person to say it to you . . . and he or she just doesn't? This vitamin will fix that problem.

Very early in marriage to Bobbie, I learned a painful lesson about unmet expectations. No, actually, I learned many painful lessons about unmet expectations.

For example, one of the things my dad did every year was to give my mother something nice for Christmas. Only one gift and something *practical*. As kids, we watched my mother lift a bathrobe or a new jacket out of the box, hold it up with admiration, and with appreciation say, "Oh, Samuel, thank you sooo much."

Question: Do you suspect that I entered marriage with expectations about what would please my wife at Christmas?

Bobbie's dad, on the other hand, bought her mother multiple and not-so-practical and over-the-top gifts, such as an expensive silver coffee service or a sleek new convertible. Gifts she did not ask for, expect, or particularly need.

Question: Do you suspect that Bobbie entered our marriage with expectations about what gifts would please her at Christmas?

Another example: When Bobbie's family was on a road trip, her dad—who always was the driver—pulled the family car over for short diversions. "Scenic Lookout Ahead" or "Pecan Pralines at Stuckey's" or "Flea Market Next Exit" meant an immediate adventure. It was get off the interstate, find a parking spot, and enjoy. Every time.

Question: Do you suspect that Bobbie entered marriage with expectations about car trips?

My dad considered the time saved on road travel like money in the bank. Every precious minute passed at a gas station, like a lost jewel. If we kids weren't back from the potty by the time the tank was filled, we believed that the family car would leave without us. This never happened because we never dared to dawdle.

Question: Do you suspect that I entered marriage with expectations?

After a few years of silent frustration about these and other unmet expectations, Bobbie and I finally talked. "I need some help in selecting gifts at Christmas," I admitted to her. "I was sure you'd like that hair dryer. I didn't know it would make you cry. I feel as if I failed you on Christmas Day, and I need help."

That gave Bobbie the freedom, later on, to say to me, "I would like our car trips to be more fun. I need for you to stop at more rest stops even if we don't make great time."

I really wanted to please my wife, so I tried on this one. I really did.

The point is this: in every marriage and in every family, people have expectations. Often these go unmet because no one expresses them. And so we mope around, stewing over the fact that our spouses or our kids or our parents aren't doing what we need for them to do.

"I need your love" is about putting our unmet expectations into words. It's the unashamed admission that our relationship is a two-way street. I speak it with the confidence that the person I'm speaking to loves me and wants to do things that make me happy.[5]

When our daughters lived at home, one of their favorite ways to take the "I need your love" vitamin was to ask for a hug. They would walk into the kitchen or the family room with open arms stretched toward Bobbie or me and simply say the words "I need a hug."

> "I need your love" is about putting our unmet expectations into words.

We always rewarded them with wrap-up hugs for free, without ever an "Is there anything you'd like to tell us?" or "What do you want now?" The ability to ask for hugs became an invaluable help when preteen and teenage-girl emotions produced weepy outbursts such as "I don't know what's wrong with me, I just feel like crying."

We didn't ask any questions. We just gave them hugs.

When I was a little boy, my mother taught me a way to communicate "I need your love" without making a sound. She had learned this from her mother.

If we were someplace where lively chatter was inappropriate—in a church service, for example—she reached over and took my hand. Then she squeezed it four times. I squeezed her hand in return, three times. She squeezed my hand twice. And I finished the wordless exchange with one final *really big* squeeze.

Here's the translation:

"Do you love me?" Four words, four squeezes.

"Yes, I do." Three words, three squeezes.

"How much?" Two squeezes.

One last hand-crushing grip. No explanation necessary.

Some Extra Dosage

Several years ago I called one of my closest friends in the world. He lives in another state, and although we've been buddies since childhood, we don't do very well in keeping in touch. It was great to hear his voice.

But a few minutes into the conversation, I could tell something was troubling him. "What's up?" I finally asked, hiding the fact that I suspected that it was more than the Astros' four-game losing streak.

He was silent for a moment. Then he told me that he suspected—at that very moment—that his wife was packing her things into her car and leaving him. The mother of four children was running away from home.

As it turned out, he was on target. A few weeks later I received an e-mail from her. She wrote that she was not off on some short-term fling but that she was gone forever and never going back.

And she kept that promise.

In the years that followed, my friend and I talked about what had happened. In every situation like this there are plenty of complex issues and two-way failures. One of the things that was clear to me—and to him—was that my friend's wife was living with a truckload of unmet expectations.

As with many men, my friend wasn't all that adept at reading his wife's signals or subtle hints; he had missed most of these opportunities to meet his wife's needs. And she had neglected to verbalize her needs and expectations to him.

This "I need your love" vitamin is about daring to tell the ones you love that their expressions of love for you are important and then telling them what's the best way to convey those feelings. Suffering in silence or harboring resentment is not an option. You're not going to do it. Recklessly hoping for spontaneity that's a perfect match for what you need is a perilous risk.

You and your children can learn how to verbalize your needs and ask for help. If you teach them how to ask for affection when they're young, you're giving them a valuable tool to assist them in their own marriages someday.

> "I need your love" is Vitamin #2.

"I need your love" is Vitamin #2.

VITAMIN #3: "I'M SORRY; I WAS WRONG. WILL YOU PLEASE FORGIVE ME?"

Make a fist.

Yes, I mean right now. Go ahead and take one of your hands and make a fist. Now, take a look at the size of your fist and imagine taking a vitamin pill that size.

At least for me, Vitamin #3 can be this hard to swallow. It's a three-layer vitamin that must be spoken in its entirety.

Of course, you understand the purpose for this vitamin. You're to speak it when you've done something or said something that has hurt or insulted or humiliated or infuriated someone in your family. You've been caught and need to make it right.

While playing out on the street, kids might get away with saying, "Sooorrry" when someone gets hurt. But this is completely ineffective in your family. Here's why: "I'm sorry" often sounds like a cliché that expresses no sincere contrition and does nothing to elicit a response that clears the air.

When I've done something to you that needs to get squared away, "I'm sorry" only gets us started. It's important to say, but it's not enough just to leave it there. "I'm sorry" tells you that if I had it to do over again, I wouldn't. The Bible calls this "repentance," and it means that I want to turn over a new leaf, change my ways, and start again.

The problem with "I'm sorry" alone is that it is an incomplete transaction. I've told you what I think about what I've just done but nothing more.

If you listen when people say "I'm sorry," most of the time you hear "Oh, that's okay" or "Don't worry about it" coming back. This doesn't fix the problem. Worse, sometimes people say "I'm sorry" in such a way that it begs a return apology: "I'm sorry too."

Or sometimes your simple "I'm sorry" apology just falls flat: "Oh, it's nothing."

"I'm sorry" needs some companions to make it most effective. "I was wrong" pronounces the verdict where it belongs: on *you*. As a speeder appearing in traffic court and charged with exceeding the limit would say, "Guilty as charged, your Honor." It eliminates the need for any argument about who is responsible for the wrongdoing. It doesn't say "I'm sorry *if* you're sorry." It doesn't say "I'm sorry that I got caught." And it doesn't say, "I'm sorry because I know that you expect me to say 'I'm sorry,' but I'm really *not* that sorry."

"I was wrong" added to "I'm sorry" eliminates the need for any argument. You're not going to try to justify yourself, calling it an accident or saying, as our Julie used to say when she was a little girl, "But I didn't *mean* to."

Now that I've told you how I feel about what I've done and I've pronounced judgment on myself, it's time to ask you to release me from what I've done. "Will you please forgive me?" is your request for exactly that release. When you say yes to my question, the slate is wiped clean. The transaction is complete. This nullifies the wrong.

> "I was wrong" pronounces the verdict where it belongs: on *you*.

If I say only "I'm sorry," you might say, "Don't worry about it," even if I had really hurt your feelings. That's not good enough.

If I take the next step and say, "I was wrong," you might say, "You can say that again." Still not good enough.

But if I ask you a question that requires a response—"Will you forgive me?"—then you have given me a chance to start all over again. You say yes, and we're good to go.

If I use this vitamin and you don't say yes to my question about forgiveness, I'll know that I still have some work to do. However, this rarely happens. People are usually quick to forgive others who are truly sorry for what they've done.

Some Extra Dosage

Some of my closest friends are lawyers. Most of them have lovely personalities, and I enjoy riding with them in their shiny new S-Class Mercedes. Of course, lawyers do a lot of good things, such as help me with my closing documents when I buy a house or file my incorporation papers when I start a company or help draft my will.

But some of my lawyer friends would have a difficult time making ends meet if more people used this vitamin: "I'm sorry; I was wrong. Will you please forgive me?" Instead, too many people—lawyers call these folks "clients"—say, "You're sorry; you were wrong. I'll see you in court."

When I think back on arguments I've had with my wife or members of my family, disappointment fills me. If I had said, "I'm sorry; I was wrong. Will you please forgive me?" a fight would have come to a screeching halt.

Instead, I was quick to justify myself, pass my wrong-doing off as an innocent mistake, or accuse someone of being overly sensitive, even suggesting that the person "get over it." In too many instances this thoughtlessness has escalated a simple argument into an all-out war. My foolish pride has taken me where I didn't want to go. Shame on me.

I'm reminded of the wisdom of Dr. Henry Brandt, one of the pioneers in Christian marital counseling. One day he told me that he had discovered the secret of helping husbands and wives restore their broken relationships. This he accomplished with a simple question to the man and woman at the start of their counseling sessions: "What do you have to confess to your spouse?"

The thick walls separating these two adversaries began to crumble. Marriages were saved.

Vitamin #3 may feel like it's the size of your fist. At times, it may seem impossible to swallow. But when you choke and gag and finally get it down, great things will happen in your family.

"I'm sorry; I was wrong. Will you please forgive me?" is Vitamin #3.

> "I'm sorry; I was wrong. Will you please forgive me?" is Vitamin #3.

VITAMIN #4: "MAY I HELP?"

Sometimes I picture myself in a recovery group among friends. "I'm Robert," I say.

"Hi, Robert," everyone responds.

"I'm Robert," I repeat, "and I'm lazy."

As far as I know, there are no chapters of Lazies Anonymous out there, but there could be. And I would be a member.

Now before you jump to any inaccurate conclusions about my work habits, I'm actually not talking about laziness when it comes to work-work. Career work. Project work. I'm driven in these settings and sometimes tend to overwork: workaholism. There *are* recovery groups for that. That's not the laziness I'm referring to.

What I'm talking about is a propensity for laziness that involves things around the house. I know that my dad suffered from this as well, which is why he said, "Look for things to do" when he saw us not doing something productive. As you realize now that you are one, parents sometimes reveal their own weaknesses by the errant behavior they focus on in their kids.

As a grown-up with a wife and a family, I discovered that I can work like a dog at the office or on the racquetball court or building a deck on the back of the house, but when it's time to do the dishes, my motivation and energy suddenly disappear. Severe lethargy sets in.

Or when I'm watching something on TV and I get thirsty, I am tempted to holler into the kitchen to see if someone might be able to bring me something to drink.[6] That is why I love to hear somebody say, "Oh, don't be silly, I'll do the dishes," or "Let me bring you a glass of iced tea."

Vitamin #4 is an admission that having a successful family can be a lot of work. There's a pile of laundry on the floor: "May I help?"

> Working together creates a camaraderie that's unparalleled by anything else.

There's so much junk in the garage there's barely enough room for the car: "May I help?" The baby's diaper needs changing: "May I help?" There's something sticky on the kitchen floor: "May I help?"

These words work like magic in a family. And even better, working together creates a camaraderie that's unparalleled by anything else.

We Are Here to Build You Up

"Hey, let's build a house!"

The words came out of my mouth with no premeditation or forethought. I was teaching a Sunday school class at our church in Nashville when the idea blew through my mind like an unexpected thunderstorm.

"We've been meeting in this class for many years, and it's been great," I said. "But I think it's time we get busy this summer and work on something special together."

The response was immediate and unanimous. Someone volunteered to contact the local chapter of Habitat for Humanity, and in a few weeks we were standing on an empty lot, the site of "our" house. Habitat had screened and qualified a family to live in the house. They were standing there with us.

Tennessee summers can be unbearably hot and humid. This one was no exception. But no one cared. We were on a mission, and it felt great.

Volunteers showed up by the carload. Those who couldn't swing a hammer brought cold drinks and sandwiches for lunch. Eight weeks later, we had a ribbon-cutting ceremony and dedication service for our finished house. We prayed together and then all exchanged tears and hugs as we celebrated.

For years to follow, our corporate experience of "May I help?" became the most unifying thing that our Sunday school class had ever done.

The same kind of goodwill can happen in your home when you start speaking this vitamin.

Some Extra Dosage

One day as the Little Red Hen was scratching in the field, she found a grain of wheat.

"This wheat should be planted," she said. "Who will plant this grain of wheat?"

"Not I," said the duck.

"Not I," said the cat.

"Not I," said the dog.

"Then I will," said the Little Red Hen. And she did.[7]

You may remember this story from your childhood. I do. In fact, as an unusually sensitive little boy, I recall feeling so sorry for the hapless little red hen: so much to do, and no one willing to help her. Today it makes me smile to think that I had compassion on this imaginary little crimson bird.

But in real life, feeling as if no one is willing to share in the work-load around your house is no laughing matter. Working without any volunteers to help makes people feel lonely. Isolated. Used. And these feelings can escalate into unfortunate outbursts of anger and frustration, doing damage to everyone in sight.

"May I help?" turns the pain of isolated drudgery into a team sport and flimsy solos into a choir of strong voices.

Working together is a powerful way of loving each other in your home.

"May I help?" is Vitamin #4.

> "May I help?" is Vitamin #4.

VITAMIN #5: "THANK YOU"

When people buy a new car, they receive a list of features that are "standard equipment." No additional charge for the basics. Then they face lots of choices—options—to make their car extra special.

Saying thank you is not an option. It must be standard equipment in your home. We talked about gratitude in chapter 4, and we're going to talk about it again because it's so important. Gratitude is a way of seeing ourselves as recipients of blessings rather than demanders of rights. "Thank you" is our way of letting others know we notice their efforts. Even if their work might be considered ordinary, it's reason to be grateful.

Clean and folded things in your underwear drawer. Another paycheck. A delicious meal. Gas in the car. A shampooed dog. Homework finished. An emptied dishwasher. These, and many others that you could list, are all good reasons to say thank you.

> Gratitude is a way of seeing ourselves as recipients of blessings rather than demanders of rights.

Our regular expressions of thankfulness, even for the *daily* things others do for us, fill them with a sense of satisfaction and pride and keep our hearts tender and humble.

"Thank you" is a powerful vitamin that can be as wonderful in writing as it is when it's spoken. When I was a youngster, my paternal grandparents always tucked five-dollar bills in their Christmas cards to my siblings and me. Receiving this money was good news and bad news.

It was good news because of what I might have been able to buy with the money. But it was bad news because I was allowed to spend it only after I had written a thank-you note. For a reason that's still a conundrum to me, I hated writing thank-you notes. Of course, part of the reason was the way our grandma bugged us about it.

"Did you receive the money?" she asked every time we talked post Christmas. "Yes, ma'am," we said with a sigh. Her question was a request for the thank-you note she deserved, but her incessant bugging made it even more difficult to write. Eventually, however, we buckled under and wrote the note . . . and spent the money.

Many years later, when I got married, this same grandmother was still on her thank-you note jag. About a month after our wedding, Bobbie received a letter from her grandmother-in-law. She opened the letter and read the simple note inside:

Hello, Bobbie.
    I hope you're well. In this part of the country it's customary for brides to send thank-you notes for the wedding gifts she receives. I have spoken with several folks here who have also not received one from you.

Sincerely,
Grandma

Inside were a half-dozen first-class stamps.

Neither the letter nor the postage amused Bobbie. But it did give me a chance to tell some of my own stories about my relentless grandmother with the thank-you note obsession.

Fifty years later I have something to say to my long-gone grandmother, even though her tact was straight out of Attila the Hun's playbook: thank you for bugging me about writing thank-you notes. You were right.

Several years ago best-selling business author Tom Peters wrote a book called *In Pursuit of Wow*. I enjoyed the book and would like to give you a two-sentence book report right now on what I learned: Write thank-you notes. It will transform your work into business success.

He's right.

In 1994, after reading Peters's book, I remembered my inexorable grandmother's tactless admonitions. I ordered special note cards with my name printed at the top, similar to ones I had received from some thoughtful friends, and started using them to say thank you.

Then once, during a Sunday school class lesson, I talked about the importance of saying thank you. I challenged my friends in the class to take out a piece of paper that afternoon and make a list of people in their lives who needed to hear—or read—"Thank you."

The next week Dr. Anderson Spickard stopped me on my way into church. He had a twinkle in his eye, so I knew he was going to kid me about something.

Sure enough.

"Thanks for ruining my day last Sunday," Andy said, unsuccessfully trying to make me feel guilty. "After lunch I sat down and made my list, and it took me the rest of the day to make my thank-you phone calls and write my thank-you notes. You ruined my day," he playfully repeated.

Taking the same risk I took in challenging our Sunday school class that day, what would happen if you took out a piece of paper right now and made a list of people who need to hear thank you from you?

Some Extra Dosage

There may be no more exhilarating emotion for the folks living at your house than to feel appreciated. And there may be no more enriching thing to your own heart than to live with gratitude.

"Thank you" is Vitamin #5.

People living in a Christian home can experience this in full measure.

"Thank you" is Vitamin #5.

YOU MAY BE WONDERING

As I said from the very beginning, we have called these Family Vitamins. I have told a lot of people about them. I've introduced them by saying that the purpose of these vitamins is to keep one's family healthy. I've quipped about the fact that paramedics don't carry vitamins in the shiny white trucks zipping along the highway. "They carry serious drugs such as valium, hydrochlorothiazide, and morphine," I have said.[8] "Vitamins are for healthy people who want to stay healthy."

But I've changed my mind about these vitamins. Sure, they're for healthy families, but now I believe that they're also for families in crisis. They will work like a miracle cure for traumatized clans that are experiencing serious chest pains or are in a ditch along some busy highway.

So even though we call them Family Vitamins, these aren't just a collection of good things to keep you strong; they're also capable of saving your family's life.

That's why I added the "Some Extra Dosage" sections—to give you an idea of the power of these vitamins when you're in serious, 911 trouble.

And don't forget to take them every day.

There may be no more exhilarating emotion for the folks living at your house than to feel appreciated. And there may be no more enriching thing to your own heart than to live with gratitude.

7

JUST FOR LAUGHS

The Best Medicine of All

Years ago when the editors at *Reader's Digest* decided to call their humor page "Laughter: The Best Medicine," they really got it right. The most important place on earth must include this magic elixir.

HUMOR GONE BAD—EXHIBIT A

My dad was in London. Maybe it was Singapore. Or New Delhi. Regardless, he wasn't home.[1] During those times when my mother had to run the operation as a sole proprietor, she kept the family dinner hour intact. It wasn't that she was heavy-handed about it, but we knew that she'd give a complete report when dad returned, and there was no use in tempting fate. *He* was all the heavy hand she needed, even when he wasn't there.

We were sitting around the dinner table. As I recall, Ruth, my older sister, was off to college, so it was the five of us and mother. Sam, my oldest brother, was a high-school junior.

During a lull in the conversation, Sam decided that he was going to take a journey on the Starship Enterprise, going where no man had ever gone before. Apparently, he had heard a joke at school that day and since it had something of a biblical theme, he thought he'd give it a shot at dinner. Unfortunately, in addition to the positive quality of mentioning a Bible character in the punch line, the joke would have been classified as "borderline" humor. Which, in my parents' book, would have been as welcome as a dingo coming to the house to babysit.

I'll cut to the chase and tell you that over forty years later, my brother still regrets having made this decision. This one ranks up there alongside the Japanese declaring war on America and the Cubs' decision to trade Lou Brock for Ernie Broglio.[2]

"What stretches farther, rubber or skin?" my brother asked. Sam posed this question without even indicating that it was the opening line for a joke. We looked at Sam, then at each other, and then back at him. Someone must have shrugged because I don't remember any of us actually answering him with a guess.

"Skin stretches farther than rubber," Sam finally said in response to the nervous silence that was beginning to settle over the table. By that time we knew he was telling a joke, but something told us that we were in for anything but a belly laugh.

"It does not," my not-so-gullible little sister finally said. Debbie wasn't going to let her big brother get away with saying something so ridiculous.

By then Sam's ears were beginning to grow crimson. The anticipation of actually speaking the words of the punch line in this setting must have begun working on him. The story sounded so funny when he was with his buddies at school. But as he looked around the table at his three younger brothers, his little sister, and his mother (thousands of miles away from her husband), he must have concluded that this *wasn't* school and these *weren't* his chums and his timing *may* have been a little off. But like an airplane streaking down the runway at liftoff speed, Sam had passed the point of no return.

"We know that skin stretches farther than rubber because

Abraham tied his ass to a tree and walked forty miles," he said, proudly squeezing out a smirking attempt at a smile.[3]

Every sensation of apprehension that Sam may have had before telling his joke around the dinner table became pure prophecy. No one laughed. In fact, we all did exactly the same thing: we turned and looked at our mother.

The best way to describe my mother's face is to ask you to recall the last time you were blasted with a full-blown wave of food poisoning. "Oh, Sam," she gasped in the same tone of voice she would have used if he had just announced his full conversion to Islam. Mother immediately left the table and went downstairs to be alone and collect what was left of her thoughts.

As though we were watching a slow-motion tennis match, once our mother disappeared around the corner, we all slowly turned like a spotlight on my big brother.

Sam was not smiling.

THE SERIOUS BUSINESS OF LAUGHTER

Although Sam completely botched the particular selection of a joke in his attempt at humor, his intentions were valiant. We *did* have a far-too-serious family that needed strong doses of laughter. By now, you know how grateful I am for my parents and siblings. But levity *is* one thing I wish we had come across more in the early years.

This was my only experience of growing up, and I had the pure luxury of getting to do this in a Christian home. A real one. We knew how to work hard together. We sat at the dinner table, engaged in great conversation, and grew to love each other sincerely. We learned about God and read His Word as a family. Vacations were varied and interesting.

But with all these good things, there is something else that I now believe is a vital piece of the Christian home puzzle. It's the serious business of laughter.

There's no question that the Germanic air of sobriety that hung over our home was genetic. Even though my maternal grandfather, Monroe Sharpe Dourte, had a great laugh and used it all the time as I was growing up, his own eight children will tell you that he rarely employed this characteristic when they were small.

> There is something else that I now believe is a vital piece of the Christian home puzzle. It's the serious business of laughter.

As I've mentioned, we had great reverence for my paternal grandfather, Graybill G. Wolgemuth,[4] but no one would have accused him, even in his later life, of being any fun at all. One summer my brother Ken and I spent a couple weeks with that set of grandparents. Grandpa decided that we needed some old-fashioned work, as though our parents hadn't done a good enough job of training us. So he drove us to a cherry orchard. It was harvest time, and the orchard featured twenty-seven million trees, dripping with ripe cherries, ready to be picked.

"Put these city boys to work," grandpa ordered the foreman. From that moment forward we knew for sure that grandpa would have a hard time doing stand-up at the local comedy club. He wasn't joking, and we weren't laughing.

Both of my grandfathers were second-generation German, which meant that there was some serious bratwurst tucked into their collective DNA. Because of this shared heritage, our learning to laugh and enjoy the lighter side of life together didn't come naturally. We needed help, and it came not a moment too soon.

ENTER DANNY

Today, as the president of a worldwide youth ministry, he's Dan. But if he'll forgive me for using the diminutive of his name in this context, our youngest brother, Danny, was just what our family needed.

In birth order, I was number four. Ruth was born in 1941, Sam in 1943, Ken in 1945, and I was born in 1948. In 1955, seven and a half years later, mother gave birth to twins. Debbie was born first, and Dan followed four minutes later.[5]

The last kid born had a view of our family from a different angle. As a youngster, he had a happy disposition. Like a Double-Stuff Oreo, Danny was loaded with perpetual joy.

By the time he could ride a bicycle, Danny helped me with my early morning *Chicago Tribune* route. In the subzero darkness I woke up, took the bundle of newspapers from the end of my driveway, cut the wire with pliers, then sat on the garage floor, folding each paper and putting a rubber band around it. This was long before plastic bags were introduced to paper-routing.

Then I went into Dan's bedroom and coaxed him awake. "Get up, Danny," I whispered, "it's time for *your* route." The beginning of my own entrepreneurial days, I had subcontracted eight houses at the east end of Elm Street, between Gamon and Naperville Roads, as Danny's Paper Route.

Without exception, every time I woke him up, he smiled at me and crawled out from under the warm covers immediately. I don't ever recall a word of complaint. He pulled on his socks and jeans and sweatshirt, and we were off together.

Imagine how amazed the folks living in those eight houses were when a happy little boy, no more than five years old, began delivering their morning papers. Sometimes they came outside, even though it was very early, and called out their greeting to this miniature paper boy.

Actually, we didn't have to wonder how amazed they were. Around Christmastime, when people tip paperboys, Danny got more money out of those eight houses than I got from my 108. He had brought happiness to those folks too.

CHRISTMAS FOR A NONBELIEVER

In our house Santa Claus was synonymous with Satan. I can still hear my dad making *tsk tsk tsk* noises when we drove past one of those big light-on-the-inside plastic Santa replicas on a neighbor's front yard. The fact that he was waving and smiling broadly at my dad made no difference at all.

Of course, this disdain for the jolly old elf was part of his growing-up indoctrination and legend. My dad's grandfather had dressed up as Santa Claus one Christmas Eve when dad's mother was a little girl. That night their house burned to the ground. For the remainder of her life, grandma Wolgemuth considered the inferno God's judgment on the family for "having Santa Claus." And it wasn't only my father she drilled with the nightmare story. I got it in every detail as soon as I was old enough to say the words *season's greetings*.

So no one even mentioned Santa's name at our house over the holidays. The jelly-bellied man with his finger aside his nose was *persona non grata*.[6]

One Christmas morning when Danny was probably ten years old, we noticed an envelope clipped to the Christmas tree. We didn't discover it until we were finishing up our family one-at-a-time, decently-and-in-order-gift-opening ritual.

The envelope was retrieved and handed to my mother. She ceremoniously read the inscription: "To Samuel from Santa."

Every person in the room held his or her breath. *Who did this?* we collectively wondered.

Dad received the envelope as if he had been handed a booger. He pulled out his pocketknife (which he kept in his front pocket at all times, including his pajama pocket, I think), slit the envelope, and pulled out a one-dollar gift certificate from McDonald's. He haltingly read it aloud: "To Samuel. Merry Christmas from Santa Claus."

Dad looked around the room to see if we were listening.

This was history unfolding before our eyes.

There was more. Dad read on, "Consider yourself lucky. I do not normally give gifts to unbelievers."

Eyes darted. *Who had the guts to do this?* In a moment the grin on his face identified the culprit. Everyone else was in shock.

Danny, the only person on the earth's crust who could have— and lived to tell the story—had pulled it off.

In moments, we were all laughing together. Including dad.

This felt so good.

MY OWN LAUGHTER DEBUT

One month after Dan's Christmas adventure, I took a daring expedition of my own into "humorland." Every spring our Wheaton Community High School held a variety/talent show. It was called "The Varsity Show." In my memory, I'm not sure if any of my older siblings were allowed to even attend the performance, much less participate. I took a chance.

This was when the star of a brilliant comedian named Stan Freberg was on the rise. His bits played on the radio, and his albums were hot sellers at the record store. The first time I heard one of his pieces on WLS radio, I remember laughing out loud. It was a hilarious replay of George Washington's crossing of the Delaware from inside the rowboat. I was hooked.

One afternoon over lunch, I asked a few of my buddies if they'd be interested in joining me in memorizing some Stan Freberg sketches, then auditioning for the Varsity Show with a comedy routine. They thought it was a great idea.

Of course, my next hurdle was to clear this with my father. To my shock and delight, it wasn't such a hard sell. He agreed. (Thanks, Danny.)

If I may say so, my debut as a comedian was flawless. My favorite moment was getting to play the part of Thomas Jefferson.

The sketch began with my friend, Jerry Heslinga (Ben Franklin), entering stage left. "Hey, Tom," he cheerily greeted me (Thomas Jefferson). I was sitting at a table in the center of the stage.

"Oh, hello, Ben," I responded, looking up from my work. I laid the feather quill down.

"What're you doing?"

"Writing this piece. I'm calling it the Declaration of Independence."

"Really? Let me see it," Benjamin Franklin said as he walked over to my desk. He picked up the piece of parchment that I had been hand-lettering with great flourish and began to read aloud. "We hold these things to be self-evident," Ben read with great aplomb, "that all men are created equal, that they are endowed by their Creator with certain unalienable rights, that among these are Life, Liberty, and the *Purſuit of Happineſſ?*"

I put my hands behind my head and leaned back, milking the moment.

"What *is* this?" Ben asked. "Purſuit of happineſſ? Your *s*'s look like *f*'s."

"Oh, that's the cool way we do things now," I responded confidently.

"No kidding?" Ben answered, scratching his powdered wig.

We did four of these sketches, and the audience loved every one. My comedic debut was a success. I discovered that I had the ability to laugh and to make others laugh. This was a defining moment in my life.

> I discovered that I had the ability to laugh and to make others laugh. This was a defining moment in my life.

ENTER MY OWN FAMILY

Many years later, I had finished high school, moved past college graduation and my wedding day, and was into fatherhood. It had been ten years since my theatrical debut as a humorist, and, given the sobriety of life—including figuring out the daddy thing and digging out a career with my fingernails—I had forgotten most of the laughter lessons I had learned.

Fortunately I had chosen a very happy wife. And it was her directive—something like "C'mon, Robert, you're going to have to lighten up"—that got my attention. Like an old oxcart on a dirt road, I had unconsciously dropped my wheels into my genetic heredity. The furrows on my forehead were getting as deep as the plowed ruts in my grandpa's potato field.

She's right, I remember thinking. *I am boring.*

Over the next few years, with determined focus, laughing Robert reappeared. Sure, life was still serious business, but that didn't mean I couldn't play "monster on the landing" or hide-and-seek with the girls, complete with yelling and running through the house and occasionally knocking something over. Bobbie must have had second thoughts about challenging me to lighten up.

I went to a bookstore and bought a riddle book.

Why is honey so expensive in Massachusetts?
There's only one *B* in Boston.

Where do fish keep their money?
In the riverbank.

Can giraffes have babies?
No, they can only have giraffes.

I bought Groucho Marx glasses with the attached mustache and tucked them in my pocket one night when we went out to dinner. After the blessing, I turned away from the table and slipped the glasses on. "How ya doin'?" I said, as I turned around. The children squealed with delight.

I even agreed to put on a Santa Claus suit and circle the neighborhood after dark on Christmas Eve, "Ho-ho-ho-ing" at the top of my voice. Fortunately, my grandmother did not live in our neighborhood.

And now that raising our family is in the past tense, I'm absolutely convinced that humor is an essential part of a healthy Christian home. King Solomon, arguably the smartest man to ever draw a breath of air, said it this way:

> A merry heart makes a cheerful countenance,
> But by sorrow of the heart the spirit is broken. (Proverbs 15:13)

> A cheerful look brings joy to the heart;
> good news makes for good health. (Proverbs 15:30 NLT)

> A cheerful heart is good medicine. (Proverbs 17:22 NIV)

Here's my point: for a healthy family, laughter ranks right up there, being just as important as honoring each other, attending church together, and engaging in meaningful conversation.

And here's another point: unless you were born with an extra funny bone, creating laughter in your home is going to have to be part of a plan. If, for instance, you and your spouse are more like me than like Danny, it's time to do something intentional about it.

RULES FOR LAUGHTER

Laughter needs rules?

You may be thinking, *I always thought laughter was a spontaneous thing. It feels kind of awkward to actually* plan *for fun and levity in our home.*

Yes, that's what I'm saying. Since it's important, and since you may not be a natural

> Unless you were born with an extra funny bone, creating laughter in your home is going to have to be part of a plan.

comedian, planning for humor in your home is precisely what you need to do.

If you owned a retail business and were gunning for success, you could just open your front door and hope that folks impulsively walked in and bought something. Or you could put together a marketing plan that creates traffic. Which strategy gives you the best chance?

Bobbie came in one day from her favorite store, TJ Maxx. "I know why I anticipate going so often to TJ's," she said. "It's because I like the effort the managers put into their displays. Every week they change the items in the front of the store, and I enjoy looking at all the new stuff."

Great marketing? Yes. Like new display items sprinkled all over your home to make it inviting and winsome, a few lighthearted riddles and family jokes can make it a place your family is delighted to live in.

Okay, so if you're going to have a home where there's laughter, you're going to have to come up with a plan. Here are some essentials to include.

Laugh at Yourself

A century and a half ago, a French priest named Henri de Tourville wrote: "It is a splendid habit to laugh inwardly at yourself. It is the best way of regaining your good humour and of finding God without further anxiety."[7]

I guess the challenge of laughing at ourselves has been going on for a long time.

When Bobbie encouraged me to lighten up, this is what she was really saying: "I want to enjoy being in your presence. I need some happy showcase items to draw me in."

In order to be a person she enjoyed being with, I had to realize that the inability to laugh at myself is usually caused by two things. My focused sobriety on the tasks at hand and my unwillingness to laugh at my own foibles are caused by work overload: too much to do and not enough time to do it. You can identify this malady when you feel that knot in your stomach, a frantic sensation. This can actually make you feel out of breath.

"Why did I say yes to one more thing?" you say out loud. "I'll never get everything done," you sigh. "What's the matter with me?" And you stop laughing.

And what often happens is that everyone around you pays the price for your stress.

If you've ever had someone try to joke with you during these times of frenzy, you know how unsuccessful he can be. And *he* knows he's been unsuccessful because you barked or snarled in response to his lightheartedness.

When Missy was engaged to be married to Jon, she gave me permission to coordinate the wedding activities—much like Franklin Roosevelt gave George Patton permission to coordinate America's military activities in Northern Africa in 1942.

I say that she "gave me permission," but actually I begged her for the job. It was shameless. I had been to so many weddings that had been managed, in my opinion, of course, like day-care playgrounds. I was interested in having a wedding that snapped with the heavy starch of regimented perfection.

In mid-September 1994, as the wedding party was gathering for the rehearsal, an unexpected and huge thunderstorm rumbled through the south side of Nashville. This thunderstorm was not on my schedule. With a flash of lightning and a huge boom, the church went black. Fortunately, there was still enough daylight so we could at least walk through the processional sequence. Unfortunately, the organ in our big church was electric, not the pump kind, so the practice had to continue without the piped anthem.

What a great opportunity for fun. Except that I didn't see any of it. I had been put in charge; I had planned out each moment; I had printed a guide booklet for each participant to follow, complete with time marks . . . and we were running late. I was going to fix that problem.

True to form for a bunch of twenty-somethings, the wedding party, and, if I might say so, the youthful minister, were whooping it up, celebrating the fun of the unplanned silent darkness.

"Would everyone *please be quiet*!" I roared in my best outside voice.

At that moment the bride—also my daughter—burst into tears. Her mother—also my wife—tried to console her. I took command, all right. An hour of harsh unpleasantness followed.

In retrospect, shame on me. Double-dip shame on me for trying to get through the situation with the precision of the Blue Angels at the speed of sound . . . only to lose the hearts of the people I wanted to please in the first place.

> What a great opportunity for fun. Except that I didn't see any of it.

I learned this lesson the hard way. And although it's been reduced to funny family folklore by now, the sting of the memory and my daughter's horrified embarrassment still make me cringe. Stress is one great enemy of laughing at yourself.

Another reason people like me have a hard time laughing at themselves is pride, pure and simple. If I make a mistake—especially a public one—it's my pride that keeps me from stepping back and creating a moment of levity that everyone can enjoy, even if it's at *my* expense.

Less than a year after Bobbie and I moved to Orlando, she was asked to sing a solo in both Sunday morning worship services at our church. Her first presentation went perfectly. Even though I've heard her sing hundreds of times, I got a serious lump in my throat as she sang "The Love of God."

I eagerly sat on the front row again for the second service. The organist finished his musical introduction, and Bobbie stepped to the microphone. When she opened her mouth, a squeaking glottal sound I've never heard before came out. If you've ever heard a squirrel holler to his buddy in the next tree, that's about as close as I can come to describing what went through the sound system that morning at *the* First Presbyterian Church of Orlando.

In an unexpected instant, Bobbie faced an opportunity. If she had been counting on her performance as a chance to impress a thousand people and advance her musical career, rather than what it truly was, an experience of service and worship, she would have been embarrassed. Crushed by the failure.

"Oh, whoops," Bobbie whispered with a smile. A sympathetic wisp of laughter wafted over the congregation. She turned and nodded to the organist, who repeated the last few notes of his introduction. The next time her first note was on target, and she finished the song as beautifully as she had in the first service.

I was stunned. A proud person—no one comes to mind at this moment—could have been decimated by this. But because her heart was set with humility and gratitude, Bobbie was thoroughly unaffected by the faux pas . . . a very public faux pas.

Your challenge as a parent is to set aside pinpoint agendas and the temptation toward self-focused embarrassment and enjoy a good laugh with one of the world's strangest people. You.

Strange . . . like this: Many years ago I was alone for seven days and six nights while Bobbie was in Charlotte with our kids and grandkids. Even though I fixed at least one decent meal for myself per day, I did not run the dishwasher a single time. Why? I reused plates and found wonderful ways of substituting a paper towel for dinnerware. Toss it in the trash when I'm finished, and the kitchen is clean again.

I've compared notes with friends on this and discovered that many men do the same. We've concluded that our wives, in the same solo situation, would never use a paper towel instead of a plate for a sandwich or a piece of toast or a serving of pasta. Never.

While I was working on the manuscript for the first edition of this book, Bobbie walked into my

> Enjoy a good laugh with one of the world's strangest people. You.

office and offered me a slice of apple. When I saw how she served the apple, it made me smile. With a simple flick of her wrist, she was able to turn a single apple into a fanned squadron of uniform slices, like really thin hockey pucks. The apple slices were carefully lined up, like leaning soldiers on a crystal dish. This is not something I would even think of doing, much less actually do. If I want an apple, I pick up one and take a bite. (I'm certain that the grocer washed it well enough to remove worm droppings.) I don't dirty the sink, a knife, a cutting board, or, for goodness' sake, a crystal dish that cannot be wadded up and thrown in the trash.

Most women would never think of drinking directly out of the orange juice container or spitting in the kitchen sink when no one is looking. Of course, my male comrades would *never* do this either.

This is what I mean by "strange."

In a family—and you may have noticed this yourself—self-humor is wonderfully contagious. When our children observe our ability to *be* the brunt of our own jokes and to laugh at our own quirks and eccentricities, they'll have a pattern to follow for themselves.

This results in far less touchiness and fewer broken hearts and angry outbursts . . . and more fun at home.

Homemade Laughter

Once we catch the vision for adding a solid dose of laughter to our families, you may be tempted—especially if you tend more toward lackluster than sizzling—to try exclusively to *buy* laughter and fun rather than create it.

Yes, such as my admission that I bought some riddle books early on. You may decide you need some commercial help with this. But the best kind of laughter in your home is always the homemade kind.

We made up "the kissing monster is coming to get you" and hide-and-seek at our own house, and I've been reminded of the value of homemade laughter again as a grandfather. I noticed this on a recent visit to our older daughter and son-in-law's home. They're terrific at encouraging homemade happiness.

Because of the construction of a new addition to their home, there was a delectable dirt pile in the backyard. There was also a big gravel hill. Both of these entertained the children, and their friends, for hours. Because I was helping with the construction, I had a bird's-eye view of it all. At one point my granddaughter proudly called up to me and asked if I was interested in some "mud pudding" she was making in one of her mother's good mixing bowls—with her mother's unqualified permission.

"Yum, yum," I called from the second-floor window. "Maybe some for lunch."

"Okay, granddaddy." Abby giggled and went back to stirring.

The day before, our kids and grandkids had rendezvoused with their good friends, who also have young kids, at a local playground for a whole afternoon of swinging, sliding, and sandboxing. Homemade fun.

Almost every evening between dinner and bath time, my sons-in-law tussle on the living room floor with their children. This inspires lots of laughing and shrieks of joy, as well as the predictable "Hey, what's going on out there?" from mom in the next room.

None of these activities were plugged into power outlets. None of them required batteries or had to be put back in the box when they were finished.

As creative as store-bought toys can be, homemade laughter is more fun than anything else.

Go ahead and think back to the happiest times of your own childhood. Even though I'm not a gambling man, I would be willing to bet that those things that come to your mind didn't include your gazing into a television screen or enjoying something store-bought that was invented to give you some kind of childhood enjoyment.

As creative as store-bought toys can be, homemade laughter is more fun than anything else.

The best kind of happy memories are almost always the result of creative, interactive play.

Laugh with Your Kids, Never at Them

Earlier in this chapter, I told you of Bobbie's admonition for me to lighten up, to laugh at myself. You and I need to do things that allow ourselves to be the subject of the laughter. And our example helps our kids to laugh at their own occasional silliness too.

But be careful. Yes, you should laugh at yourself. Your children may laugh at you, and you should encourage your children to laugh at themselves. But you never laugh *at* your children. You laugh *with* them.

Aw, come on, you might be thinking. *Aren't you getting a little technical here?*

When Harper, our granddaughter, was one year old, Julie taught her animal sounds. The next time Harper and her parents visited us, Julie let her demonstrate some lighthearted play.

"Harper, what does a duck say?" her proud mother asked.

"Quack," Harper replied with a huge smile on her face.

Granddaddy and nanny were, of course, delighted.

Little Harper went through the list with accurate and animated sounds for each animal. We got cow, dog, cat, and tiger.

Then Julie set Harper up for the zinger: "What does a *squirrel* say?"

"Nuts," Harper dramatically announced.

Of course we all broke into spontaneous laughter. And Harper was thrilled. We could tell this wasn't the first time she had wowed an audience. Harper had learned something that actually made grown-ups laugh. Harper's mom is smart enough to know that when a child is able to create a "laugh with" moment, it's a powerful boost to her confidence.

But what if, when she was asked what a doggy says, she had responded with "Moo"? And what if we had laughed and made a snide comment? Can you envision the look on the toddler's face as her audience mocked her error? You've witnessed this, haven't you? You've seen how teasing—even if it's not intended to hurt—has the power to wound and close a child's spirit.

It's just a bad idea. Don't laugh *at* your children. Encourage them, instead, by being a front-row cheerleader.

Do you remember when we talked about the power of words to inspire the heart of a youngster, how critical words could destroy a kid's esteem? Laughing with your child has the same possibility for inspiration—laughing *at* your children has a weighty, devastating potential. "I was just kidding," when you've broken your youngster's heart with a mocking laugh, isn't going to fix it. If you've ever experienced this mistake, you know exactly what I'm talking about.

> Teasing—even if it's not intended to hurt—has the power to wound and close a child's spirit.

Even though you didn't intend your thoughtless laugh to be vicious, its impact is undeniable. And once mocking has been turned loose in your home, its effects can be horrendous. Apparently this was also a problem a few thousand years ago:

> The eye that mocks a father
> and scorns to obey a mother
> will be picked out by the ravens of the valley
> and eaten by the vultures. (Proverbs 30:17 ESV)

Eyes that mock becoming bird food: now there's a graphic word picture.

SARCASTIC HUMOR AND CYNICISM ARE POISON

I mentioned this briefly in chapter 3, but it's worth repeating here. Sarcasm is disrespectful and has a nasty first cousin: cynicism. Where mocking is usually attached to a specific event—like the dog mooing

I just mentioned—cynicism is an attitude. It's a person's way of coloring almost everything with a crayon of scorn.

Because of its dangerous contagion, by choice, I have no close friends who are cynical. I cannot afford to hang out for long periods of time with people who are sarcastic. Their influence in relationships can be poisonous.[8]

> A scoffer does not love one who corrects him,
> Nor will he go to the wise.

> A merry heart makes a cheerful countenance,
> But by sorrow of the heart the spirit is broken. (Proverbs 15:12–13)

By choice
I have
no close
friends who
are cynical.

For sixteen years, I lived in Orange County, Florida, a reminder of one of the state's most important industries: oranges. (The talking Mouse is the other one.) There are orange trees everywhere, in groves, in people's backyards, and in city parks, right next to baseball fields. Annual orange revenues in Florida are more than $10 billion.[9]

Every once in a while, especially during the late winter and early spring, we read something in the newspaper about a disease called the orange canker. Canker is a bacterium that causes unsightly brown blemishes on the fruit and can cause it to drop prematurely from trees. It doesn't harm humans, but it destroys orange trees. A new state law has stepped in to put an end to this disease. When a tree is found to have canker, the agriculture department can cut down every tree within nineteen hundred feet of the infected tree. And they can do this *without the permission of the owner!*[10]

You'd think that this law would be devastating to orange growers, wouldn't you? But it's not. "This is *very good news* for citrus growers who have, over the past ten years, lost 2.1 million citrus trees due to the spread of this devastating disease," said Andy LaVigne, Florida

Citrus Mutual's executive vice president/CEO. "This ruling will allow the state to do its job and eradicate citrus canker from our state."[11]

Folks who grow orange trees know the power of a bad tree and are willing to sacrifice every tree within a quarter of a mile to eliminate its deadly influence.

Although I would discourage the actual use of chainsaws in your family, the principle should be clear. Laughter in your home cannot be tainted with cynicism. Do everything you can to stop its spread.

Scornful laughter does nothing to bind your family together. It has the potential of tearing you apart.

> Scornful laughter does nothing to bind your family together. It has the potential of tearing you apart.

SO GO AHEAD AND LAUGH

If someone put a hidden microphone in your home, how much of that recording in an average day would include the sound of joyous laughter? It's the sign of a healthy home. A home where lighthearted people enjoy making each other smile and laugh. A home where snide and derisive comments are never heard.

And just in case you need a little material for your next meal, see if this summary of some new dog breeds helps:

What do you get when you cross a pointer and an Irish setter?
A Pointsetter, a wonderful Christmas pet.

What do you get when you cross a Pekinese with a Lhasa apso?
A Pekapso, a dog who constantly hides from you.

What do you get when you cross a collie and a malamute?
A Commute, a dog who's willing to travel long distances to get to work.

What do you get when you cross a bloodhound with a Labrador?
A Blabrador, a dog who never stops barking.

There. Now, don't you feel better?

8

DISCIPLINE IS
NOT A DIRTY WORD

It's the Stuff of Champions

Think about the word *discipline* for a moment. People use it in different contexts, don't they? For example, in a book such as this, your first thought about discipline may have been in the direction of what parents do to disobedient kids, *discipline* as in *punishment*. Certainly that's a legitimate use of the word, but there's another. You may watch the Boston Marathon on television and marvel at the discipline of the lead runners clicking off their sub-five-minute miles.

In spite of sounding as if I'm taking you back to grade-school English class, here's the difference between these two uses of the word *discipline:* the first is a verb—like run, jump, swim, the discipline you employ with your naughty child is something you *do*. But in the second case, the word is used as a noun—as in, "That person over there, she has discipline."

Now if you'll just hold on for one more minute before we break for recess, I want you to know something that's critically important about these uses for the word *discipline*. The noun is the goal, and it's the result of the verb. In fact, the noun is the great reward of the verb.

A person disciplines (verb) himself—or is disciplined by a parent or coach—so that one day that person can enjoy the sheer luxury and joy of having discipline (noun).

Who's having more fun after running the Boston Marathon, the person who won or the guy sitting on his La-Z-Boy eating Cheese Whiz out of the jar with a spoon?

Exactly.

So as you and I consider the subject of disciplining (the verb) our children, please don't forget the goal.

SO YOU WANT TO BE A GREAT PARENT?

When the game show *Who Wants to Be a Millionaire* hit our television screens in the late 90s, it became an instant success. Even Regis Philbin's solid-color ties became an overnight standard.

You may remember the format. Each question had four possible answers. The first ones were easy. "For two hundred dollars, how many tires do most automobiles have in their trunks? (a) four, (b) six, (c) one, or (d) seventy-three?" But as the dollar amounts increased, the difficulty of the questions also rose slightly. "For five hundred thousand dollars, what was the nickname of Mahatma Gandhi's seventh-grade substitute gym teacher?" (Answer: Bubba)

What if you had been a contestant on the show and Regis had asked the following question: "What is the most important ingredient in a Christian home? (a) good works, (b) church attendance, (c) laughter, or (d) discipline?"

If I had been given these four choices, I'd *still* be sitting there, and Regis would *still* be filling time while that death-dirge music played on and on.

Because "all the above" wasn't choice (e), there's no right answer to the question. In fact, a Christian home is a place where there's balance and integration between all of these things—including (d) discipline.

OUR VIEW OF GOD

Of the more misunderstood dimensions of our Christian faith are the disciplinary demands, such as obedience to God's law and punishment for sin. Many want to debate "God is love" versus "God is nice." This view has a profound impact on how we manage our Christian homes.

You sometimes see proponents for each of these views debating their positions on cable television talk shows. Unfortunately, the guys taking the "God is love" stand look as though they're about to punch somebody's lights out, and the guys promoting "God is nice" look like complete limp-wristed wimps. Neither of these images is helpful.

> My son, do not make light of the Lord's discipline, and do not lose heart when he rebukes you, because the Lord disciplines the one he loves, and he chastens everyone he accepts as a son. (Hebrews 12:5–6 NIV)

The writer to the Hebrews got it right. God's example is worth emulating. When you and I discipline our children, we're not *interrupting* our commitment to love them. We're actually *demonstrating* it. Proving it.

In putting the things in this book down on paper, many times I've wished I could actually sit with you over a cup of coffee and talk, face-to-face. This is one of those times. What you'd quickly identify is that my strong admonition for you to discipline your children is not about proving your superiority or even getting them to toe the line. My brow is not furrowed in anger, nor am I grinning at the chance, once and for all, to put children in their places. Parents who view discipline this way are perilously close to danger and may need some professional help.

The look in my eye is one of compassion

> When you and I discipline our children, we're not *interrupting* our commitment to love them. We're actually *demonstrating* it.

and understanding. From experience I know that doing discipline right can be a very difficult and challenging task.

The subject of discipline is also very controversial.

Many child-raising experts disagree on fundamental issues, such as what discipline and punishment look like. Let's take a look.

EFFECTIVE PUNISHMENT: EXHIBIT A

I received my final spanking during my senior year in high school; it was one I would never forget.

As it happens sometimes with boys about that age, I was certain that I was in love. I had first met her at church when we were in grade school, but it wasn't until my senior year that I really *noticed* her, if you know what I mean.

The commercial photography company I worked for was holding its annual Christmas party, and I could bring a date. Not as prolific a dater as some of my friends, I needed a while to think of whom to ask and even longer to gather the courage to make the presentation.

As I said, one Sunday at church I saw her. She stood out for several reasons: first was the urgency of my need to find a date for the Christmas party; second, she wasn't going out with anyone at the time; and third, all at once she looked really cute to me.

The next night I phoned to see if she might be willing to go to the party. She agreed on the spot. Our date the following weekend was better than terrific, and for the next few months, we did our best to see each other as often as possible, which was the problem.

Although my parents liked the girl, they were concerned at the speed with which I had been smitten. My dad was particularly troubled because in a few months I was headed off to college, and he thought it would be best for me to go to school without a romantic attachment back home.

My parents had identified an appropriate curfew for my brothers and me. I knew the rules and was expected to follow them. Yet one weekend, early the following spring, I missed my curfew. My first indication that my dad had noticed this was the fact that he was sitting on the front steps as I pulled the family car into the driveway at 11:30, one half hour late. I can still feel what my heart did when the headlights of the car swept across the front yard and landed on my father. He was not smiling.

What I remember about that night was that my dad didn't meet me at the garage door or stop me on my way to my bedroom. He went straight to bed and let me suffer. I didn't see him until the following morning, which, for me, came after a night of serious tossing and turning.

The bathroom where my dad took his morning shower was connected to my bedroom, so hearing him in the morning was standard fare. That particular morning, he didn't have to waken me when he walked in. I was awake.

My memory of dad's disposition is very clear. He was not angry. He didn't seem upset. (He probably knew that my restless night had already prepared me for my verdict.) With a calm and resolute voice, he spoke my sentence. For the first time in my life, I was grounded for two weeks. That meant no driving the family car and no going out at night.

The fact that this seventeen-year-old was "in love" classified this punishment as cruel and unusual. However, since I believed that love conquers all—including a silly impediment like my dad's grounding—I decided to see if I could somehow beat the rap.

In a few days, my dad left for a long business trip. That was my chance. Slipping out of my room after everyone was asleep, I mounted my bicycle, which I had cleverly hidden in the bushes late that afternoon. The dangerous journey to my girlfriend's home took me several miles completely across town, but the adrenaline in my system made it feel like just a block or two.

Four hours later, I sneaked back into my room. In the shadows, on the edge of my bed, someone appeared to be in my room. I stepped closer. *It was my mother.* Tearing a page from her husband's playbook, she stood, and without a word, walked out of my room.

In a couple of days, dad returned from his trip. For this intentional infraction, my punishment included *more* than grounding. I got a spanking. I accepted my punishment without an argument.

Before the boom of reprisal lowered, however, my dad talked to me. There was no hollering or demonstrable anger. But his jaw was set, his eyes narrow and focused. He explained how it felt to receive a call from my mother and to hear the news of my willful insubordination. He used the terms "blatant disobedience" and "disrespect for your mother." He told me how he counted on me to be a responsible young man, especially when he was gone. And he told me how disappointed he was in me.

The pain of the spanking was real, but something else was more painful. The weight of my own rebelliousness crushed me. Having broken the rules and gotten caught was bad enough, but to disappoint someone who was depending on me made my mutiny unbearable.

> To disappoint someone who was depending on me made my mutiny unbearable.

After he had spanked me, my dad invited me to stand. He firmly took my shoulders, and then he hugged me. Then he wrapped the words around me, "I love you, son."

Many experts would say that children that age are too old for spankings. But because of the gravity of the infraction, my dad decided that this was appropriate. The fact that I remember it so well— and am thankful for it—was exactly his point.

A fool despises his father's instruction,
But he who receives correction is prudent. (Proverbs 15:5)

My dad wasn't a talker. More often than not, his disciplinary lectures came to me by way of what he *did* rather than what he *said*. This is why my memory of this lesson is so vivid.

RULES FOR DISCIPLINE

Beginning with lessons I learned from my parents as a youngster and running through my own experience as a father, a number of discipline non-negotiables have developed. As a recipient of a kind of discipline that shaped my character, and as a practitioner in partnership with a wife that shaped our children's lives, I urge your careful consideration of each of these in your Christian home.

Discipline Must Be Direct

When your children are disobedient or they commit another kind of blatant infraction of the rules, your response must be without equivocation. It is no time for diplomacy. Like a laser, you must focus on the issue.

Do you remember when David slept with Bathsheba, then arranged for her husband to be killed in battle? Nathan the prophet approached King David with the daunting task of calling him to account: "Then Nathan said to David, 'You are the man! Thus says the LORD God of Israel . . . "Why have you despised the commandment of the LORD, to do evil in His sight? You have killed Uriah the Hittite with the sword; you have taken his wife to be your wife, and have killed him with the sword of the people of Ammon"'" (2 Samuel 12:7, 9).

Can you hear the resolve in Nathan's voice? It didn't matter that he was speaking to his country's absolute monarch, who could have ordered his execution for such insubordination. He was not intimidated. Like a surgeon's scalpel, Nathan's words found their mark. Let your words be direct. Get to the point.

Early one cold morning, after he got the fire in the wood-burning stove going in his workshop, my grandpa Dourte gave me a sweet portion of my inheritance: "Be careful, Bobby," he said as he picked up a knife and a sharpening stone. "Nothing is more dangerous than a dull knife."

Like Nathan and my wise grandfather, when you discipline, you call it as you see it. It is no time for hedging. No time for being indirect. The "knife" must be razor sharp.

It's your job to say, "Excuse me, that's unacceptable behavior." It is no time for, "You know, honey, it seems to me that you might want to take another look at what you're doing, and, perhaps, if it's not too much trouble . . ."

You and I must model Nathan's courage, calling the king to task immediately. Our children must be the recipients of this kind of direct discipline.

Discipline Must Be Painful

The intended painfulness of discipline is certainly the most controversial part of this picture.

> He who spares his rod hates his son,
> But he who loves him disciplines him promptly. (Proverbs 13:24)

Of course, spanking is the major focus of this controversy, and for good reason. Child abuse in America is epidemic. Parents who are physically much larger and stronger than their kids wield unmistakable physical superiority. And sometimes they use it harmfully. It stands to reason that this horrific fact, in contrast to Solomon's sobering admonition regarding spanking, must have a logical explanation. I believe it does.

My dad's response to my teenage disobedience is why I called the story "Exhibit A." He was direct and deliberate. His punishment issued enough pain to make every detail perfectly memorable more than fifty years later. But his love for me was never in question.

Given what you and I read and see in contemporary media, we might suspect that American moms and dads have decided against spanking. This is not true. According to a recent survey, 81 percent of the parents said that spanking ought to be used, given the right circumstance, with their children at home.[1]

Why do four out of five parents believe in spanking? It works. It's painful enough to give the child a vividly unpleasant experience linked to his unacceptable behavior. *Wow, that hurt*, a smart child will think. *I'll think twice about doing* that *again!*

Mission accomplished.

Of course, the opponents of spanking are plenty vocal. And I believe their voices need to be heard. Would you be surprised to hear that I agree with some of what they say?

Why? Sometimes parents, in fits of rage, hit their children, then call it spanking. A parent's doubled fist or a slap to a child's face is unthinkable behavior. This is a serious problem, one that should *never* be condoned. I strongly believe that there's a huge difference between *spanking* and *hitting*.

> Why do four out of five parents believe in spanking? It works.

A major leaguer *hits* a baseball. A tennis player *hits* the ball. A housekeeper *beats* a rug. But a good parent never hits—or beats—his child. Never.

We spanked our children, but we did not hit them. And the times when Bobbie and I determined that spanking was the right choice for punishment, we were extremely careful. We went to a private location—usually a bedroom. We never spanked in public. What should be a private moment when we deal with what has happened cannot become an open exhibition. Adding embarrassment to the equation can be lethal to both you and your child. You do not want to go there.

As my father had modeled with me, once we had found a private location, we talked. We clearly described the behavior our children had displayed. There was no question as to why we were taking this kind of serious action.

The actual spanking was not violent, but it *was* repetitive—ten to fifteen spanks to the rear end.[2] Discomfort was guaranteed. When the spanking was finished, we turned their tearful faces toward us and always hugged our children—a full arms-around-you-and-hold-you-a-few-extra-seconds hug—and then we told them that we loved them. As you would imagine, they didn't always eagerly return the hug. Back then, the linkage between what we had just done—spank and assure them of our love—didn't readily compute. Today, in retrospect, it does.

> Adding embarrassment to the equation can be lethal to both you and your child.

Our grown children punish their own children, spanking them if necessary, very similarly to how we disciplined them: They are direct and make the punishment appropriately painful. And they make certain they connect punishment to a hug and reassuring words.

Today your children may not appreciate your commitment to these things. Someday they probably will.

For children from toddler age to five or six, spanking is usually the most effective pain-inducing punishment when the infraction is serious enough to warrant it: open defiance, disobedience, hurtful actions or words. As your child gets older, there are other forms of "painful" discipline besides spanking. Sometimes the loss of a privilege can be effective.

What's important is that the punishment is direct and painful. For most kids, a ten-minute time-out or a parent's counting to three are about as effective as a spanking with a piece of kite string.

> Punishment is not an interruption in the process. Spanking, done properly, is love's testimony.

For Bobbie and me, until our children were nearing teenage years, spanking seemed to be the most effective way to create a that-was-not-fun-at-all-so-I-won't-be-doing-that-again-very-soon experience.

Remember the keepsake from the Scripture: "For the LORD disciplines those he loves, and he punishes each one he accepts as his child" (Hebrews 12:6 NLT). Punishment is not an interruption in the process. Spanking, done properly, is love's testimony.

Discipline Must Be Swift

One of the reasons parents are tempted to overreact and even hit their kids is accumulated inaction from their children's past wrongs. Rather than keeping short accounts and "nipping it in the bud"—as Barney Fife used to screech to Andy Griffith—sometimes parents wait too long to deal with problems, allowing them to build up.

Like youngsters stacking blocks on top of each other, they collect infraction after infraction. Then, as that last disobedience gets set on the top of the wobbly tower, the blocks clatter to the floor. You've had enough, and *now* it's time to do something about it. But because of your inaction—laziness—for previous problems, your emotion is tied to them *all*, and you find yourself out of control.

You can spot out-of-control parents at shopping malls or grocery stores. You know that their kids are "stacking blocks" because of the way the parents are whining. "Aw, Trevor, would you pleeease stop begging for candy?" "Come over here, Tiffany. How many times have I told you not to wander away from me? Pleeease come back here."

Children certainly aren't conspiratorial enough to plot on purpose. Actions that could be avoided by wise parental preplanning—quick word games, small intriguing objects, toys, portable drinks or snacks—happen when parents do not employ any diversionary tactics. But there must be some level of entertainment for a misbehaving child as they watch grown-ups turn into helpless beggars. Of course, their amusement turns sour the moment their parents stop talking and begin getting physical.

This is an unfortunate, and completely unnecessary, scene. Swiftness in discipline means keeping kids from stacking the blocks. It's focused, painfully effective, and then it's finished.

Again, remember that this is the chapter when I wish we could be sitting somewhere together and talking. What I just said may sound as if you've invited Captain Von Trapp to your home to get things back in shipshape. You blow the whistle, and the kids snap to attention and shout their names.

Tweep. "Liesl!"

Tweep. "Louisa!"

Tweep. "Friedrich!"

This is *not* what I'm talking about.

In the last chapter we said that a Christian home is a place where laughter is frequently heard. If you'll remember, until Julie Andrews came along and started singing "Doe, a deer, a female deer," there was nothing fun about living in the Von Trapp home. The surly captain was all whistle and no joy.

What I *am* saying is that the discipline *tug-of-war* is absolutely unnecessary. You let your children know the rules of your family. Then when you ask them to do something, or to stop doing something, you expect obedience. You do not communicate this to them with your face as tight as a trampoline, the veins on your neck bulging, and your eyes popping out of their sockets. You communicate this to your children with the same unemotional steadiness you use to instruct the bag boy at the grocery store to use paper or plastic.

"Be prepared in season and out of season; correct, rebuke, and encourage—with great patience and careful instruction" (2 Timothy 4:2 NIV). Aren't these great words to describe this conversation we have with our kids about obeying "the first time"? *Correct* [persuade], *rebuke* [scold], and *encourage* [exhort], "with all longsuffering [forgiveness] and [good] teaching [paper or plastic?]" (NKJV). No screaming and yelling. No bullying or foolish threats, just a simple, thorough explanation of the rules and your expectation that your children follow them.

When our girls were youngsters, Bobbie and I asked them in moments like this, "When do you obey?"

Their response was, "The first time."

Even though we didn't turn the question around, they could have asked us, "When do you discipline us if we *don't* obey the first time?"

Our response would have been, "The first time."

Swift discipline keeps the blocks from piling up.

Discipline Must Be Participatory

No screaming and yelling. No bullying or foolish threats, just a simple, thorough explanation of the rules and your expectation that your children follow them.

Have you ever seen a special on TV that shows how a particular movie was made? You get a look at what actually happens on a movie set while a scene is being shot. You've seen the director. Sometimes he's sitting on one of those chairs with the X-legs and canvas seat and back. Sometimes he's peeking through one of the cameras so he can see exactly what the shot looks like. Or he's calling out directions—hence his title—to the actors or the crew. If it's an outside scene and the shot is a long one, with cameras and director perched some distance from the actors, you'll often see the director with one of those handheld bullhorns.

Of course, the most important word in his lexicon is "Action!" The essence of what he does, he does from a distance.

Now that you have this image of a movie director firmly in your mind, I want you to make an important decision about your role as one of the parents in your Christian home. I want you to resolve that you will *not* make a habit of acting like this.

You are not your family's director. You do not call out orders to your children as a dictator would to his minions. Effective discipline in your home must include *participation*. To be most effective, it's going to take a lot more than your verbal orders flung here and there: "Stop that incessant arguing." "Clean up your room." "Do your homework." "For the last time, put down your cell phone and look at me."

Do you remember the story of my father-in-law, Raymond

You do not call out orders to your children as a dictator would to his minions.

Gardner, sneaking out to visit the roller-skating rink? The reason the discipline and the lesson were clearly visible to him sixty years later was the fact that his mother stepped into the scene and got involved. If cell phones had been available in the early forties, a scalding call from his mother would not have had the same effect.

I have already told you a bit about Dan, my younger brother. What I didn't mention was that, as joyful as he was to have around, one day a powerful streak of rebellion virtually detonated in this person. This was the day Dan decided to run away from home.

He was five.

Mother was standing at the kitchen sink, looking out the window, when she saw her little boy walking north, along the east shoulder of Main Street, which led to busy Roosevelt Road. She could tell by the slump of his shoulders and the droop of his head that he was very upset. Even his shuffling pace revealed something about his demeanor.

Mother quickly left her post and hustled out the back door to intercept her young traveler. A capable athlete in her day, she took no time to reach him. He hardly looked up. Kneeling down next to him—a familiar position when she was speaking to a youngster—mother asked where he was going.

Dan did not speak.

"Are you running away from home?" mother asked in the same tone of voice she would have used in asking the grocer if the canta-loupe was ripe.

Dan slowly looked up into his mother's face and nodded. Running away from home was exactly what he was doing, but her seeming lack of urgency surely surprised him.

Then my mother said to her miniature prodigal, "But you didn't pack your suitcase." Her voice sounded perfectly sincere.

Again Dan looked into his mother's face, searching and hoping for any glimpse of sadness that she was losing her son for good. She seemed resolved, perhaps pleased with his decision.

Throwing his arms around his mother's neck, Dan began to cry—deep sobs coming from his broken heart. Although I didn't see this when it happened, I can clearly picture it . . . a mother kneeling in the roadside gravel just a few hundred feet from the house, holding her contrite little boy.

Of course, she could have hollered invectives at neighbor-alerting decibels from the back door. "And where do you think you're going, young man? You come back here *right now!*"

Like a director, she could have used her "bullhorn" to shame or threaten him from the back porch. But she became a participant and secured a suitable ending to the rebellion.

Getting personally involved in the discipline of your children is a lot of work. And let's face it: you've had a busy day yourself. You're exhausted. So you pick up your bullhorn and call out directions. "Did you finish your homework?" "Who's going to pick up the toys in the family room?" "Turn off that video game and do something worthwhile."

Often parents follow these directives with worthless pontifications and comparisons to their own childhoods. "This place looks like a pigpen. What's the matter with kids these days? Why, when I was a kid . . ." (*yawn*).

You are issuing these useless and thoroughly ineffective words from the comfort of your director's chair. Bad idea. You're the parent here. You're *not* Cecil B. DeMille.

Here's what you could do instead: "Why don't we work on your spelling words together?" "Hey, I have an idea. Let's see how fast we can clean up the family room. I'll take this half, and you take that half." "I've got some errands to run. Let's leave your phone at home, and let's go together."

> Getting personally involved in the discipline of your children is a lot of work.

Of course, there are times when participation will not be possible. You'll have no choice but to issue directives to your children without getting personally involved. Our experience was that adding a mix of participation with spoken instructions went a long way on those occasions when we had time only for words.

Again, the reason for participating was to let our children know that we were in the disciplining adventure with them.

THE HAPPY SECRET: IDENTIFY, VALIDATE, SHARE

When she was eight years old, Abby had an upcoming piano festival in which two judges sat on a panel and listened to students perform two memorized selections. For weeks Abby had been working on the songs her teacher, Mrs. Musterman, had chosen for the judging. They were titled "Joyful Bells" and "Happy Secret."

One day after school Abby tried to rush through her practice session in the living room and made several whopping mistakes. In frustration, she lowered her hands and sank into a whining explosion. "I'm not good at piano," she cried. "I'm good at gymnastics and singing, but I'm *not* good at piano. I don't want to play anymore."

Listening to the stormy outburst from the kitchen, her mother stepped into the living room. Instead of lecturing Abby and commanding her to just keep practicing until she got it right, Missy wisely helped her daughter to *identify her feelings*. "Tell me why you're so upset," she said.

"I just don't like piano." Abby continued, "It's not what I'm good at."

Missy was careful to *validate her feelings* with the next words. "I understand. You've worked so hard, and it *is* frustrating when you make so many mistakes. I'll sit here and listen. You help me to *hear* the *bells be joyful* and the *secrets be happy* by playing the notes correctly. Try the whole song again, and then we'll take a break."

Abby seemed more willing to continue the practice, moving past the frustration because Missy was *sharing in the discipline* by sitting and listening.

And because her mom was available, Abby admitted something to Missy after playing it through again. "I wish you could be with me when I play for the judges. I'm scared to go all by myself."

Missy listened and again *validated her feelings*. "Why don't you tell Mrs. Musterman how you're feeling at your next lesson, and see what she says?"

The next Tuesday, Abby walked into her teacher's room with her mother. Abby asked her question right away. "Can my mom go in with me when I play at the festival?" she asked.

Mrs. Musterman, a seasoned and inspired teacher, gave an incredible response. "Well, your mom can't go in with you—it's just the two judges that are allowed to hear you." She paused. "But there is *someone else* who can go in with you."

Abby and Missy were both anxious to hear who this could be.

Mrs. Musterman continued, "Jesus can go in with you and sit right on the bench next to you when you play. In fact, I had one student who told me that it felt as if Jesus laid His hands on top of his own hands and helped him play both his pieces in front of the judges."

Abby was satisfied with the words of encouragement. What could have been the end of her journey into the world of piano playing was catapulted to a new level because her mom and her teacher identified and validated her feelings and then shared in the discipline with availability and encouragement.

Abby called Bobbie and me from the car on her way home from the judging the next weekend. "Guess what?" she said. "I got a 'Superior' for my grade from the judges!"

"Oh, that's fantastic!" we chimed back. "We prayed for you."

"I know," Abby replied. "And Jesus had His hands on top of mine the whole time!"

Identify and validate feelings. Share the moment with availability and encouragement. Because it was the title of one of Abby's piano pieces, this is the process our family now refers to as the "Happy Secret."

YOUR KID'S BUDDY?

Does the piano-practice story mean that the goal is to be your kid's buddy, using diversionary tactics to keep from ever having to lay down the law?

No.

Your child is not looking for another household friend. You're not his chum; you're his parent. And although he will not be able to verbalize this until he's at least your age, what he *is* looking for is your leadership: dispensed fairly, swiftly, and lovingly.

One afternoon, Bobbie and I were in a conversation with a young dad at church. Even though I'm not a clergyman, I've had enough years as a Sunday school teacher that sometimes people treat me as if I'm their minister.[3]

> Your child is not looking for another household friend. You're not his chum; you're his parent.

In this case, the dad was complaining about his son not wanting to come to church and Sunday school. "He always has an excuse about how tired he is on Sunday morning or how he doesn't enjoy the sermon," the dad whined. On and on the guy groused about this problem.

"How old is your son?" Bobbie asked.

"Eight."

Although it wasn't the time or the place to make a scene, we were stunned. Eight years old? Driving home, Bobbie and I discussed our conversation with the dad. "I think some parents are scared of their kids," she said. "They are so eager to be their son or daughter's best friend that they're afraid to *be* the father or the mother."

I agreed.

DOING LEADS TO HAVING

Until now we've been talking about "doing" discipline in your home. You may have never looked at it this way, but this discipline activity starts with clearly stated boundaries. Then the focused, painful, swift, and participatory disciplinary action equips the child to honor adults and, ultimately, experience happiness. It really *is* a gift that keeps on giving.

Here it is again, the verb and noun uses of the word. *Doing* discipline leads to the sheer pleasure of *having* discipline.

Everything in life underscores this principle. When you think about it in these terms, it's at work everywhere: *doing* homework leads to *having* good grades, doing daily exercises leads to *having* fitness, *doing* annual budgets leads to *having* financial control.

When you invest your time and energy in enacting fair and predictable disciplinary activity in your home, you are giving your children the gift of discipline—*self*-discipline.

Because we were hopeless competitors at home, we made child's play out of some very adult-sounding stuff. We called it "the no game."

Bobbie and I knew not to wait until our children were teenagers to teach them to pull in the reins on their impulses and urges. Because we were involved with teenagers at our church for the first several years of our marriage, we saw what it looked like for teenagers not to be able to say no to their drives. There was one fifteen-year-old girl whose parents had not taught her self-control, so she was unable to stay away from promiscuous sexual activity, even with boys she hardly knew. "I don't know why I can't stop it," she told Bobbie tearfully. "I guess nobody ever told me how *not* to."

> *Doing* discipline leads to the sheer pleasure of *having* discipline.

"Where were her parents when she was three and five and eight?" Bobbie asked one night. "I wish I could really help her. If only I could just pour some discipline into her."

We came up with a way to help our kids make wise choices—to say no to their first urges and impulses. Over dinner Bobbie and I challenged our family to play "the no game" between that night and the next.

Here's how it worked. From the time of dinner one night until dinner the next night, each person looked for one chance to say no to himself or herself over some urge, no matter how small, and make it stick. We then reported to the family what we had conquered.

I know this sounds strange, but stay with me here.

The next day Julie was looking for her opportunity to play the no game. She and her friends were sitting at their lunch table when someone began saying unkind things about another girl. Julie was tempted to jump on the pile and add her own juicy two cents. *No,* she thought to herself. *That's not the right thing to do.*

As most youngsters, Missy loved to talk on her phone. After school she and her good friend were talking away when Missy remembered that she had a lot of homework to do. "I can only talk for five more minutes," she said. The five minutes ended, and she signed off the phone.

I reported that I had a late-night conference phone call. It meant getting to bed at almost midnight. Normally I get up early and jog a few miles for exercise. But that morning arrived prematurely. The faint dawning light woke me, and I lay there quietly for a few minutes. In my semi-comatose state, there was some serious negotiating going on.

As though I was carrying on a conversation with myself, I weighed the sumptuousness of staying in bed against the torture of going for a jog. Then I remembered our game. What a great time to say no to myself.

With that, I turned and sat up; my feet landed on the floor. I went on my jog.

Finally it was time for Bobbie's no-game report. She told us that right after lunch, she had dashed off to her favorite store, the one where the clerks smile and call her by name. As she walked the aisles, she found a belt she really liked, except that it was almost exactly like one she already had, and she really didn't *need* it. "But it's on sale," she had noticed. "No," she whispered. She returned the belt to the rack and walked on.

That night at dinner we celebrated our victories: the lunchtime restraint, the shortened telephone call, the morning jog, and the belt that continues to hang at the boutique. We cheered about Julie's decision to be kind at lunch, Missy's telephone control, my lacing up the running shoes, and Bobbie's unbought belt.

Silly game? Sure. But developing the ability to rein ourselves in made this little dinnertime amusement a huge endowment down the road. *Doing* self-discipline becomes *having* self-discipline. And having self-discipline is one fantastic asset, especially when the stakes are much higher.

Missy's ability to tell herself to end her phone call could become a decision to say no to the advances of a boy she really likes. Julie's restraint over lunch could become a resolve to say no when her friends invite her to experiment with drugs. Bobbie's unpurchased belt could help her stay on target with her vacation savings plan. My successfully staring down the urge to sleep in may become the self-discipline I need to steer clear of Internet pornography.

"But the fruit of the Spirit is love, joy, peace, longsuffering, kindness, goodness, faithfulness, gentleness, self-control" (Galatians 5:22–23). The occupants of a Christian home are not alone in this quest for self-discipline. They have a permanent resident in their guest room—the Holy Spirit of God. And, as a bonus, self-control is one of the things He promises to give.

THE DISCIPLINE OF WORK

Work while you work, play while you play.
That is the way to be happy each day.

Things that you do, *do with your might.*
Things done by half are never done right.
—QUOTED INCESSANTLY BY MY GRANDMA WOLGEMUTH

In chapter 3, I told you a little of my work history, beginning with a paper route when I was in the fourth grade. An honor student in the school of hard knocks, my dad had insisted that I have work to do, so I always had a job. In addition to paid employment, I also had my share of chores around the house: washing the family car, mowing the lawn, cleaning my room and the downstairs bathroom. My brothers and sisters had their own chores as well.

My dad was not comfortable seeing his children sitting idly around the house between all of the official work. "Look for something to do," he said when we were headed for some downtime, or if he walked through the family room and we were watching the Cubs on TV. Since I was interested in keeping up with my favorite baseball team, I learned how to fill that time with work that could be done right there in the family room. My mother taught me how to iron, and since we had a big family and permanent-press clothing had not been invented, there were baskets full of ready-to-iron laundry. I also learned how to use a needle and thread, hemming dresses or mending for my mother. When there wasn't ironing or mending to do, I learned how to polish shoes, becoming one of our county's finest spit-shiners.

ESTEEM AND BELONGING

Taking this work ethic to my paying jobs offered me measurable rewards: esteem, belonging, and success.

Several years ago, Bobbie and I met Daniel Lapin, an Orthodox rabbi, best-selling author, and father of seven. He was speaking at a conference we attended a few hours from our home. The rabbi's brilliance and insight, especially on issues related to the family, gripped us: "Work, not play, gives children a strong sense of self-respect."

The rabbi had put words to a mystery I had sensed for a long time.

Of course, I never could have understood this when I was young, but my ability to work hard and accomplish tasks began to build my confidence as a young leader. Surveying our tightly manicured lawn, or standing back and admiring my dad's spanking-clean car, filled my young heart with a sense of pride and accomplishment.

> "Work, not play, gives children a strong sense of self-respect."

The self-discipline I developed from my parents' strict authority coupled with the self-respect that came from their teaching me to work hard were powerful influences in shaping me. And because Bobbie and I believed self-respect and hard work made for a great partnership, we did the same with our children. Thumbing through our photo albums would show you some of the wonderful moments of working-together family projects.

SAYING WHEN

You're sitting with a friend over a cup of coffee at your favorite breakfast place, and the server approaches with a fresh pot of steaming coffee. You've had plenty, but you can't turn down the aroma of the brew. "I'll take a half cup," you say to your waitress.

As she slowly begins to pour the dark freshness into your waiting cup, she puts you in charge of how much coffee you're going to get. "Say when," she says with a smile.

A conversation about discipline wouldn't be complete without mentioning the discipline of moderation, the "say whens" in your life and mine.

Moderation About Food

There may be no more challenging discipline than the one related to what we eat. This is true because unlike some vice that we swear to avoid completely, we have no choice on this one. We *have* to eat. Moderation about food means that you and I exercise our self-discipline when it comes to choosing nutrition over convenience, reasonable amounts of food instead of overeating. Planting seeds of consumption self-control in your children—by your own example—when they're young can spare them from lives of frustration standing on the bathroom scales.

Teach them to "say when."

Moderation About Other Things

You and I could talk about how much time we spend on our cell phones or sitting in front of our computer screens, how much we drink, how we spend money, the language we use, or how fast we drive on the freeway. *Moderation* is a marvelous word to apply to each of these things. As adults, we may feel free to overindulge. But keeping these things under control is an important expression of self-discipline. It's a terrific opportunity for us to say when.

Modesty

A close relative of the word *moderation* is this word *modesty*. Because this was my grandmother's favorite from her guilt-inducing glossary, I cannot believe what I'm about to say . . . but she was right. Modesty *is* a crucial expression of self-discipline. Even among Christians, it's an art form as endangered as the snail darter. *What are their parents thinking?* you may wonder after seeing the way some teenagers are dressed.

Although I'm not suggesting that anyone completely abandon stylishness, I am suggesting that *thinking* is a terrific idea when it comes to helping your children choose—and wear—their clothing. Our friend the late Zig Ziglar used to say that kids act the way they're dressed. A visit to a hallway at your local high school between classes might give you an idea of what he was talking about.

Have you heard the expression "dress up if you want to go up"? It is one of the first things taught to young job seekers in business schools. Appropriate and attractive clothing and a neat appearance go a long way toward landing the right job. Wise parents don't wait until the first job interview to encourage their children's clothing choices. People judge kids by the way they are dressed, and you do your children a favor when you send them out making a statement of self-worth.

> *Thinking* is a terrific idea when it comes to helping your children choose— and wear—their clothing.

Don't be afraid to say when.

A Good Look in the Mirror

We have one of those terrific retractable dog leashes. Ours extends to twelve feet. I know this because when I take my little dog for a walk, that's how it is most of the time: fully extended.

Even though I'm a grown-up, I understand my dog's need to see how far the leash will go before it comes to an abrupt stop. The expression *pushing the edges* was coined for people like me. Even though, as a parent, I stand by the things I've said about discipline, as a member of the human race, I find the struggle to maintain personal discipline increasingly powerful.

This means that, in my heart of hearts, there are times when I'd really rather toss aside self-discipline. As an adult with all the freedom I need, I have the capability to cheat on my taxes, gossip about "losers," and look at all the Internet lewdness I can feast my eyes on. And I live in a culture where shame has lost its . . . well, all its shame.

Not long ago I read about a twenty-six-year-old man named Barry Landis who lives in Lancaster County, Pennsylvania—the region of my own conservative ancestry. Barry's car is seven years old, but it still has plenty of giddyap. Phillip Matson, the Pennsylvania state trooper assigned to Lancaster County, clocked Barry doing 109 miles an hour and pulled him over.

Because of a rash of hundred-plus speeding violations, the state decided to post "century club" speeder's names in the local newspaper. You're ahead of me on this one, aren't you?

Unfortunately, the old vice-squad tactic that attempts to embarrass men who visit prostitutes by posting their names in the paper backfired on them. Barry's friends celebrated by presenting him with the newspaper clipping for his scrapbook, telling of their own ultrahigh-speed brushes with the law. "It sorta made me a celebrity," Barry admitted.[4]

As I said, shame isn't what it used to be, so my own propensity toward wrongdoing has lost much of its sting.

> For we know that the law is spiritual, but I am of the flesh, sold under sin. I do not understand my own actions. For I do not do what I want, but I do the very thing I hate. Now if I do what I do not want, I agree with the law, that it is good. So now it is no longer I who do it, but sin that dwells within me. (Romans 7:14–17 ESV)

Can you believe this candor from the apostle Paul? I can imagine some of the folks in Rome who received these words in the first century were taken back by their hero's unvarnished admission. But as you and me, Paul *knew* what he needed to do, even agreeing on what was the right thing to do, but he *still* had trouble getting it done.

What are Paul and you and I going to do?

Thank Goodness for Jesus

In a Christian home, everyone—mom and dad included—understands that the forces keeping us from self-discipline are powerful. We don't default to submission to God's Word and right living. Like a magnet near a pile of metal shavings, our sinful natures tug and pull and draw us away from what we know is pure and right and good. "Who will deliver me from this body of death? Thanks be to God through Jesus Christ our Lord!" (Romans 7:24–25 ESV).

It's a profound conundrum. Jesus Christ calls us to the discipline of obedience, nothing short of perfection. He cannot tolerate anything less. No sorry excuses will count. And then, when we find ourselves completely overwhelmed by these impossible demands, Jesus Christ Himself provides the answer.

His holiness lays down the unreachable standard. Then His grace pardons our sin and gives us a chance to go for it again.

> As we know Jesus better, his divine power gives us everything we need for living a godly life. He has called us to receive his own glory and goodness! And by that same mighty power, he has given us all of his rich and wonderful promises. He has promised that you will escape the decadence all around you caused by evil desires and that you will share in his divine nature.
>
> So make every effort to apply the benefits of these promises to your life. Then your faith will produce a life of moral excellence. A life of moral excellence leads to knowing God better. Knowing God leads to self-control. Self-control leads to patient endurance, and patient endurance leads to godliness. (2 Peter 1:3–6, author's paraphrase)

What's remarkable to me about what the apostles Paul and Peter have said in these last few pages is that these men had no access to cable television or the Internet. They never conceived of an internal combustion engine that would propel them through the air or down a busy freeway, but their diagnosis of our twenty-first-century hearts is precise. And their remedy is still impeccable.

But just in case you need one more shot of encouragement, listen to this: "And let us not grow weary of doing good, for in due season we will reap, if we do not give up" (Galatians 6:9 ESV).

You may want to write this one out on a card and post it by the kitchen sink or on your bathroom mirror. Maybe it'll help on those days when you say to yourself, *You know what? I'm sick of this discipline stuff!*

When all is said and done, your Christian home is a place where discipline, external and internal, is standard fare; where there are no apologies for strictness and hard work; where expectations for obedience are very high.

> Knowing God leads to self-control.

And it's a place to which people are mysteriously attracted. Who *wouldn't* want to live in a home like that?

REVISITING THE VERB AND THE NOUN

You'll remember the comparison of *discipline* the noun and *discipline* the verb at the beginning of this chapter—how the goal of the verb (receiving discipline) was the noun (having discipline). Here's another powerful example of this verb/noun principle.

"Do not be deceived, God is not mocked; for whatever a man sows, that he will also reap" (Galatians 6:7). Here sowing and reaping are word pictures of the perils and rewards of discipline. Like the word *discipline, harvest* can also be a verb and a noun. You harvest a crop (verb), then you sit down and enjoy the yummy harvest (noun).

Sowing acts of discipline creates a harvest of self-discipline. The rewards—harvest—of discipline are tangible. Or as your coach used to say when he ordered your squad to take another lap, "No pain, no gain."

It's the stuff of champions.

9

SAFE AT HOME

The Refuge You Are Looking For

From the time you and I were small, we lived with a healthy sense of fear. We didn't approach snarling dogs or step onto a busy highway without the help of a grown-up. But most of the time we had a sense of security: there were responsible adults who could help us when we called on them, local and state police patrolled our streets, and our military kept tabs on the world outside our borders.

The morning of September 11, 2001, changed this for every law-abiding person in the world. From that day and probably for the remainder of our lives, two words hang over you and me like the gleaming cusp of a guillotine's blade: *not safe*.

In the face of this unmistakable anxiety, one place stands like a fortress against this nagging sense of fear and dread. This place is your home.

> One place stands like a fortress against this nagging sense of fear and dread. This place is your home.

FASTEN YOUR SEAT BELTS

I love to fly. I do it all the time. But I hate to fly in bad weather.

If you fly, you know what I mean. It's completely white outside the windows. You cannot see any cloud shapes. You cannot see blue sky. You cannot see the ground. It's like staring at an unspoiled snow bank—you see no images or shapes or anything.

Then the bumps come. Some are light and choppy, as if the plane were flying over a washboard. Some are heavier. You take hold of your ginger ale and try to keep it from sloshing over the edges. Then there is turbulence that literally jolts your body. You know it's coming because the captain asks the flight attendants to "please discontinue service and take your seats."

The passengers grow quiet. People put their books down and fold their newspapers. Some make desperate gasps when the plane drops a few split seconds in a free fall. The engines whine, then roar as the captain does business with what he cannot see.

Like you, I know the numbers—my drive to the airport was statistically far more perilous than that flight. But for the moment, my heart is pounding. I put my head back, close my eyes, and thank God for my family. Often I'll quietly sing an old hymn. These things help.

I can summarize exactly how I feel during these dreadful moments in two words: *not safe.* And, as I said, I do *not* like the way this feels. I'm not a big fan of not safe.

"PEACE, BE STILL"

Jesus' disciples didn't like turbulence either. Their craft, of course, was a fishing boat.

> And a great windstorm arose, and the waves beat into the boat,
> so that it was already filling. But He was in the stern, asleep on a

pillow. And they awoke Him and said to Him, "Teacher, do You not care that we are perishing?" Then He arose and rebuked the wind, and said to the sea, "Peace, be still!" And the wind ceased and there was a great calm. (Mark 4:37–39)

Take just a moment and reflect on how it felt in that boat before "Peace, be still." The disciples—the passengers in the boat—had given up hope. In the seamless darkness of the storm, they were terrified.

Jesus spoke into the night of their frightened hearts. "Now you are safe."

SAFE AT HOME

Think about your kids' worlds. If they're in school, their days are filled with frenzy: academic pressure, competition for acceptance or status, and verbal grenades from their peers.

And think about your world: anxiety about your children's welfare, financial stress, strained relationships, and/or pressures at work.

So where can you go?

One of your goals in establishing your Christian home must be to provide a place of safety for your family. When you and your children step across the threshold of your house and the door closes, you need to feel safe. Like kids touching home base when they're playing hide-and-seek, the running and chasing and hiding and fear must be over.

In chapter 3, we talked about how we need to make people feel welcome when they walk through our front doors. As when faithful customers enter a store, we hear the little electronic chirp that signals to us that someone very important has walked in.

Safety at home is what happens between the comings and the goings. It involves the way we treat each other, honor each other.

And this kind of safety begins with the freedom to speak.

A SAFE PLACE TO TELL THE TRUTH

Safety at home . . . involves the way we treat each other, honor each other.

It was high noon. And it was hot. If you've ever been to the Middle East, you know how brutal the sun is in the middle of the day. You also know how precious water can be.

Apparently Jesus had gotten separated from His disciples, because the Scriptures tell us that He sat down next to Jacob's well alone. He was tired and thirsty. Presently a woman approached the well with a large clay pot, and Jesus asked her for a drink.

It must have been the structure of his face, or maybe a telltale Galilean accent, but the woman—a Samaritan—knew that the man was a Jew. "'How is it that You, being a Jew, ask a drink from me, a Samaritan woman?' For Jews have no dealings with Samaritans" (John 4:9).

Over the next few minutes, the dialogue between Jesus and the Samaritan woman revealed some intimate facts—secrets—about her life. Jesus told her He knew she had gone through five husbands and was currently living with a man who wasn't her husband. Can you imagine the shock of hearing this brutal truth from a complete stranger?

What was even more remarkable about this conversation was that somehow the Samaritan woman was drawn to Jesus. It would have been predictable for her to be outraged by His directness. Incredibly, she wasn't. In fact, she left her water pot and ran into town to tell everyone she could find about her amazing encounter. "He told me all that I ever did!" she said (John 4:39 ESV).

Right there, next to Jacob's well on a hot day in Samaria, Jesus created a safe place for truth-telling.

When our children were growing up, Bobbie and I made a pact with them. We told them that when they faced a possible "situation," we would not punish them if they told the truth . . . the first time. They may have had to deal with consequences—replacing the broken vase or apologizing to a sibling—but if the answer to "Hey, how did this get broken?" was an immediate "I did it!" there was no punishment. (There was also no punishment for accidents or honest mistakes.) We decided that our home had to be a safe place for truth-telling.

"What you said hurt my feelings" was something that anyone could express freely and without fear of reprisal. The truth gave recipients of the message a chance to explain what they had said or had intended by what they said.

The summer after Julie's sophomore year in college, she told me over breakfast that she felt spiritually dry. "It's nothing major," she confessed, "but I'm not as excited about my relationship with Jesus as I should be."

Two thoughts came to me simultaneously. First, I was really glad that she felt safe in disclosing her feelings. She had every confidence that I wouldn't whip out a Sunday school lesson, and I was grateful for that. But second, what was I going to do with that information?

"I'm really not sure what to do," I admitted, taking my own turn at truth-telling.

Then something popped into my mind. "I have an idea," I said to Julie. "Let's get together at seven thirty on Tuesday and Thursday mornings this summer. I really don't know what to say to you, but I'll bet if we read the Bible and pray together, God will show us what we need to do."

That simple prediction turned out to be right. Twice a week we rendezvoused in our family room. We sat on the floor and read passages of Scripture, we discussed areas of our lives that were discouraging or especially challenging, and then we knelt at the ottoman in front of a big overstuffed chair to pray. Our summer together renewed our relationships with God and deepened our love for each other.

Julie had been honest about her spiritual doldrums.

WE'RE ON YOUR SIDE

Since I was a young boy, I have been drawn to baseball. As a grade-schooler, in order to pick up the newspapers I was being paid to deliver, I had to ride my bicycle past a Pony League field. Often on spring and summer weekday afternoons, a game was going on there. For me to ride past that field without stopping for an inning or two was almost impossible.

Since those days I've been to many baseball games, including the major-league kind. I've also watched hundreds of games on TV.

Unlike any other professional sport, the manager of a base-ball team has unrestricted access to the umpire. You cannot name another sport where this is true. Sure, you've seen a football or hockey coach jawing at the referee from the sidelines or a basketball coach taking a couple steps onto the court to express his conster-nation over a call. But in baseball, it's not uncommon to see the manager run from the dugout onto the field to go nose to nose with the umpire.

Every once in a while, the manager—just before he's ejected from the game and just before he's fined a hefty sum by the league—is so upset that he kicks dirt onto the umpire's shoes.

Not counting the possibility that the manager stubbed his toe stepping out of the shower that morning, why does he do such an out-rageous thing? Does he do it because he may get his way and convince the umpire to change his decision? Never. Then why?

The answer is amazingly simple. He does it to let his players know that he's on their side. Sure, he really *is* disputing the call on the field, but why the theatrics?

The enraged manager is saying to the umpire, "I don't approve of your decision. And don't mess with my players. I will always defend them. And I'm willing to look very silly out here and get kicked out of the game to make my point."

I am not advocating that you and I act this extreme in order to make our point with our kids, but when it comes to whose side you're on, your kids should never have any doubt.

> Plead my cause, O LORD, with those who strive with me;
> Fight against those who fight against me. (Psalm 35:1)

Imagine that your three-year-old son comes running into the house with a bump on his head. Of course, he is crying. Through his tears, he tries to explain what happened. You piece together the fact that he fell off his bike . . . because he was trying to ride it sitting backward on the seat.

Our "adultness" kicks in. Here's an opportunity to teach our little boy a lesson. The folks who engineered this bicycle did not take into consideration the dynamic weight-shift ratios should the rider choose to mount the seat facing backward. So we begin to explain to our weeping child why he shouldn't have attempted such a daring and foolish thing.

> When it comes to whose side you're on, your kids should never have any doubt.

All the while it's *his* head that's pounding. A lecture on the physics of proper bicycling isn't helping with the pain.

At this low point in his day, our little boy doesn't need a symposium from Mr. or Mrs. Science; there may be time for this later. Right now, he needs the unqualified embrace of someone who's on his side.

I'm not advocating that we become limp and weepy parents, babying our kids whenever they're upset. Folks who do this are inviting their children to become limp and weepy, wailing at every opportunity and manipulating everyone in sight. What I *am* talking about here is doing things that give your kids the confidence that comes from knowing with absolute certainty that you're on their side. Your knee-jerk reaction is not in opposition to them. You're their advocate, their champion.

If I were your kid, this would make me feel safe.

A SAFE PLACE TO MAKE MISTAKES

Where would science and technology be if researchers were unable to make mistakes in the laboratory? In a controlled environment, miracle drugs, cell phones, and even toilet bowl cleaners are the result of trial and error. Can you imagine if supervising scientists told their understudies, "Don't do anything unless it's perfect"? How silly.

Your home—a laboratory about life—needs to have an environment where people are allowed to fail.

In February 1992, my net worth dropped to zero. No, actually, *our* net worth dropped to zero. The publishing company that my business partner and I had started five years earlier had just folded. At that moment, because I had pledged all my (our) financial assets to the venture, my (our) family's financial situation crumbled.

Bobbie and I took our car back to the dealership and asked for mercy. We called our daughter in college and told her that she wouldn't be able to return after that semester. With no equity to be able to buy a home, we looked for a place to rent.

All of this became an enormous inconvenience—and potential embarrassment—for my wife. In five years I had gone from the presidency of a highly respected company in our town, living in a home with five fireplaces in a lovely neighborhood . . . to this.

"How *could* you do this to us?" she could have moaned. "What are we going to do now? Why can't you be like other husbands and just get a regular job?"

But she didn't. Bobbie took my side, treating me like the little boy with a bump on his head. She didn't give me a documentary on what I had done wrong and how it was going to send our family into the pit. She told me that she still believed in me. She reminded me that we were in this together, and we would get out of this together.

For the first seventeen years of our marriage, I was free to succeed. Then, after five years of risk and daring, I was also free to fail.

As my most faithful cheerleader, Bobbie gave me the courage I needed to deal with my failure, learn from it, and begin again.

In chapter 4, we talked about your Christian home being filled with grace. "We love Him because He first loved us" (1 John 4:19). Here's another example of that. God didn't wait to love us—even die for us—until we were successful. His love for us was in full force *while* we were utter failures.

Our kids need the same thing we need. When they forget their lines in the school play or strike out in Little League, they feel the loss, just as I did when my business fell apart. They need

> For the first seventeen years of our marriage, I was free to succeed. Then, after five years of risk and daring, I was also free to fail.

our honest support—"Honey, I'm proud of you for trying"—and our hugs and encouragement. It won't fix the mistake, but it will make it bearable. It also will give them strength to try again.

One mom we know says to her kids, "A mistake means you're trying something. And that's good. If you never try anything, you never make mistakes. I'd rather see you try."

Many years ago Bobbie watched twelve-year-old Sabrina compete at Disney's Wide World of Sports in a national gymnastics meet. Bobbie was impressed at how her coach responded to the girls after each event. Everyone got a smile and a side hug or high five every time she competed. Bobbie remarked to Sabrina's family how consistently the coach affirmed the girls, regardless of their performance. The mother sitting down the row overheard and agreed that the girls really did have an outstanding coach.

Then she said something that took Bobbie a while to get over. "I've seen parents turn their faces away in disgust or not speak to their kids after the meet if they missed a move or fell off the beam. I've seen a father walk out the gym door in an angry fit to punish his daughter for not sticking a landing."

"These are kids," Bobbie told me later. "They need to feel safe."

A SAFE PLACE TO ASK ANYTHING

We've talked about the importance of creating a safe place for truth-telling. Your Christian home also needs to be a safe place for truth-asking.

Because you and I have electricity in our homes and because it allows us to have televisions, radios, and computers at the ready, images and ideas that are almost too horrible to contemplate bombard our families. From the time they are old enough to wonder, our children are exposed to things that our grandparents could never have imagined.

Your home must be a place where questions about the unthinkable are acceptable, where discussions are open and free.

> Your home must be a place where questions about the unthinkable are acceptable.

I cannot remember making a strategic decision about this early in my marriage with Bobbie. Perhaps we just fell into it because we were working with teenagers when our children were born. These adolescents showered us with plenty of questions. Our home was a perpetual town-hall meeting. Other teenagers often asked us about issues they wouldn't dare discuss with their own parents. This was a privilege, although we always encouraged them to seek their own parents' counsel and wisdom.

We wanted to set in motion a free and open forum for our own small children so they would come to *us* when they were older. Our first serious opportunity came along when Missy stepped out of the bushes one afternoon. She had been playing hide-and-seek with the little neighbor boy; Missy was four, and Jimmy was six. Bobbie detected a possible problem when Missy emerged, her shorts quite askew.

"Jimmy wanted to see what girls' bottoms look like," she reported innocently.

Having been found out, Jimmy headed for home in a dead run, possibly revealing less virtue on his part.

Bobbie remained completely calm as Missy explained that Jimmy had offered the classic curious child's quid pro quo: "You show me yours, and I'll show you mine."

Bobbie headed straight for our public library. After some searching, she found a book appropriate for children that explained body parts and their functions. She called Jimmy's mother, Mary, a close neighbor-friend, and told her what had happened. Asking for an opportunity to turn it into a teaching moment, Bobbie told Mary that she had found a book at the library and would like to go through the book with Missy and Jimmy together. Mary gave her unequivocal permission.

In less than twenty-four hours from the bushes episode, Bobbie was sitting in the flower-print stuffed chair in our living room with Jimmy on one arm and Missy on the other. Reading each page and giving the kids enough time to look at the illustrations, she solicited questions from the children. Missy was full of them. Jimmy was far more sedate.

We're not sure what the long-term impact of the experience meant to Jimmy, but for our daughter, it was a precursor of things to come.

When I got home later that day, Bobbie asked me to run to the grocery store for a few things. I asked if Missy could come along. Until she was too old to fit in the kid seat on the shopping cart, riding in the grocery store was one of our high-speed favorite adventures—NASCAR at the supermarket.

Once we had located our assigned items and I had double-checked the list, I found an aisle that looked as if it was moving along nicely. When it was our turn, I walked around to the front of the cart to unload our purchases onto the moving belt.

By this time a gentleman in a business suit—obviously on a similar errand for *his* wife—took his place in line behind our cart where our four-year-old was parked. Missy sat there for a while, staring at the man, her eyes at about his belt buckle height.

"Mister," I heard her ask as I set a half gallon of 2 percent milk onto the moving food sidewalk, "do you have a penis?"

Her question was as sincere as if she had asked the man if he liked Cocoa Puffs.

I turned and looked at the dismayed shopper. After a long day at the office, he was mercilessly unprepared for that question. His gaze dropped to the green and black vinyl-tiled floor. Neither of us spoke.

As Missy and her sister grew, our children learned that in our home, no topics or questions were out-of-bounds. As preteens and teenagers, when their questions turned tough, Bobbie and I did our best not to make any judgments as to *why* they were asking those things. We dealt with questions about drugs, sex, alcohol, or cheating in school at face value.

Although sometimes it wasn't easy, Bobbie and I did our best not to overreact, not making assumptions that the *asking* of these questions meant something. Our children often heard their friends say, "I can't believe you talk to your parents about *that*!"

This kind of openness will come with the decision to make your home a safe place for questions. Make a promise to treat each honest query—scary though they may be—with respect.

And honest questions from them will also give you a chance to be transparent with your children about your own insecurities and fears and foibles.

THINKING IS BEING

For as [a man] thinks in his heart, so is he.
—PROVERBS 23:7

Consider the power of these words King Solomon wrote over three thousand years ago. The character traits you embrace determine who you become. Zig Ziglar underscored this idea when he said that "a person cannot consistently perform in a manner that is inconsistent with the way he sees himself."[1]

198

Because this is true, you can take this to the bank: members of your family are likely to become what you think they'll become.

Of course, I'm not talking about your kids becoming doctors or lawyers or ministers just because you think that's best for them. That conscription will be theirs—and theirs alone—to determine.

"Finally, brothers, whatever is true, whatever is honorable, whatever is just, whatever is pure, whatever is lovely, whatever is commendable, if there is any excellence, if there is anything worthy of praise, think about these things" (Philippians 4:8 ESV). What I *am* talking about are these kinds of things: truth, honor, rightness, and purity.

> You can take this to the bank: members of your family are likely to become what you think they'll become.

If, in my heart, I think of my daughter as a truthful person, then that's how I'll act toward her. It's my presupposition, my default screen: *My daughter is a truth-teller.* When she tells me something, she sees no cynicism on my face. I trust her stories.

Then, on those rare occasions when she fails to live up to this standard, my reaction is absolutely predictable. "You didn't tell the truth. That's not *like* you."

I have just put words to the goal that I have for her. I expect high marks in honesty. And I *know* that she can do better than compromising statements. My preconception—my bias—is, *this girl is an honest person.* What she did was a momentary hiccup. And a corrective adjustment, coupled with my forgiveness, puts her back on track.

Even if your child is really struggling with chronic untruth-telling, I encourage you to continue affixing strong truth-telling character in his or her mind. Speak "This isn't like you" again and again. You may also want to use the no-punishment-if-you-tell-the-truth-the-first-time approach.

This takes us back to Bill Glass talking to the prison inmates, doesn't it? What those prisoners heard was what their parents believed about them, what they *thought* of them. And many of them became what their parents thought they'd become.

> A safe home is a place where people always think the best of each other.

A safe home is a place where people always think the best of each other. And even when unacceptable behavior interrupts this, the default goes right back to truth, honor, rightness, and purity.

WHO DID THIS?

One of the fascinating things about our culture is the seemingly rampant outbreak of the "blame game." For every negative nuance in a person's life, someone is at fault.

One day Jesus and His disciples were walking along a road when they passed by a man—probably a beggar—who was blind.

"Now as Jesus passed by, He saw a man who was blind from birth. And His disciples asked Him, saying, 'Rabbi, who sinned, this man or his parents, that he was born blind?'" (John 9:1–2). "Who's to blame for this?" they asked Jesus. "Did this man do something awful to deserve this, or was it his parents' fault?" The disciples gave Jesus two selections to choose from: (1) the blind man, or (2) his parents. Jesus chose (3) none of the above.

His answer may be confusing to you. Jesus said, "Neither this man nor his parents sinned, but that the works of God should be revealed in him" (John 9:3). In a Christian home, we understand—at least we accept—this mystery called the sovereignty of God. This is not a fatalistic thing. We don't throw our hands up in despair and say, "We're just puppets on a string. What's the use?" Rather, God's providence provides comfort and hope.

"Are not two sparrows sold for a copper coin? And not one of them falls to the ground apart from your Father's will" (Matthew

10:29). Do you see it? In saying these words, Jesus was assuring His followers that they were far more valuable to God than a tiny bird. And if God's sovereignty keeps track of these little creatures, imagine how carefully He watches over you and your family.

Your home is a safe place, where, regardless of what happens, no one ever needs to panic. Remember the storm? Remember the frenzied disciples? Remember Jesus' words to the storm?

In the story of the blind man, Jesus was telling the disciples that they were asking the wrong question. It was not about who was to blame. The question was: What is God saying to us because this *has* happened?

Is this experience or crisis or accident or trauma a chance for us to examine our own hearts and perhaps repent? Is this an opportunity to draw closer to Him, to trust Him in new ways? Is this a way for us to demonstrate to others how important God is to us and how faithful He has been to our family?

> Is this an opportunity to draw closer to Him, to trust Him in new ways?

Can you feel the calm? I can too.

A SHELTER IN THE NEIGHBORHOOD

As wonderful as my family was when I was a kid, we did not grow up thinking much about our neighborhood. It wasn't that we were unfriendly—we weren't. It wasn't that we didn't kill the dandelions in our yard. We did. We just came and went without much thought about the folks who lived close by. Perhaps this was a carryover from my parents both growing up on farms where their closest neighbors were a quarter of a mile away.

To make my point: one of our family's favorite stories is about the day a huge moving van pulled up in front of our neighbor's house, two doors to the east. The Strandquists (whom I mentioned in chapter 1) were leaving the neighborhood. My dad saw the van and decided to walk over to say good-bye. He summoned my brother to go along.

Dad caught Mr. Strandquist as he was walking to his car. "We're sorry to lose you from our neighborhood, Melvin," dad said with loads of genuine sincerity.

"Aw, thanks, Bob," Mr. Strandquist replied, matching my father's aplomb. "We'll miss you too." He then looked at my brother and said, "So long, Tom." He smiled and his eyes narrowed, underscoring his genuineness.

My dad and my brother shook Mr. Strandquist's hand and walked back to our house. A few minutes later, as we sat down to the table for dinner, they gave us the report of their visit. We would have been impressed except that Mr. Strandquist's first name was Larry, my dad's first name was Sam, and my brother was Ken.

Our family exploded in laughter. The story still makes me smile. In retrospect, however, we concluded that what had happened really wasn't something to joke about. With all due respect to my parents, this was less of a joke and more of a missed opportunity.[2]

Of course, I enjoyed playing ball with my buddies from the neighborhood and met many of the grown-ups from delivering newspapers to their houses or washing their cars,[3] but this was pretty much my mind-set . . . until I met Bobbie.

My first visit to her home in McLean, Virginia, was in December 1967. When I walked into the kitchen, she was putting the finishing touches on a beautiful birthday cake. I didn't think that either of her sisters or her parents were celebrating a birthday. "Who's the cake for?" I asked.

"It's for General Illig," she replied. "It's his fiftieth birthday."

"Who's General Illig?" I asked.

"He's our neighbor," she replied.

Although I didn't reveal to her my complete shock, I can tell you that I was amazed on several levels: first, that she knew the day of her neighbor's birthday; second, that she did anything about it; and third, that she went to *that kind of trouble.*

More than four decades later, I can tell you that Bobbie

transformed the way I saw our home in the neighborhoods where we lived. And, to her complete credit, I can tell you that over the years, many of our neighbors and their kids have looked upon our home as a safe place. They may or may not have directly connected this with our residence being a Christian home, but if you were to survey most of them, you'd discover that they knew something good was inside, and they were comfortable there.

When our children were still living at home, this provided them with a great sense of security. Their home was not only a place where they felt safe but where their friends were always welcome. Like landing on the safety square on a board game, they were confident in bringing their buddies to our home.

LITTLE CITIES OF REFUGE

Did you know that "safe places" are not a new idea? Way back in the Old Testament, as Moses was laying out the territories in Canaan, God instructed him to set aside cities for a special purpose.

> When a man goes to the woods with his neighbor to cut timber, and his hand swings a stroke with the ax to cut down the tree, and the head slips from the handle and strikes his neighbor so that he dies—he shall flee to one of these cities and live; lest the avenger of blood, while his anger is hot, pursue the manslayer and overtake him. (Deuteronomy 19:5–6)

First, there were three "cities of refuge." Then, as the nation of Israel grew, three more cities were added. The law of the land was that people who were guilty of manslaughter, but not murder, could be safely exiled there until the frenzy of the crisis settled and cooler heads prevailed. Even their families were safe there. The national courts had no jurisdiction in those cities.

Although you and your kids probably don't need protection from the long arm of the law, you do need somewhere to go that's out of harm's way. A home where there's safety in telling the truth and asking any question, where people are on your side, where you can make a mistake and still be loved . . . a loving place inside, and a safe place in your neighborhood.

> He who dwells in the secret place of the Most High
> Shall abide under the shadow of the Almighty.
> I will say of the LORD, "He is my refuge and my fortress;
> My God, in Him I will trust." (Psalm 91:1–2)

> **A Christian home is a safe place because God is there.**

Taking Moses' idea and running with it, the psalmist announced that refuge—safety—was no longer a matter of geography. A Christian home is a safe place because God is there. He turns your home into a fortress. Your home, wherever it is, can be a city of refuge.

RELAX; YOU'RE JUST THE PARENT HERE

The purpose of reminding you of these important things is to underscore your primary responsibility in your Christian home. You're the parent. You're not a policeman, patrolling the family room, looking for a chance to issue a citation. You're not a hall monitor or a driving instructor or Santa Claus, making a list and checking it twice. You're not a boarder, coming and going at will. And you're not a librarian, making certain that all desks are in straight rows and no one speaks above a whisper.

You're the parent. And your job is to create a place—a happy and safe place—for your family, an atmosphere that assures everyone that he is *really* home.

PEACE ON EARTH

You've probably never heard of Bernie Felstead. But the firsthand account of his experience near the village of Laventie in northern France provides a wonderful picture of what a safe place looks like. It's a story Bernie recalled to a reporter as crisply as if it had happened last year. Even though Bernie was 102, the only living eyewitness, his eyes sparkled when retelling an experience that had taken place more than eight decades before.

It was a bitter-cold morning, December 25, 1914. A twenty-one-year-old private in the Royal Welsh infantry, Bernie was holding his ground in a trench, along with hundreds of brothers-in-arms—young men longing to be home at Christmas. Hostile German troops were barely a hundred yards away.

The evening before, Christmas Eve, the gunfire had begun to subside. Just before dawn, silence suspended itself like a great mist over the battleground. A lone German soldier began singing the Welsh lullaby, "All Through the Night." His silken tenor voice pierced the darkness as he sang the words in perfect English.

> *Sleep my child, and peace attend thee*
> *All through the night.*
> *Guardian angels God will send thee*
> *All through the night.*
> *Soft the drowsy hours are creeping*
> *Hill and vale in slumber sleeping*
> *God his loving vigil keeping*
> *All through the night.*

Bernie Felstead and his comrades listened in amazement. Ten months of relentless gunfire had, for that moment, been replaced with a song their mothers had tenderly sung to them as little boys. Deep emotion filled their hearts.

"The Germans came out of their trenches and walked over to us," Bernie remembered. "Nobody decided for us, we just climbed over our parapets and went over to them. We weren't afraid."

Bernie remembered how foreboding the Germans looked with their strange spiked helmets. Very few British troops knew any German, and hardly a German spoke a single word in English. "But," said Bernie, his leathered face hinting a trace of the emotion that must have filled his heart that morning, "without any spoken orders we all agreed we would not fight that day."

The soldiers exchanged greetings and shook hands, wishing each other a "Happy Christmas." For a few hours, armies of angels hovered over the battlefield. "Peace on Earth" had its way. And Bernie Felstead lived to tell the story.[4]

Even though these troops went back to war, that night provided a respite for battle-weary soldiers. This could be a picture of your home: an oasis from life's relentless battles. No fear, incessant arguments, thoughtless interruptions, general disorder, or armed guards at the ready. This is a safe place to live. And this is something you can do.

Jesus said it this way: "Whatever house you enter, first say, 'Peace to this house.' And if a son of peace is there, your peace will rest on it" (Luke 10:5–6). Exactly as He did that night on the Sea of Galilee, Jesus stretches His hands over your heart and your home. And He speaks, "Peace, be still."

Take a deep breath. Suck in a big draft of air and let it out.

Relax. You're home. *This* is the refuge you were looking for.

206

10

PARENTS AS PRIESTS: PULPITS OPTIONAL

Mom and Dad, Why the Robes?

Don't curse the darkness; light a candle.
—CHINESE PROVERB

*I have no greater joy than to hear
that my children walk in truth.*
—3 JOHN 1:4

A handful of Chinese Christians huddle in one of their modest homes for worship. Together they softly sing hymns and simple choruses. And although their hearts are overflowing with praise to their heavenly Father, their voices are hushed. One of them leads in corporate prayer, then a study of God's Word. A few have Bibles. Most share unbound pages of Scripture.

What they are doing is against the law.

These brave believers know the price they would pay if government forces found them out: certain imprisonment and maybe death. Since the revolution in 1949, the number of those executed

207

for holding services in their homes is estimated in the hundreds of thousands.

This persecution has not dampened the house-church movement in China. When the communists seized the country over six decades ago, there were less than one million Christians. Today some have set the number of believers at well over fifty million.[1]

These courageous saints know, every time they meet, that their world does not welcome what they believe. Their culture is hostile to their undying love for Jesus Christ. It's a nation where children are educated in a system that has been stripped of anything that speaks of God or hints of religion.

Sound familiar?

Don't worry; I'm not going to climb up on a soapbox. This isn't the time or the place. Suffice it to say, however, you and I know that our culture does not embrace those things that we, as believers in God and His Word, consider precious: truth, honor, rightness, and purity. When we walk out of our homes, we're bombarded by messages that are hostile to what we know to be true and precious.

But we should not despair.

It helps to get some perspective. In the United States, there are about 120 million homes. These homes were originally established by grandparents or parents—baby boomers. In a recent survey of baby boomers, one-third of them described themselves as born-again Christians. That means in this country alone, there's the possibility of forty million house churches![2]

CHURCHES EVERYWHERE

The plane I was riding was screaming into the sky directly south from the Nashville airport. We were headed to the West Coast, so as the plane banked sharply to the right, I got a glimpse of the area of the city where we lived, southwest of downtown.

purpose of repentance and worship. His was a house church, and Noah was the spiritual leader.

For centuries, until Moses received the Ten Commandments on Mount Sinai after God delivered the Israelites from Egypt, fathers were the priests in their homes. In fact, the first Passover celebration that saved the children of Israel from the tenth plague—the death of the firstborn—was performed *in every single home*. This was the *official* beginning of house churches on a grand scale, and it continues right up to today in your home and mine.

In the New Testament, Jesus Christ, God's perfect Son, came to earth as our Priest.

> Seeing then that we have a great High Priest who has passed through the heavens, Jesus the Son of God, let us hold fast our confession. For we do not have a High Priest who cannot sympathize with our weaknesses, but was in all points tempted as we are, yet without sin. Let us therefore come boldly to the throne of grace, that we may obtain mercy and find grace to help in time of need. (Hebrews 4:14–16)

Following His death and resurrection, Jesus commissioned His followers, including you and me, with a grand assignment: "But you shall receive power when the Holy Spirit has come upon you; and you shall be witnesses to Me in Jerusalem, and in all Judea and Samaria, and to the end of the earth" (Acts 1:8).

Of course, you and I live in freedom, so we have plenty of regular churches in our towns and are able to come and go as we please. But as I said in the first chapter, we cannot assign the spiritual training of our children to anyone else. As clever and winsome as the youth specialists on our church staffs might be, our *homes* are where our children's spiritual lives will make up their minds. Not our churches.

As we observed in Job's and Noah's homes, before God assigned priests to official duty, heads of households were priests in their homes. Then, through the tribe of Levi and family of Aaron, God authorized official priests to bring the nation of Israel before the throne of God. Then Jesus Christ stepped in as our Great High Priest, and at the close of His ministry, He passed the responsibility of the priesthood back to us in what we refer to as the Great Commission, which you just read.

Soon after this, the apostle Peter put this priesthood thing into words: "But you are a chosen race, a royal priesthood, a holy nation, a people for his own possession" (1 Peter 2:9 ESV). Peter wasn't lecturing down at the seminary in Jerusalem when he wrote these words; he was speaking to ordinary folks like you and me. Home-builders. And he was right.

We are the proprietors of the most important place on earth. We are the specialists. No one can do this better than we can. No one is more qualified.

More than forty years ago, God blessed Bobbie and me with babies. As if it were last week, I can remember an overwhelming, anxious feeling as we brought our bundled newborns home from the hospital—one in 1971 and another in 1974. *What in the world am I going to do now?* kept rolling over and over in my mind. Bobbie and I were parents, but what did that really mean?

Thankfully, because of what we had seen from our parents and learned from others, we knew that we had just established a house church, a little sanctuary in our neighborhood.

And the same is true when you bring your first baby home. You don't actually put up a sign in your front yard, but if you did, it would read:

A Christian Home
Dad and Mom, Priests
Worship Services Daily

INSTANT ACCESS

The role of the Old Testament priest was to connect sinful people to a holy God. Once Jesus had accomplished His assignment, the need for a human mediator came to a screeching halt.

> For there is one God and one Mediator between God and men, the Man Christ Jesus. (1 Timothy 2:5)

Because of what Jesus did, you and I have access—instant access—to God, our heavenly Father. This means that you and I as priests can approach God's throne as we are. And we can usher our children right into His presence as well.

So here's the picture. Even though some of my more doctrinaire friends may press back on this just a bit, I believe that our homes are self-contained sanctuaries, and we're the priests. Although we don't actually erect steeples on top of our houses, we could. These are miniature temples. Each one. (Can you imagine what fun it would be to fly over our neighborhoods and see every Christian home complete with a white tower and cross on top?)

We're ready to go, conducting worship inside our house churches right in our neighborhoods. We have been given this right and privilege—and the authority—to bring our families to God's holy throne, with confession of sins, teaching, prayer, and song.

A PRIEST . . . REALLY?

Since this may be the first time that you're hearing about this responsibility, you may be interested in knowing what it is that priests are supposed to do. What's the job description? Stay with me here; this is very important to understand.

The primary responsibility of the Old Testament priest was *to conduct worship and be the connecting link between the people and their God.* He did this by way of sacrifices. People brought precious things to the priest—usually a special animal from their flocks—and he killed the animals as symbols of the people's contrition for their sin. It was a reminder of how seriously God treats sin. Death was the ultimate payment for it.

The priest offered prayers of confession, repentance, and thanksgiving for himself and for those who had come. He held the head of the animal in his hands as he confessed the wrong actions, words, and thoughts of all the people. Families watched as their special animal was killed and the priest dipped his hand in the blood and sprinkled it on the altar. Then the priest declared to the people that their sins were forgiven.

But the death and resurrection of Jesus Christ—our High Priest—eliminated forever the necessity of more animal blood sacrifices. The innocent Lamb of God was the final sacrifice.

> Not with the blood of goats and calves, but with His own blood [Jesus] entered the Most Holy Place once for all, having obtained eternal redemption . . . And for this reason He is the Mediator of the new covenant, by means of death, for the redemption of the transgressions under the first covenant, that those who are called may receive the promise of the eternal inheritance. (Hebrews 9:12, 15)

Throughout this book, I've mentioned some of your job description as your family's priest. God has charged you with building a home where He lives, a place where you celebrate each individual's life, a place where you treat words with care, a safe place, and a place filled with joy.

YOUR PRIESTLY JOB DESCRIPTION

Remember the Bible's description of the house priest Job, "blameless, a man of complete integrity"? And Noah, "a just man, perfect in his generations"?

These epithets give us a clue as to what you and I need to do as priests in our homes. In fact, we don't have to speculate at all. God, through Moses, was very specific about what priests were supposed to do. Read this carefully; it lays the foundation for your important tasks.

> When you [the priest] offer a *sacrifice* of *thanksgiving* to the LORD, offer it *of your own free will* . . . Therefore you shall *keep My commandments*, and perform them: I am the LORD. You *shall not profane My holy name*, but *I will be hallowed* among the children of Israel. I am the LORD who sanctifies you. (Leviticus 22:29, 31–32)

Sacrifice

You remember that under the old covenant, priests offered sacrifices as a symbol of the people's confession of sin. Now that you're a priest, you are required to bring *your own sin* to the Father. David, the king of Israel and a sinful man, understood this very well:

> The sacrifices of God are a broken spirit,
> A broken and a contrite heart—
> These, O God, You will not despise. (Psalm 51:17)

One of my earliest memories of my dad is the way he prayed. Every morning, he went to the basement of our home and knelt at a chair. Although my siblings and I could not hear his actual words, the deep timbre of his voice sent a thin vibration through our house. In humility, our dad entered the Throne Room of God—remember, instant access?—and confessed his sin. He did this as our family's priest. It was part of his job.

On the Day of Atonement—*Yom Kippur*—the high priest entered the most holy place in the temple to perform the sacrifice alone. On all other days he wore the colorful, jewel-encrusted vestments that set him apart from the people as their spiritual leader. But on that day he wore simple clean white linen; in God's perfect presence, he was an ordinary sinner.[4]

As my dad's son, I am my own family's mediator. And when I enter God's presence on my knees, I'm regularly overwhelmed by my sin and my unworthiness to be the priest in my home. I tell Him about my heart: selfishness, pride, impatience, thoughtless words spoken, lust. And as my dad did, I thank God for Jesus and His gift of forgiveness.

This prepares you and me to lead our whole family in prayer. In chapter 2, we looked at some of the opportunities to do this, such as bedtimes, mealtimes, and riding along in the family car.

As your family's priest, this is the "sacrifice" you must offer as well. The sign out front reads "Worship Services Daily."

Thanksgiving

By *thanksgiving*, I'm not referring to turkey and dressing or the voyage of the *Mayflower* or the landing of the pilgrims or the Wampanoag Indians who helped them survive in the New World. What I am speaking of is a spirit of gratitude that is essential for all priests.

Many years ago in our Sunday school class, I spoke of the need for gratefulness. I looked into the bright faces of those gathered together and said, "There's nothing you have that's not been given to you as a gift." I read from Paul's first letter to the believers at Corinth: "You are not your own, for you were bought with a price" (1 Corinthians 6:19–20 ESV).

Given the fact that many of these people were successful and wonderfully accomplished in their own endeavors, they greeted this truth with some sense of surprise. But it's true. In spite of the fact that you may consider yourself "self-made," you're actually indebted to many, many people who have cared for you.

As your family's priest, you understand that from the day of your birth, everything you have, God has given to you. I've mentioned the importance of gratitude before, but this is especially important to you as your family's spiritual leader.

When you think about it, thanksgiving is really a matter of having a good memory. Looking back on God's protection and blessing should fill your heart with humility and wonder . . . and gratitude.

"I am the LORD who sanctifies you, who brought you out of the land of Egypt, to be your God: I am the LORD" (Leviticus 22:32–33). Here God was reminding the Hebrews that they once had been slaves, common chattel in the hand of the pharaoh. Then they were free. Over and over again, God told His people to recall His covenants and promises and to celebrate His goodness. You can find the word "remember" dozens of times in Scripture.

Of course, priestly thanksgiving includes gratitude for your children. Their birth is a blessing from God . . . an indescribable miracle. And your response to this miracle is to celebrate their talents and unique gifts, even if they're very different from your own. Be thankful for the treasure of your children.

I've told my family that the epitaph I want chiseled on my tombstone is "He had a grateful heart." If at the end of my life I get only five words, those are the ones I want.

I want to be a thankful priest.

Gratitude is something you must have as well.

The sign out front reads "Worship Services Daily."

Offer It of Your Own Free Will

Generosity is thanksgiving's first cousin. It, too, is a prerequisite for the priest of your home. "So let each one give as he purposes in his heart, not grudgingly or of necessity; for God loves a cheerful giver" (2 Corinthians 9:7).

The instructions for priests included offering sacrifices to the Lord "of [their] own free will." Do not, as the apostle Paul said, take this important role as some kind of duty, foisted on you against your will. Being your family's priest is a privilege, not an obligation to be resented. When you see it like this, you can be generous—even happy—with the assignment.

I come from a long line of generous people, starting with my parents. Regardless of how much—or how little—money, food, clothing, or time they had, they gave to others generously. As missionaries with lots of friends in Christian ministries, their resources were always available. At the end of the month, they gave away most of the excess of their bank balance. They, of course, learned generosity from people with grateful hearts—their parents.

My father's parents lived on a farm in Mount Joy, Pennsylvania. During their younger years, they traveled extensively to Christian conferences or on mission assignments. When they left their house for the journey, they *did not lock their doors*. Their explanation was remarkably simple. "If someone is coming by and needs a place for the night, or something to eat, he's welcome to come in and help himself." Pure generosity.

In addition to their "open home" policy when they were out of town, these grandparents also gave of their resources when they were home. My dad was an only child and when he was young, his parents were famous for taking in "strays"—youngsters who had no homes. And there was never any obligation for the kindness.

On my mother's side, her parents' generosity—and frugality—was legendary. Sometimes evening visitors went calling on grandma and grandpa Dourte, then left, thinking they weren't home. A completely unlit home was their clue. But grandma and grandpa *were* home. They preferred saving money for missions rather than burning electricity they didn't need. So they walked around their house in almost complete darkness.

At his funeral, my mother's father left a written will that one of his sons read. "I give to my children and grandchildren and great-grandchildren and great-great-grandchildren something that I can share with all of them in full; there is no need for dividing. I give them my love for Jesus Christ and my life's desire to serve Him. I want them all to have it in full measure."

No wonder my parents learned the fine art of generosity.

Of course, generosity isn't only about money. It includes other resources such as your time. Priests hold everything they have—their treasures, their time, and their families—with an open hand. As you'd do if you borrowed your next-door neighbor's brand-new car, we priests take good care of these things because they do not belong to us—they are gifts from Jesus, the Great High Priest. The New Testament calls this *stewardship*.

Priests give of their own free will. Their nature always leans in the direction of generosity.

As your family's priest, generosity is something you must practice as well.

The sign out front reads "Worship Services Daily."

Keep My Commandments

Even if you didn't grow up in a Christian home and you're new to the Bible, you've probably heard about this verse: "Children, obey your parents in the Lord, for this is right" (Ephesians 6:1). Don't you just love this one? I do too. In giving us instructions on how families are supposed to work, the apostle Paul minced no words when it came to obedience. "Just do it," he said to our kids, "because it's the right thing to do." What a terrific arrow to have in our parental quivers.

Because Bobbie and I loved this verse and believed it to be true, obedience was a non-negotiable in our house. Early in our parenting we decided that the argument over whether or not to obey was foolish. But wait. Even though parents often treat obedience as age-specific— something for kids—it's not at all. Obedience is for grown-ups too. Including priests.

The instructions God gave to the priests that we just read leave no room for argument. "Keep my commands and follow them" (Leviticus 22:31 NIV). Obedience is for everyone.

Question: How old were you when you took your first steps? My kids and grandkids were all walking by their first birthdays. That's about normal. Now here's a sobering truth. It was true about you and me, and it's true about our kids: from the moment they take their first wobbly steps, slowly but surely, your children are headed for the door.

These first steps eventually become their first big wheel, which become their first days at school, which become their first steps on the gas pedal in the family car, which become their first steps across the platform in their graduations from high school, which become their first steps onto a college campus (or whatever they do after high school), which become their steps to the altar of your church for their wedding vows, which is the end of the line for you.

Your children's obedience to you follows the same kind of measured process. When they're tiny, they really have no choice. But the older they get—and the more adept they become at negotiating—obedience becomes more of a struggle.

Your goal is to gradually transfer your children's obedience from you as their parent to God, their heavenly Father. And how will they learn the secret of obedience to God? From the family priest who "keeps God's commands and follows them."

Priests are obedient to God's voice.

As your family's priest, obedience is something you must do as well.

The sign out front reads "Worship Services Daily."

No Profanity

As we've seen, the Old Testament instructions to priests included the following command: "You shall not profane My holy name, but I will be hallowed among the children of Israel. I am the LORD who sanctifies you" (Leviticus 22:32).

When you read "no profanity," you're thinking possibly about nasty four-letter words you might hear from drunks hollering at each other in a bar. Sure, priests must stay away from these words. But the kind of profanity that God commanded priests to avoid is far more pointed.

Let me ask you a question: Which historical figures, not counting biblical men and women, are your heroes? Mine would include people such as Martin Luther, Abraham Lincoln, and C. S. Lewis. What names would you include?

Now let's pretend that tomorrow afternoon, you're going to spend a full hour with one of these people. Sixty minutes, one-on-one—no interruptions—with Marie Curie or Winston Churchill or Susan B. Anthony. Does the thought of this take your breath away? How well would you sleep tonight, knowing what you're going to be doing tomorrow? Not very well. The anticipation would surely fill your arteries with pure adrenaline.

When tomorrow afternoon arrived, imagine how your heart would race as you entered the room where this person was waiting for you. Imagine how your words would be respectful, your behavior impeccable.

The job of the priest was to take his little flock on this kind of fabulous journey. He had the privilege of literally ushering his young charges into the presence of a holy God, the Creator and Sustainer of the universe, the Eternal One who "was, and is, and is to come" (Revelation 4:8 KJV).

The "profanity" that priests were to avoid at all costs was neglecting to escort the people into God's hallowed presence or, worse, the utter sacrilege of taking this journey casually rather than respectfully—begrudgingly rather than willingly.

"Whoever of all your descendants [of Levi] throughout your generations, who goes near the holy things which the children of Israel dedicate to the LORD, while he has uncleanness upon him, that person shall be cut off from My presence: I am the LORD" (Leviticus 22:3). I once thought that my job as a parent was to make certain my children's character was clean and their conduct was exemplary. But I soon learned that these were *not* the most important things I could do. I was commanded to be clean. Shaping our kids' hearts is God's work, and He accomplishes it as we bring our children to Him.

Our primary task as our family's priest is to demonstrate to our children what it means to stand in the presence of a holy God. The thought of this should make our hearts race.

The sign out front reads "Worship Services Daily."

Hallow His Name

When Bobbie and I prayed with our children, they heard "We love You, Heavenly Father," and "We praise Your holy name," and "We worship You." They heard us confess our sinfulness, and they heard us plead for God's grace and mercy for them.

"Thank You for loving Missy with a perfect love. Thank You for dying on the cross and forgiving her sin. Thank You for protecting her as Your precious child."

"Thank You for loving Julie with a perfect love. Please give her wisdom today. We ask You to fill her with Your Holy Spirit. Go before her today. Let her feel Your presence."

We didn't have to go on and on about how to be reverent in God's presence. They couldn't help but catch this in our spirits and hear it in our voices. They saw their mom and dad "walk" into God's presence. They were witnesses to the effect this had on us and on our behavior. They experienced the awe and wonder, and it had the same effect on them.

Honoring and revering God when you bring your children into His presence will have a profound effect on them and their conduct. As your family's priest, showing deep respect for God in your children's presence is something you must do as well.

The sign out front reads "Worship Services Daily."

Music

Although this isn't listed in the Leviticus 22 job description, music was—and still is—a very important part of worship in your house church.

Introducing your family to hymns and Christian music is an important part of your assignment as the family's priest. If you've studied world religions, you know that our Judeo-Christian faith is the only one that celebrates worship in beautiful melodies and harmonies. For centuries, great masters wrote, performed, and conducted music to the glory of God: Handel, Mendelssohn, Bach, Liszt, Beethoven, and other great composers.

More recently, inspired hymn-writers tucked sound Christian doctrine into the lyrics of their timeless work. And the melodies have sealed these truths into our memories forever.

> *Amazing grace! how sweet the sound*
> *That saved a wretch like me!*
> *I once was lost, but now am found,*
> *Was blind, but now I see.*[5]

> *Fairest Lord Jesus, Ruler of all nature,*
> *Son of God and Son of Man,*
> *Thee will I cherish, Thee will I honor,*
> *Thou my soul's glory, joy, and crown.*[6]

God is serious about music. When we open our Bibles to the center, we find a complete hymnal: the Psalms. And King David was its primary lyricist: "Then David spoke to the leaders of the Levites to appoint their brethren to be the singers accompanied by instruments of music, stringed instruments, harps, and cymbals, by raising the voice with resounding joy" (1 Chronicles 15:16).

My grandparents loved music—grandpa Dourte's tenor voice was legendary. My mother was a singer and Bobbie was a singer, so music has been part of our family life from the very beginning. Music has provided a beautiful backdrop for our priesthood. We sang the miles away on car trips as our children grew up, and we passed along a love for music to the grandchildren.

When each of our grandkids visited our home, learning a new hymn was part of the fun—Bobbie called it "Camp Nanny." She neatly programmed learning the words to "Holy! Holy! Holy!" "This Is My Father's World," and "How Firm a Foundation" into the festivities.

Two years before her death, we visited with my 103-year-old grandmother.[7] Hymn-singing was the only way we could communicate. Because of her advancing years, she could not speak in sentences, but she *could* sing. And she did—remembering every treasured word as we sang with her.

Play a hymn or praise-song CD in the car on your way to school in the morning, and sing along. Another wonderful time for music is when your kids are going to bed.[8]

You weren't born with a voice like Pavarotti's. Neither was I. But it doesn't matter. The Scripture doesn't specify *how* we are to sing, just that we *should* sing.

> Make a joyful shout to the LORD, all you lands!
> Serve the LORD with gladness;
> Come before His presence with singing. (Psalm 100:1–2)

The music we make when we sing may more closely resemble "joyful noise" than beautiful music. That's perfectly acceptable. As the priest, it's your responsibility to bring good music into your home. The sign out front reads "Worship Services Daily."

THE PRIEST AS GENERAL CONTRACTOR

If you've ever built a home, you know about construction sequence. The subcontractors who are to execute their specialties—framing, heating and air conditioning, plumbing, electrical, and so on—must come to the construction site in a specific order. In fact, the job of the general contractor is essentially making certain that "subs" arrive when they're supposed to, not too early and not too late. If the guys who hang the drywall show up before the plumber and the electrician are finished, you're going to have a problem.

It shouldn't surprise you that all of creation has a sequence. King David spelled it out this way. This is basic training for priests.

> When I consider Your heavens, the work of Your fingers,
> The moon and the stars, which You have ordained,
> What is man that You are mindful of him,
> And the son of man that You visit him?
> For You have made him a little lower than the angels,
> And You have crowned him with glory and honor.

> You have made him to have dominion over the works of Your hands;
> You have put all things under his feet. (Psalm 8:3–6)

Did you catch the pecking order? God is first, then the angels, then us—mankind—and then animals and the earth itself.[9]

In the same way, there is an important sequence—an organizational chart—to the way priests organize their house churches, their Christian homes. God is first, the parents are next, and then the kids. To completely unpack this would use up more space than my editor will let me take here, but let me summarize it this way.

God First

As the mother or the dad—the priest—your primary allegiance is to the Lord. There is no way that you'll be successful meeting every one of each other's needs. That's God's work. Only He is capable of this, so you must love Him most. Some have called this the "transcendent third." When you love Him first, He draws you to each other.

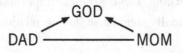

Your Spouse Next

Next, your love for each other takes precedence over your love for your kids. One of the most foundational texts about this in the Bible appears in Paul's letter to the Ephesians. His first admonition was for a husband and wife to love each other (Ephesians 5:22–28). *Then* he spelled out instructions for the parents' relationship with their children (Ephesians 6:1–4).

This is a tough one for some dads and moms to understand, but children who are the top priorities in their families live with a deep sense of insecurity. And kids who are put in this position unconsciously feel the responsibility for happiness and harmony, a weight no kid should ever bear. A mom and dad's strong love for each other creates confidence and self-esteem in their children.

Bobbie and I encouraged young parents to invest in babysitters on a regular basis. One Christmas we gave our daughters and their husbands a three-day getaway, all expenses paid. This gift was complete with visits from Bobbie (Nanny) to cover all the duties at home while our grandchildren's parents were away. The best thing we can give to our grandchildren is parents who love each other. And that happens when they take time to focus on each other alone.

In order to leave no room for misunderstanding, the apostle Paul outlined it this way. He first called husbands and wives to live in mutual submission (Ephesians 5:21). Then he told us exactly how to do it: wives are to submit to their husbands, and their husbands are to love their wives and be willing to die for them.

When women see that their husbands are willing to lay their pride and ambitions and passions aside—die—for their wives, they happily submit, which makes husbands *more* willing to die, which makes wives *more* eager to submit, which makes husbands even *more* willing to sacrifice, and so on.

Humanly speaking, *nothing* is more important in your Christian home than a mutually submissive, loving relationship between you and your spouse.

After Bobbie and I first said "I do" in 1970, we lived in four different states. Each of these moves was the result of a new career opportunity for me. Did I have the "right" to announce to my wife that we were moving to Texas or Tennessee? Yes, I suppose that I could have read "Wives, submit to your own husband" out loud to her, and the discussion would have been over.

But I didn't do that. Why? My wife was one very smart woman, and her discerning opinion of my choices was very important. Also, her security and happiness are mine to protect. If I'm commanded to love her, even be willing to die for her, then pushing her around the country against her will would have been an act of disobedience.

But more than either of these reasons was how I viewed her. My wife was a spiritual resource for me. I wouldn't have thought of *not* using one of my most valuable reserves.

So I presented her with these opportunities. I told her what my desires were, but I made certain that I took *her* desires into serious consideration as well. If I'm supposed to "die" for her, I guess that could have included not taking one of these great career prospects. In each case, she heard me out, sorted out the options, and then agreed that the opportunity seemed like the right thing to do for our family. So each time we moved, she was a vital part of the decision.

And this kind of love cuts both ways.

In 1975, a record producer approached Bobbie with an opportunity to launch into a singing career. We had a four-year-old and a baby at home. Bobbie and I talked about what that would mean for our family—relentless travel and days, maybe weeks, of separation. Of course, some may inaccurately contend that because my wife is "commanded to submit to me," I could have decided that this was a bad idea and just told her to forget it.

But my job as the family co-priest meant being willing to love her as Christ loved us and gave Himself for us (see Ephesians 5:25). So we talked at great length about what the opportunity might mean. I told her that it was a decision we would make together, and if it was what she really wanted to do, and, after praying about it with her and alone and agreeing, I'd do whatever I could to help her . . . then sit on the front row and cheer like crazy.

Ultimately, Bobbie decided that she wanted to be a wife and mom first. Because she seemed at peace with her choice, I celebrated the decision with her.

Back to our building analogy: this is the foundation of your Christian home. If you and your mate are willing to love each other and live in mutual submission—she submits in love, he serves in love—your house will stand sure.

When our Julie was born with a paralyzed foot, all of our energy became instantly focused on our child. But right in the middle of our struggle, I received a note from a very wise friend. It read, "Don't forget that the most important thing you can do to be the dad Julie is going to need is to love her mother."

He was right.

As your family's priest, you must do mutual submission and shared resources in their proper order as well.

The sign out front reads "Worship Services Daily."

Then the Kids

As I said, children are next. Remember the construction order is this: your relationship with God, your relationship with your mate, and then your relationship with your kids.

Once you have the mutual submission thing with your spouse in order, the apostle Paul told kids to obey their parents. No argument there. But then he added an interesting reminder: "Fathers, do not provoke your children to anger, but bring them up in the discipline and instruction of the Lord" (Ephesians 6:4 ESV).

Once again, because the Bible commands kids to obey their parents, you could throw your weight around and force them to knuckle under . . . memories of Captain Von Trapp. But if you look carefully

228

at that verse, you'll see a very important word. It is, in fact, the opera-
tive word in the text. Can you see it?

The word is *bring*.

As I mentioned before, you and I are not *commanding* our children to discipline and instruction. We're not even *sending* them. We're
bringing them with us. This means that *they're coming along with us* to
the world of discipline and instruction. We're going first.

When God was giving instructions to the priests—parents—for the
celebration of Passover in the early Jewish house churches, he told them,
"During these seven days . . . tell your children, 'We do this because of
what the LORD did for us when we left Egypt'" (Exodus 13:8 GW).

Do you see it, "what the Lord did for *us*"? The parents didn't say
to their children, "All right, listen up. God has a few choice words for
you. This is what you're supposed to do. Now, go do it." No. They
included themselves. They reminded their children of what God had
done for *them*. Then they *brought* their children along.

The way to keep from "provoking your children to anger" is to *be*
the picture of discipline and learning yourself. In other words, family
priests never ask—demand—that their children go where they're not
willing to go themselves. Once you've done this hard work, then you
have the right to expect obedience from your kids.

GOING FIRST

I spent my first few years out of college in high-school youth ministry.
Our "mission field" was the North Shore—the suburbs directly north
of Chicago. With the idealism of an eager young man, I did my best
to understand those kids—to connect successfully with their needs.

After a few months of holding meetings and doing one-on-
one counseling, I got the idea to create a written survey. "In order
of importance, list what you need most from your parents" was the

opening question. I then put together a parents' workshop so I could report my findings to these teenagers' parents.

Can you guess what the majority of these kids put as number one? You probably guessed right. The teenagers listed "I need my parents to love me" first. Even kids living in the affluence of that part of the county told me, through the survey, that they first needed the assurance of their parents' love.

Okay, do you want to take a guess at what came in a close second to love? I tallied these surveys over four decades ago and can still recall how surprised I was at what they said next. It never would have occurred to me.

"I need my parents to be consistent," they wrote.

Over the next few months, I followed up with more questions to those young people about that answer. And what I received from them helped to shape my ministry and laid the groundwork for my own parenting. "We don't want our parents to tell us to do one thing and be unwilling to do it themselves," these bright young people wrote. "If they expect me to keep a clean room, I expect them to keep a clean garage . . . or kitchen or their own space." "It's not fair for them to tell me not to swear and then use that same language themselves."

Parents—priests—must be willing to live what they speak and do what they preach. Priests do not demand anything of their children that they are not willing to do themselves. Parents go first.

My mother grew up with seven siblings. She was number three— she had two older sisters. Allon, the first boy, was number four. As it turned out, Allon became the family daredevil. Perhaps he first caught the thrill of daring when his mother snatched him up as he was crawling across a freshly dug open well on a single board when he was eighteen months old.

Regardless of how it began, my Uncle Allon knew no fear. His brothers dared him, as a youngster, to stand on his head at the peak of the barn roof, forty feet from certain death. Allon willingly obliged, laughing at the risk. Even with the most dangerous proposals, he was always willing to go first. And his raw bravery not only made for great entertainment, Allon's daring gave his family a sense of confidence. *If Allon can be brave, then I can be brave.*

I must have been ten or twelve years old when one day my uncle showed me a scar in the center of his chest from being gored while "wrestling a bull." He met my wincing at the sight with a good strong laugh.

In 1998, my uncle, the Reverend Allon Dourte, died after several years of battling cancer. All of his siblings survived him, and they collected written memories of their brother and read them during his funeral service.

My mother wrote that it was just like Allon to show his family that death was not something to fear. As a Christian, Allon did not let the ultimate dread of his own mortality keep him from going first . . . again, just as he had done from the beginning. His love of life and his smiling at death made all of us feel brave.

Whether it's the example you set by the way you speak or take care of your things, by your willingness to bring your children to church, or by the way you face *your* final curtain, as a Christian parent, you should be willing to say to your children, "Let me show you the way you do this." "Follow my example." "I'll go first."

As your family's priest, going first is something you must do as well.

ONE FINAL WORD ABOUT YOUR CHRISTIAN HOME

Remember my vision of house churches from the airplane? If I were flying over your town and looking down at your neighborhood, your home would be one of them.

Yours is a house church, a Christian home: the most important place on earth. And you are the priest.

Now you know what to do.

You're ready to go.

EPILOGUE

In the introduction to this book, I encouraged you to treat the experience of reading it like a visit to a cafeteria—picking and choosing those ideas that looked especially tasty, knowing that you can come back and pick something else another day.

I trust that you've been able to do just that. And I hope those things that you've already placed on your tray have been helpful.

In spite of sounding lighthearted about this experience, I believe the health and preservation of the Christian family—*your* Christian family—is a deadly serious subject. You *know* that in North America, the family is under incredible assault. And you also know that the best way for you to stand against this attack is to recommit yourself to your *own* family, doing the right things with your kids day after day after day.

Your home *is* the most important place on earth.

In his book, *I, Isaac, Take Thee, Rebekah*, Dr. Ravi Zacharias underscores this fact:

The home was instituted before the Church was brought into being . . . God intended the home to be the seed from which the culture flowers and history unfolds.[1]

As I was finishing the original manuscript for this book in 2003, Bobbie came across a letter that she had written to me in August of 1969. We were engaged to be married the following March and she was getting ready to leave America for a tour of Europe and the Middle East as part of a singing group—a Teen Team, sponsored by Youth for Christ, International.

We were separated by half a country. She was with her family in Washington, DC, and I was in Chicago, working in my first job as a youth minister. We had talked many times—especially since our engagement the previous May—about our marriage, our future, and the children that we hoped God would send our way.

In her letter, after greeting me in her usual way,[2] she wrote:

I just finished reading chapter 11 of Romans . . . the first verse I underlined was the 16th: *And since Abraham and the other patriarchs were holy, their descendants will also be holy. . . . For if the roots of the tree are holy, the branches will be, too* [NLT]. It made me think of how we want our children someday to be real children of God . . . if our roots are deep in Him . . . our children will grow. There is nothing so exciting as to think that someday, if the Lord lets us, we will create life, and we'll love and cherish that life and want to give it back to God.

Bobbie wrote this in 1969. God did bless us with children and grandchildren. Through these years we were reminded of our need as parents to walk obediently before God. This was a daily experience of failure and triumph. We were challenged to teach our children, reminding them of God's grace in our lives and bringing them along in the faith. And it has been a thrill to watch them do the same with their kids.

She wrote her letter to me the year before we were married. But what neither she nor I could have ever forecast was that her earthly life would end just before her sixty-fifth birthday. Yes, Bobbie was able to celebrate the birth of our two daughters, their weddings, and the glorious births of five grandchildren. But all ten of us said good-bye to this remarkable woman still in the prime of her life.

Her letter made reference to Romans 11:16. I'm guessing that Bobbie didn't stop reading with that chapter but continued on to chapter 12. Verse one of that chapter challenges us as followers of Jesus to present ourselves as a "living sacrifice." This is exactly what Bobbie did. She lived, and she died. Her funeral service ended with a verse posted on the large screens in front of the church:

> Unless a kernel of wheat fall to the ground and dies, it remains only a single seed. But if it dies, it produces many seeds. (John 12:24 NIV)

Whatever your past may be and wherever you are in your own personal experience of God's grace and however old your children are, please be encouraged. Listen carefully to this from our friend, the apostle Paul:

> Brothers, I do not consider myself yet to have taken hold of it. But one thing I do: Forgetting what is behind and straining toward what is ahead, I press on toward the goal to win the prize for which God has called me heavenward in Christ Jesus. (Philippians 3:13–14 NIV)

My prayer is that God will give you—your home's priest—great confidence and wisdom. God bless you in this wonderful adventure.

ACKNOWLEDGMENTS

Not until my first job in book publishing, in January 1979, did I ever pay attention to the acknowledgments. Truthfully, when I was reading a book, I always enjoyed getting to them because it gave me a chance to turn a page or two—making solid headway into the book—without even pausing to see who, or what, the author was "acknowledging."

Now, as an author, although I still understand why most people skip these pages, I know why they're here. Even though there's only one name on the cover of a book, the process of writing it is clearly a team effort.

When I first met with the folks at Thomas Nelson regarding this book, I seriously considered adding my late wife, Bobbie, to the cover as a coauthor. If you knew how our marriage had been a collaborative effort since our "I do's" in 1970, you'd understand. Although the decision was made to leave her name off the cover, you've seen that her love for Christ, her love for me, her love for our kids, and her creativity as a wife and mom fills its pages. Now, since her death in 2014, I look back on the impact she had on me and my parenting and am so grateful for Bobbie.

My parents, Samuel and Grace Wolgemuth, first gave me a snapshot of what a Christian home looks like. This wonderful image was indelibly seared into my heart. My parents are already in heaven, and until her death in 2010, my precious mother was a great encouragement to me. My love and thanks go especially to her, the woman whose name and life is Grace.

I've dedicated the book to my nieces and nephews and—for those who are married as of the writing of the book—to their spouses. I'm deeply grateful to the parents of these nieces and nephews, my brothers and sisters—Ruth, Sam, Ken, Debbie, Dan—who not only invested in me during our growing-up years but are my friends today. Because this book contains some of the stories of our lives as siblings, I asked them to read the manuscript and give me their input and ideas. They did. I'm thankful to them for this.

I'm also thankful to my niece Kristin Fitzgerald and my nephew Andrew Wolgemuth and his wife, Chrissy, for combing through the manuscript and making some great "catches."

Having spent most of my career in the world of book publishing, I know few authors understand the important role a publisher makes in the life of a book better than this author. My former business partner and one of my closest friends on the earth, Mike Hyatt, was the first to invite me to write a book to encourage Christian families. My gratitude goes to him.

The editorial and marketing teams at HarperCollins Publishing are first class. I am grateful to them all, especially Matt Baugher, Joel Kneedler, and Paula Major. And in this business, having a great agent is like having a solid health insurance policy. Ann Spangler is all of that and more. I'm very thankful for each of these friends and consummate professionals.

In 2015, I married again. Nancy Leigh DeMoss was a good friend to Bobbie, and right before stepping into heaven, Bobbie told two of her closest confidants that she wanted me to marry Nancy. They did not tell me this until two months after Nancy and I began dating in 2015. As Nancy mentions in the foreword, soon after we started our relationship, she found a copy of the original edition of *The Most Important Place on Earth* and read it in order to get a picture of who this man was. Ironically, I picked up a copy of Nancy's book, *Lies Women Believe*, and learned a lot about her too.

Nancy told me how much she appreciated this book, and when I told her that my publisher was going to update and rerelease it, she asked if she could write the foreword. I said yes.

Marriage to this special woman has been a joy. She is a treasure. God's gift of grace. His sweet provision. I'm grateful to add Nancy DeMoss Wolgemuth to this list of friends and family who have encouraged me in the writing and rewriting of this book.

Finally, I'm thankful to my heavenly Father, whose grace has been extended to me in countless ways, and for you . . . for allowing me to share a few hours with you.

APPENDIX A

How to Lead Your Child to Christ

Then Jesus called for the children and said to the disciples, "Let
the children come to me. Don't stop them! For the Kingdom
of God belongs to those who are like these children."
—LUKE 18:16 NLT

The scene is familiar. Jesus is teaching a group of grown-ups when
a handful of kids begins to make a ruckus. The disciples, no
doubt embarrassed that the Master's oration has been interrupted, do
their best to corral the children so Jesus can continue.

Jesus disrupts the disruption. He tells the disciples—turned
bouncers—to back off. Not only does He not mind the extra noise of
the little ones, He turns the table and invites them to come to Him.
He takes the initiative.

But it's not the first time.

We love Him because He first loved us. (1 John 4:19)

From the beginning of time, long before our great-great-grand-
parents were even conceived, God knew us and loved us and wanted
to draw us to Himself. This is true for you and me. And as we read in
the story above, it's true for our children as well.

241

There's *nothing* more important for Christian parents than to be certain that their kids have made their own profession of faith in Jesus Christ. Moms and dads cannot wrap their own experience of salvation around their kids like a sweater on a cold day. God has no *grandchildren*. Every child must make the transaction on his own.

Although I'm going to highlight the key points in helping your child understand the need for salvation and how to make his or her own profession of faith, the delightful truth is that in a Christian home, this transaction is also a process. In many ways a child's receiving the gift of God's grace is *truth*, settled in a *moment*, confirmed through *daily experience*, and stretched out over a *lifetime* between parents and their children.

WHO IS GOD?

Your child's experience of the wonder of an awesome God comes first.

The feeling of absolute awe when you and I first laid our eyes on our baby—whether through natural birth or adoption—is one that we'll never forget. This was God's blessing, and we knew it. We were spectators to a miracle.

From that moment forward, in the presence of our child, that very same sense of wonder needs to fill our hearts whenever we're reminded of God's creation, His gifts, and His love. In chapter 2, you read about saying to your children, "Isn't God amazing?" when you see a sunset or watch ants tromping in single file across the sidewalk in front of your house.

> The heavens declare the glory of God,
>> and the sky above proclaims his handiwork. (Psalm 19:1 ESV)

The most important thing you can do in the process of leading your child to a personal relationship with Christ is to give him or her a sense of your own reverence for God. *He* is the most important Person in the world to you. As your children grow and discover the truth of God's love and His provision of grace for them, they'll be familiar with Him because of how you have obeyed and adored your heavenly Father.

As I mentioned in chapter 10, "Our primary task . . . is to demonstrate to our children what it means to stand in the presence of a holy God." This is something you and I can do every day.

SIN

Although sin is an ominous concept to discuss with our kids, they are more aware of their own limitations and wrong attitudes than we may think. And they can be taught what it is that displeases their heavenly Father.

The Bible makes it abundantly clear that mankind is sinful from the moment of our birth.

> For all have sinned and fall short of the glory of God. (Romans 3:23 ESV)[1]

Sinfulness shows up in our families every day—greed, angry outbursts, disobedience, selfishness. These reveal our sin nature, that part of us that's owned and operated by Satan himself.

The apostle Paul explained it this way:

> It is no longer I myself who do it, but it is sin living in me. (Romans 7:17 NIV)

We have friends whose little girl was having a particularly naughty day. By midafternoon, in complete frustration, mom sat down with Vickie and explained to her that our lives are in a tug-of-war between God—the One who wants us to be kind and obedient, and Satan—the one who doesn't. In careful detail, Vickie's mother told her that she needed to be obedient to God, who wants her to be a good girl.

The rest of the day, Vickie was as close to perfect as a six-year-old could be. Her words were kind, she obeyed the first time, and she even shared her toys with her little brother.

But the next day was another story. From the moment Vickie woke up, it seemed as though she had completely forgotten yesterday's resolution. Soon after breakfast, Vickie's mother sat down with her to ask about her pitiful behavior.

Looking at her mother, Vickie announced, "I've decided to go with the other guy."

The story makes us smile, but the reality of sin's power over our children is not funny. Tell your kids how Satan wants to hurt them and make them do bad things. Tell them how Satan wants to pull them away from God's love. Then tell them that Jesus' power is stronger.

THE CROSS AND THE EMPTY TOMB

Jesus loves me, this I know, for the Bible tells me so.
Little ones to Him belong;
They are weak, but He is strong.

It's a common thing for children to count on the strength of others to bolster their own confidence. "My daddy can beat up your daddy."

The lyric of the first Christian song that most children learn is profound. "He is strong" isn't a statement of His physical strength, it's a *spiritual* truth. It means that Jesus' death and resurrection conquered Satan and the sin he peddles.

For the wages of sin is death, but the gift of God is eternal life through Christ Jesus our Lord. (Romans 6:23)

Yes, Jesus lifts you and me from sinful activity. That's good. Jesus' power also saves us from the evil one who relentlessly haunts us and tries to lead our hearts astray. That's very good. But Jesus' death and resurrection from the grave seal our relationship with God, our heavenly Father, forever. That's fantastic.

THE GIFT OF SALVATION

Like nicely wrapped packages we open on our birthdays, the salvation that Jesus offers is a gift to be received.

In the first century, the apostle Paul and his friend, Silas, were imprisoned because they were preaching the good news of Jesus—the Cross and the Resurrection. Late one night, a huge earthquake rocked the ground, throwing the prison doors open and even loosening the men's shackles. When the jailor realized what had happened, he pulled out his sword and prepared to kill himself. Paul and Silas stopped him, assuring him that they had not escaped. The jailor was overwhelmed by the witness of these great men. He fell to his knees and asked what he needed to do to be saved.

So [Paul and Silas] said [to the jailor], "Believe on the Lord Jesus Christ, and you will be saved, you and your household." (Acts 16:31)

Did you catch the promise of receiving the gift? For the jailor and then for his family.

That's why Paul challenged parents to "bring" their children up in the faith. Parents who go first have the privilege to invite their children to follow along.

WHEN DO MY CHILDREN NEED TO RECEIVE JESUS AS THEIR SAVIOR?

Because you're a parent, you know that the state of moral awareness and spiritual accountability comes to children at different ages. Certainly selfishness and disobedience are hardwired to their DNA very early—not wanting to share toys with the neighbor toddler or refusing to obey you. This behavior can be credited to a sin nature that is conceived in every human being.

The issue here is the time and place when our children "understand" their own sinfulness.

You discover this when you see that your child has the capacity to make a choice between obedience and disobedience, between kindness and greed, between impetuousness and self-control. You may also recognize a readiness when you observe that your child feels a sense of sorrow and shame after being punished for doing naughty things.

I know that my own children and grandchildren have come to this place of maturity at different times, anywhere from about four to seven years old.

Perhaps the best way to begin the discussion about your child's need to receive the gift of God's grace is to tell him or her about your own journey of faith. Then remind your children:

- How great and good their heavenly Father is . . . how much He loves them;
- They need God to forgive them for things they do that displease Him;
- Jesus' death on the cross and resurrection from the grave pays for their sin and saves them from Satan's power over them and brings them into a new lifelong friendship with God; and
- God loves them so much that He wants to live in their hearts and take them to heaven when they die.

Some parents take their children through these steps by way of praying with them. My mother did this with me when I received Christ as my Savior as a small boy. She prayed a prayer on my behalf, one phrase at a time, that I repeated after her. It went something like this:

Dear Heavenly Father—thank You for loving me—I know that I am a sinful boy and need You to save me—thank You for dying on the cross and rising from the dead—I receive Your gift of forgiveness—thank You for coming to live in my heart for the rest of my life—and thank You for the promise of heaven when I die—Amen.

Whether you help them with the words of their prayer or give them enough information that they can come to Christ on their own, the important thing is that they hear themselves speak the words of worship, repentance, acknowledgment of God's grace, and affirmation.

Just in case anyone ever wondered if speaking these words, one person at a time, is an important part of the transaction between sinful mankind and a holy God, the apostle Paul leaves no room for doubt.

Because, if you confess with your mouth that Jesus is Lord and believe in your heart that God raised him from the dead, you will be saved. For with the heart one believes and is justified, and with the mouth one confesses and is saved. (Romans 10:9–10 ESV)

ONLY THE BEGINNING

Even though this transaction is the completion of your child's acceptance of God's gift of salvation, it's the beginning of something else: a life of discipleship. Many of the ideas you've read in this book are intended to guide you and your children in that direction, including Bible reading, prayer, confession of sin, and church attendance.

Your children will also need reassurance of their place in God's kingdom. Even though the transaction is completed, there will be times when they will wonder if they need to go back and do it again. Like your wedding vows, the matter was settled when the words were spoken. Your child needs to know that God will never let them go.

Here's what Jesus said:

My sheep hear my voice, and I know them, and they follow me. I give them eternal life, and they will never perish, and no one will snatch them out of my hand. My Father, who has given them to me, is greater than all, and no one is able to snatch them out of the Father's hand. (John 10:27–29 ESV)

These words assure you that your child's adoption into God's family is eternally secure. Of course, just as is true with you, your child will be in a continued process of spiritual growth through the confession of sin and a renewal of his or her desire to follow Christ.

Because of the struggle we know they will encounter from this moment forward, it is important to continue to pray for our children for the remainder of our lives.

A few months before he died, I sat with my dad in his home. He was suffering from a rare neurological disease that rendered him quiet and withdrawn. He had a hard time talking or listening. His eyes were failing so he couldn't read the newspaper or watch the Cubs or Bulls on television.

"Dad," I said to him, "how does all of this make you feel?"

He looked straight into my eyes. "Useless," he said.

"Dad," I finally said after a few minutes, "do you remember how you used to pray for us?"

"I still do," he returned with a faint smile.

"Do you know what a difference that makes in our lives? Do you know how thankful we are?"

He nodded.

"Even if you were able-bodied and strong," I continued, "there still is nothing more important—more useful—that you could do than to keep praying."

"You're right. Thank you, son," my dad added.

"No, thank *you*," I said as I walked over to his chair. Kneeling down in front of my dad, I put my arms around him and hugged him.

"Thank you," I repeated, kissing him on the cheek. I held him for just a few more moments and kissed him again.

> And I am sure of this, that he who began a good work in you will bring it to completion at the day of Jesus Christ. (Philippians 1:6 ESV)

Finally . . .

Bringing your children to Jesus is a natural part of what needs to happen in your Christian home. Praying for them is something you will do today and tomorrow . . . and the next day. And growing in your own relationship to Christ is a lifetime adventure.

Remember that this place you call home is also a "house church." This is just the right place for ordinary and holy things to happen.

APPENDIX B

Grace Wolgemuth's 26 Bible Verses

In chapter 2, I told the story of my mother, Grace Wolgemuth, teaching our daughters twenty-six Bible verses, each beginning with a letter of the alphabet. Over the years she has taught these verses to many, many children, including most of her twenty grandchildren and many of her eighteen great-grandchildren.

Here are the verses, just in case you'd like to teach them to your kids:

A All we like sheep have gone astray. Isaiah 53:6

B Be kind one to another. Ephesians 4:32

C Children obey your parents, for this is the right thing to do.
      Ephesians 6:1

D Don't fret or worry; it only leads to harm. Psalm 37:8

E Every good and perfect gift is from above. James 1:17

F "Follow me," Jesus said, "and I will make you fishers of men."
      Matthew 4:19

G God is love. 1 John 4:16

H He cares for you. 1 Peter 5:7

I "I am the Bread of life." John 6:35

J   Jesus said, "Let the little children come to Me." Matthew 19:14

K   Kind words are like honey, enjoyable and healthful. Proverbs 16:24

L   Love one another. John 13:34

M   "My sheep hear My voice, and I know them, and they follow
    Me." John 10:27

N   Now is the time to come to Jesus. 2 Corinthians 6:2

O   Obey God because you are His children. 1 Peter 1:14

P   Pray about everything. Philippians 4:6

Q   Quick Lord, answer me, for I have prayed. Psalm 141:1

R   Remember your Creator now, while you are young. Ecclesiastes
    12:6

S   Sing a new song to the Lord. Psalm 98:1

T   Thank God for Jesus, His gift too wonderful for words.
    2 Corinthians 9:15

U   Underneath are God's everlasting arms. Deuteronomy 33:27

V   Visit the orphans and widows. James 1:27

W   We love because God first loved us. 1 John 4:19

X   Except a kernel of wheat fall into the ground and die, it remains a
    single seed. But if it dies, it produces many seeds. John 12:24

Y   You must be born again. John 3:7

Z   "Zacchaeus, you come down; for I'm going to your house today."
    Luke 19:5

NOTES

Introduction

1. Some purists would contend that 4:30 doesn't qualify as "evening."
2. Nothing edible can ever come from something that, before it's cooked, looks like a fender of a Packard.
3. Alan Wolfe, *The Transformation of American Religion: How We Actually Live Our Faith* (New York: Simon and Schuster, Inc., 2003), 2.
4. My maternal grandfather ate all his meals with a flyswatter lying next to his fork. He could crush one of those critters in midair. You can't always count on the dependability of flypaper.

Chapter 1: Why a Christian Home?

1. Disneyland in Southern California was the first "Happiest Place on Earth." When Walt Disney World was built in Central Florida, it shared this moniker. And now Walt Disney Worlds around the globe do the same. Linguistic purists will argue against having more than one "happiest." But Disney doesn't worry about it. These purists are down the hall in engineering and have no input in marketing.
2. Walt Disney, A Detailed Biography, JustDisney.com, accessed February 8, 2016, http://www.justdisney.com/walt_disney/biography /long_bio.html.

3. "Orlando Becomes First Destination to Surpass 60 Million Visitors, Sets New Record for U.S. Tourism," Visit Orlando, April 9, 2015, http://media.visitorlando.com/pressrelease/index.cfm/2015/4/9 /Orlando-Becomes-First-Destination-To-Surpass-60-Million-Visitors -Sets-New-Record-For-US-Tourism.

4. Walt Disney, Walt Disney Quotes, JustDisney.com, accessed February 8, 2016, http://www.justdisney.com/walt_disney/quotes.

5. C. S. Lewis, *Mere Christianity* (New York: The Macmillan Company, 1943), 174.

6. Tacitus, *The Histories*, trans. Alfred John Church and William Jackson Brodribb, http://classics.mit.edu/Tacitus/histories.html.

7. Ibid.

8. "10 Facts About America's Churchless," Barna Group Research, accessed February 26, 2016, https://www.barna.org/barna-update /culture/698-10-facts-about-america-s-churchless#.

9. "New Marriage and Divorce Statistics Released," Barna Group Research, accessed February 26, 2016,, https://www.barna.org/barna-update /family-kids/42-new-marriage-and-divorce-statistics-released#; "American Lifestyles Mix Compassion and Self-Oriented Behavior," Barna Group Research, accessed February 26, 2016, https://www.barna .org/barna-update/donors-cause/110-american-lifestyles-mix-compassion -and-self-oriented-behavior#.

10. Young Life is an international youth organization. Through weekly meetings in kids' homes, camps, and inner-city ministries, Young Life has been a powerful force in loving teenagers and introducing them to Jesus Christ. In 1941, Jim Rayburn, Young Life's founder, said, "It's a sin to bore a kid with the Bible," and Young Life—currently with a worldwide staff of over eighteen hundred—was born.

11. Mark DeVries, *Family-Based Youth Ministry* (Downers Grove, IL: Intervarsity Press, 1994).

12. George Barna, "Spiritual Progress Hard to Find in 2003," December 22, 2003, https://www.barna.org/component/content/article/5-barna -update/45-barna-update-sp-657/132-spiritual-progress-hard-to-find -in-2003#.

13. These three Bible chapters, Matthew 5, 6, and 7, my mother recited

every morning from memory, between the time she woke up and the time her feet hit the floor. No wonder the Lord answered her "Please stop the rain" prayer.

Chapter 2: A God Place

1. After my grandfather had sold his farm, he took up painting and wallpapering. There wasn't a single surface in his home that didn't have a coat of either one or the other.

2. One summer our landscaper sprinkled mothballs around the begonias in front of our house to keep vermin from dining on them. After my first whiff, I was tempted to install a screen door with a long spring that made it screech when we opened it and smack when we let it go, just to complete the experience.

3. Incense is often made from the dried sap of a frankincense tree. Remember that this was one of the gifts the wise men brought to the Christ child? Going all the way back to Moses (Exodus 30:22–25), God instructed His people to use fragrant oils and incense in worship (Leviticus 4:7). Mary poured expensive and sweet-smelling oil on Jesus' feet (John 12:1–8) as a symbol of her sacrificial love for Him. When Isaiah entered the temple and was overcome with the presence of a holy God, the place became "filled with smoke" (Isaiah 6:4).

4. Many churches, especially the larger ones, have options for "Sunday worship," including Saturday night, Sunday afternoon, or Sunday night. These count!

5. "A strip across Central Florida, from Tampa to Titusville, is considered the lightning capital of North America and is known as 'Lightning Alley.' Through that zone, there are at least 150 lightning flashes per square mile annually, with 30 or so striking the ground." Joe Callahan, "Florida is nation's hot spot for lightning," Ocala.com, June 18, 2014, http://www.ocala.com/article/20140618/ARTICLES/140619732?p=2&tc=pg.

6. Dr. Henry Blackaby is the co-author of *Experiencing God: Knowing and Doing the Will of God* (Nashville, Tennessee: LifeWay Christian Resources, 1990), the study course that has been used by millions of people around the world and translated into over fifty languages.

7. Richard, Tom, Melvin, and Norman Blackaby all have doctorates

in different biblical disciplines. Richard is the president of Blackaby Ministries International; Tom pastors a church in Vancouver, British Columbia; Mel pastors a church in Jonesboro, Georgia; and Norman is a professor at Dallas Baptist University; Carrie Blackaby Webb has her master's degree in Christian education and is, along with her husband, a career missionary in Germany.

8. There are some good family devotional materials available at your local Christian bookstore. The best we ever saw was a multimedia experience called *Family 15*, Thomas Nelson Publishers, 2004.

9. Martin Luther, "The Large Catechism," (1530), in *Triglot Concordia: The Symbolical Books of the Evangelical Lutheran Church*, trans. F. Bente and W. H. T. Dau (St. Louis: Concordia Publishing House, 1921), 565–773.

Chapter 3: The Most Important People in the Most Important Place

1. The breeder Bobbie bought our Yorkie from, a German woman with a heavy accent, told her in broken English, "Yoakies like little beebies."

2. Jacques Charles, Channing Pollock, Albert Lucien Willemetz, Maurice Yvain, "My Man." Copyright 1965, EMI Music Publishing.

3. Thanks to the advent of caller ID, you can know exactly who is calling. I'm not suggesting that you treat random telemarketers with the same kind of loving care.

4. If you're working during the day, do your very best to give yourselves over to your kids during the evening and on weekends. Say no to things that will take you away during these times. Spend as much time with your kids as you can without jeopardizing your employment.

5. Marcella Hazan as told to Janis Frawley-Holler, "The Sacred Table," *Family Circle*, October 8, 2002, 210.

6. Before our girls could read, Bobbie tried to tell them that this verse really said, "Be kind, one to a mother."

Chapter 4: Amazing Grace

1. Irving Berlin, from *Annie Get Your Gun*.

2. From "The Blind Men and the Elephant" by American poet John

Godfrey Saxe (1816–87). Ironically, the moral of the poem was theological. Saxe believed that although people argue about God, they are, in the end, all blind: "Not one of them has seen!" Christians, of course, take issue with his premise. In Jesus, God—the subject of theology—became perfectly visible.

3. Ken was such a good boy most of the time that when my aging parents broke up housekeeping, he got the new spoon permanently.

4. Dwight Stones won Olympic bronze medals in 1972 and 1976.

5. Although he didn't mention it in the gospel bearing his name, Luke, the writer of the book of Acts, gave attribution to Jesus for having said this.

Chapter 5: The Power of Words

1. I also talk about this in *The Most Important Year in a Man's Life* (Grand Rapids: Zondervan, 2003). Established in 1859, this agreement provided for the neutrality of military hospitals, the protection of people who helped the wounded in battle, and the return of prisoners to their country. It also adopted the use of a white flag with a red cross on hospitals, ambulances, and evacuation centers whose neutrality would be recognized by this symbol. Even though the Geneva Convention has gone through several revisions in the past 150 years—including the denunciation of chemical weapons in battle—it has stood like a sentry over hundreds of battles. And tens of thousands of soldiers have been saved because of its protection.

2. This identification with our earthly father has profound spiritual implications too.

3. Our children used to brace themselves when I started a sentence with those words. What was certain to follow was some story about trudging to school in waist-deep snow with my feet bound in rags or some other heart-wrenching narrative.

4. Bobbie Wolgemuth and Joni Eareckson Tada, *Hymns for a Kid's Heart*, vols. 1 and 2, Crossway Books/Focus on the Family, 2003, 2004.

5. In Tennessee they called these multi-kids rides to school "hookups," but they did not refer to the things kids hung their coats on as "car pools."

6. Because we've lived in the South, we know that when you say "Bless his heart," you are at liberty to say anything you want about the

person and get away with it. Schoolteachers have been quoted as saying, "But Benedict Arnold, bless his heart, was such a traitor."

Chapter 6: The Power of Words Part II

1. Since I'm only an ordained elder in the Presbyterian Church and not an authentic, ordained minister, I can't conduct weddings without a real clergyman standing next to me. In this case it was Rev. Richard Freeman, our pastor.
2. Coming to Orlando is nothing unusual. In 2003, more than forty-five million people did the same. Eventually, *everybody* comes to Central Florida (2003 estimate from Global Insight Research, Inc., 1000 Winter Street, Boston, MA 02451).
3. I didn't say "love the Cubs" because, as far as I'm concerned, this *is* a legitimate use of the word *love*.
4. Gary Smalley and John Trent, *Love Is a Decision* (Dallas, TX: Word Publishing, 1994).
5. Imagine how frustrating it would be to tell someone that you need him to welcome you home, and he tells you that it just isn't a good time.
6. Someone has described televised sports as "men and women on the court or the field desperately in need of rest, being watched by millions of people desperately in need of exercise."
7. Felicite Lefevre, *The Little Red Hen* (New York: Henry Altemus Company, 1920).
8. I have no idea what hydrochlorothiazide is. I think that it's an emergency cardiac life-support medication. Or maybe it's something people put in their swimming pools to control algae.

Chapter 7: Just for Laughs

1. One time my dad was gone for *three* months on a missionary assignment.
2. I know. You've heard of Lou Brock, one of the greatest base-stealers in the history of baseball, but you've never heard of Ernie Broglio. Exactly my point.
3. No scriptural reference has been found to support this punch line.
4. His middle name was also Graybill. But if you think we ever dared

joke with him about having a double name—like, "Did your mother stutter?"—you're not getting the picture of what he was like.

5. Mother was almost forty when the twins were born.

6. The same wasn't the fate of the Tooth Fairy. Somehow it fit into our family's doctrinal statement and left a coin under our pillow with each pulled tooth. We were even told that if we woke up when the fairy was making its delivery of the coin, it would instantly perish. Thanks for not noticing the Santa-Tooth Fairy inconsistency here.

7. Henri de Tourville, quoted in Hannah Ward and Jennifer Wild, *The Doubleday Christian Quotation Collection* (New York: Doubleday, 1998), 196.

8. If you're married to a cynic, show this chapter to him or her and tell your spouse how a poisonous attitude has a chance to ruin your family. Plead with your cynic to begin working on this.

9. "USDA Decreases Estimate of Florida Orange Crop," Florida Citrus Mutual, http://flcitrusmutual.com/news/pr_estimate_120915.aspx.

10. Since the first diseased tree was discovered in Miami in 1965, more than 640,000 trees have been cut down on people's private property. Associated Press, *The Orlando Sentinel*, February 12, 2004, 6 (italics mine).

11. Ibid. (italics mine).

Chapter 8: Discipline *Is Not a Dirty Word*

1. As a result of 118,000 respondents to a 2004 survey from www .familyeducation.com, 59 percent said "yes" to spanking, and an additional 22 percent agreed but said it should be used rarely. Only 16 percent said "no."

2. Experts disagree on whether a neutral instrument should be used—a hairbrush, a yardstick, and so on. Bobbie and I used our hands. We did this in order to monitor the actual pain inflicted.

3. Mostly this means that people who haven't been to Sunday school immediately start apologizing when I see them at Home Depot. Also, when they find Internet humor with some religious reference—Saint Peter at the pearly gates or "A rabbi, priest, and minister were golfing"

jokes—they e-mail it to me. I don't appreciate this, not because of the religious themes but the fact that the jokes are never funny.

4. Rick Hampson and Paul Overberg, "Speeders Outgun New Limits," *USA Today*, February 23, 2004.

Chapter 9: Safe at Home

1. Zig himself says that he learned this from Dr. Joyce Brothers. John Maxwell has also been given attribution. But most sources give credit to Zig. It doesn't matter *who* said it first. Truth has a way of finding a voice.

2. Later in his life, my dad became Mr. Neighborhood. Perhaps the encounter with Mr. Strandquist got his attention.

3. A dollar to wash the car, twenty-five cents extra if it had whitewalls.

4. I first told this story in the introduction to the book *O Come, All Ye Faithful: Hymns of Adoration and Joy to Celebrate His Birth* (coauthored with John MacArthur, Joni Eareckson Tada, and Bobbie Wolgemuth), from the Great Hymns of Our Faith series (Wheaton, IL: Crossway Books, 2001). I retell it here with the publisher's permission.

Chapter 10: Parents as Priests: Pulpits Optional

1. The estimated number of Chinese Christians comes from Xenos Christian Fellowship, Columbus, Ohio, 2004.

2. "According to University of California-Santa Barbara researcher and author Wade Clark Roof, 1 / 3 of American's [*sic*] 77 million baby boomers identify themselves as born-again." Quoted from "Born-again Doesn't Mean What It Used To: ...," text illustration shared by SermonCentral, January 2006, http://www.sermoncentral.com /illustrations/sermon-illustration-statistics-basicsofchristianity-23966.asp.

3. The historical books of the Old Testament include Joshua, Judges, 1 and 2 Samuel, 1 and 2 Kings, and 1 and 2 Chronicles. These record the return of the Israelites to the promised land and the establishment of the kingdom.

4. "In the morning [of the Day of Atonement], [the high priest] would put on his priestly clothes and go about the daily morning service, including the morning's sacrifice, the lighting of the menorah and the burning of incense. Then he would wash his hands and feet

in a golden basin. Afterwards, he took a bath, a ritual he repeated throughout the day.

"Then, the High Priest would change into a simple robe made of white linen and walk over to a young bull and recite for himself and for his family the first of three confessional prayers. Three times during the prayer he pronounced the *Shem Hameforash* (the name by which G-d identified himself to Moses at the burning bush, and to this day, remains unpronounceable), instead of the usual 'Adonai,' meaning Lord." Amy J. Kramer, Everything Israel, "Yom Kippur 101," accessed February 9, 2016, http://www.everythingisrael.com/yom-kippur-101/.

5. John Newton, "Amazing Grace." Public domain.

6. Anonymous, "Fairest Lord Jesus." Public domain.

7. Yes, you read that correctly. She passed away one month prior to birthday number 106! We had the fire department on notice in case the candles got carried away.

8. There are some wonderful hymns or praise music CDs available for kids at your Christian bookstore. Our favorite is *Hymns for a Kid's Heart*, vols. 1, 2, and 3, by Bobbie Wolgemuth and Joni Eareckson Tada (Crossway Books).

9. The folks who have "The Earth Is Your Mother" bumper stickers aren't familiar with Psalm 8.

Epilogue

1. Ravi Zacharias, *I, Isaac, Take Thee, Rebekah* (Nashville: W Publishing Group, 2004), 17.

2. Which I will not include here.

Appendix A: How to Lead Your Child to Christ

1. Other Bible references that speak to the universality of sin include Ecclesiastes 7:20: "For there is not a just man on earth who does good and does not sin;" Job 25:4: "How then can man be righteous before God? Or how can he be pure who is born of a woman?"; and Psalm 51:5 ESV: "Behold, I was brought forth in iniquity, and in sin did my mother conceive me." This material formed the foundation for a book Bobbie and I wrote with the same title, *How to Lead Your Child to Christ*, published in 2005, by Focus on the Family.

QUESTIONS FOR DISCUSSION
AND APPLICATION

The subtitle of this book announces, "What a Christian Home Looks Like and How to Build One." But merely reading an architect's drawing doesn't get the house built, does it? So let's get to work!

The questions for each chapter will help you . . .

Familiarize yourself with the blueprints for a Christian home. You'll talk about what you've read, discuss the principles that have worked for our family and many others, and wrestle with the truth of Scripture. And that's a worthwhile exercise in light of God's promise that His Word will not return to Him empty but will accomplish all that He desires (Isaiah 55:11).

Build a Christian home. Along the way you'll be encouraged to respond to and act on what you've read; to be doers of the Word, not just hearers (James 1:22). You'll be challenged to pick up the tools you need for building a Christian home and, relying on the power of the Holy Spirit, to use them. The key tool is prayer—prayer for wisdom, for grace, for a teachable spirit, for God's transforming Spirit to work in the lives of every family member—and sometimes prayers of confession. The importance of prayer cannot be overemphasized. After all, "unless the LORD builds the house, they labor in vain who build it" (Psalm 127:1).

Stay on top of home maintenance projects. Making our house a Christian home calls for parents to be vigilant, conscientious, and energetic. After all, there's always something to be done around the house, and the projects range from fixing things that are broken to brightening up rooms with a fresh coat of paint to even knocking down walls to make the place more livable. But fortunately none of those tasks are do-it-yourself projects. The Lord is with you always (Matthew 28:20) as you seek to raise your kids to know and love and serve Him (Deuteronomy 6:4–9).

Remember to pick and choose the ideas from both the text and the following questions that are most significant and relevant for where your family is today—and safely file away other ideas for when the time is right for them. Also, whenever you seek to apply one of these ideas, be sure to ask God to help.

1

WHY A CHRISTIAN HOME?

Different Is a Very Good Thing

1. Is your family normal? Is it different? Is it cool? First, explain why you answered as you did and then comment on the significance of your family being either normal, different, or cool *or* not normal, not different, and not cool. Now look at this same issue from another angle: In what specific ways is your home too "culture-friendly"—and what do you think God might want you to do about that similarity?

2. Why is "the most important place on earth" a good description of your home? List some of the life-determining comments, events, and interactions—both good and not good—that can happen there.

3. You get only one chance at this home-building deal, and time is not on your side—but my message is not shame and blame. It is instead urgency, focus, purposefulness, intentionality, and care. Why is it easy to lose this sense of urgency and a sharp focus on the importance of our home-building efforts? What can we do to prevent that shift away from the essential?

4. Parenting is relentless, and there are times—whether we're dealing with the little ones' constant diaper changes and loud tantrums or our teens' relentless testing of limits and annoying attitudes—that we are going to feel like giving up. Why do we parents get to that point? What can we do to avoid getting there or, perhaps more realistically, to rebound when we do find ourselves there? What good would come from retreating and giving up on our kids? What bad would come from giving up?

5. The ingredient that makes a Christian home special and different in a good way is grace, and grace means salvation, forgiveness, hope, genuine happiness, purpose, and power. What evidence of grace do you see in your home? Ask everyone who lives there for specific answers.

6. Mom or dad, did either of you grow up in a Christian home? Does your family have a real-life model of a Christian home in your extended family, at church, in the neighborhood, or someplace else? If so, what lessons learned when you were younger or what specific examples from today are helping you build a Christian home? If you answered "no" to those first two questions, what have you learned about the kind of home you want from not being raised in a Christian home and/or not being able to watch one in action?

7. Remember the plastic-jug-making machine that I saw at the salad-dressing factory? In what specific ways is your family being pulled, if not reshaped, by the immoral world? And what can you do—what will you do—to defy that pull?

8. Close your time with prayer. Read Romans chapter 12, verses 1 and 2 and let it be the starting point for some prayer time for your family. Also ask God to grant you knowledge, wisdom, patience, spiritual understanding, joy, and the ability to lead a life that pleases Him as you parent.

2

A GOD PLACE

God Lives in Your Home. What Does that Mean?

1. Except for the kitchen and the bathroom, every single room

in my grandparents' house smelled like mothballs, and most houses do have a distinct smell. What do you think your house smells like? Does it smell like friction, chaos, criticism, and tension or calm, warmth, and happiness?

2. Filling your house with the smell of God is, at least in part, a matter of following simple directions. When you do, the smell is automatic. Whose house smells like God to you? To what do you attribute that sweet aroma? Be specific. Your home will have the aroma of God when He is invited to be part of your day-to-day life together. Then He is able to work in each person's heart and add His love and grace to your family.

3. You can make God more a part of your family life—more present in your home—when:

a) You go to church. "Assembling together" is God's idea, and it's essential to Christian health and growth for individuals and families (Hebrews 10:25).

b) Every family member has a Bible. Why would anyone be without his or her own flashlight in this dark world of ours?

c) Family members read the Bible and memorize Scripture. The Bible alone provides the only antidote for the greatest problem our children will ever face—the poison of sin (Psalm 119:11).

d) Your home is bilingual, and one of the two languages is God talk. Such statements as "Isn't God amazing!"; "Thank You for this food"; "The Lord willing"; and "What did God say to you today?" are part of everyday conversation.

e) You have family devotions (study a book of the Bible, memorize Scripture, learn all the verses of a classic hymn)—and never let on that these family devotions are anything but great fun!

f) You pray together. After all, prayer is the glue that affixes your heart to your heavenly Father. So . . . pray at bedtime. Choose some prayer roads (see pages 42–44). Identify some prayer hooks (see pages 46–48). Colossians 1:9–12 is a good starting point for praying for your kids.

4. Remember that these are just suggestions. They're not a magic formula, a scorecard, or a do-everything-or-it-doesn't-count list. These are simply ways to allow your relationship with God to impact your family life.

   a) Which of these intentional habits are already a part of your family life? What benefits do you enjoy as a result?

   b) What will you do this week to revive or reenergize one of the habits that already is or once was part of your home? Brainstorm together. Be specific—and ask group members to hold you accountable.

   c) Which of these habits, if any, are you most hesitant to try to establish? Why?

   d) As you may have heard said, genuine faith is caught rather than taught. So what will you do to overcome your own reluctance, nervousness, or fear?

   e) Which of these habits seem better for a different season of your family's life? Explain.

   f) Which habit will you work on adding to your home this week? What specific steps will you take? Be sure to pave the way with prayer.

5. When you commit yourselves to a church, use God talk, and "pray without ceasing"(1 Thessalonians 5:17)—when you allow your relationship with God to be more present in the everyday activities of your family—God will take care of the smell.

6. Close your time in prayer, this time letting Colossians 1:9–12 guide your prayers for your children and yourselves.

3

THE MOST IMPORTANT PEOPLE IN

THE MOST IMPORTANT PLACE

What Is It Like to Walk into Your Home?

1. Think about a place where you feel special, important, and perhaps even honored. What prompts that feeling as you cross the threshold? Be as specific and thorough as possible, focusing especially on the people—and perhaps mentioning the pets—in that place.

2. What can you do to make every family member who walks into your home believe that his or her arrival is the best moment of your day? Consider words ("I'm so glad you're here"), affection (a bear hug), or focused attention (look into the person's eyes). And why not ask everyone what would work best for him or her so that the coming-home celebration is a good fit for them?

3. The basics of a Christian home are simple enough—respect dad, love mom, and nurture the kids—but you've probably found that they're not always easy to implement.

   a) Mom, what keeps you from respecting dad—and what are you going to do about it?

   b) Dad, what keeps you from nourishing and cherishing your wife? What changes could your answer prompt you to make?

   c) Parents, what keeps you from nurturing your kids—from loving, disciplining, affirming, correcting, and providing tenderness? Remember that when it comes to attitudes, conduct, or instruction of every kind, you go first. Also, your goal as a parent isn't perfection; it's transparency.

4. Review "The Two Blue Chairs" (see pages 61–63). What are the blue chairs in your life? What goal or priority is bumping your kids farther down the list than they probably should be?

5. What counts to a child is a parent's presence. Think of all the opportunities you have to be with your kids. When you are physically present, what interferes with your being completely present mentally and emotionally? What can and will you do to reduce, if not eliminate, that interference?

6. Which of the around-the-house items listed below need some maintenance? Describe your plan for specific home improvements—these or your own ideas:

   a) Having no-interruption, no-TV family dinners a minimum of _____ (you fill in the blank) times a week
   b) Verbally and physically welcoming each family member who walks through the door
   c) Speaking enthusiastically and supportively to each other on the telephone

7. Spend some time praying about the directive to "Be kind to one another" (Ephesians 4:31–32) as you work on a little remodeling of your most important place on earth.

4

AMAZING GRACE

It's What Sets Your Home Apart

1. What are you consciously doing to give your children, whatever their age, glimpses of grace—and what specific actions might you add to your repertoire?

2. What can parents do to help their home be a place where genuine repentance and wholehearted forgiveness are generously extended to one another? You might start by having everyone practice saying out loud "I'm sorry. I was wrong. Will you please forgive me?" When family members struggle to say those words (and we all do!), talk together about why that statement and request are so hard to make. Brainstorm now in your small group but also later with your family some ideas about how to become more comfortable saying those words.

3. What sin in your child(ren) are you not correcting because you yourself are guilty of it and don't want to be accused of being a hypocrite?

4. That magical attitude of thank you can be sprinkled throughout your home in a variety of ways. Add to the following list some specific ideas:

   a) Just say it!
   b) Random symbols of gratitude
   c) Thank-you notes
   d) A sense of wonder

5. In your small group—and perhaps later with your family—discuss why God considers not being thankful a sin (1 Thessalonians 5:16–18).

6. Tenderness is preplanned and deliberate, so spend some time right now telling your group one or two great things about each member of your family. As you identify positive traits in every family member, enjoy the feeling of being drawn toward those people God placed in your family. It's not an accident, you know. Your family is His design!

7. To encourage a spirit of generosity in your most important

place, what can you as a family do to remind yourselves that "it's more fun to give than to have"?

8. Cultivate a grateful heart by spending much of your prayer time thanking God for all His blessings, tangible and intangible (Psalm 100:4). Then thank Him that He can help you fill your Christian home with repentance and forgiveness, tenderness, and generosity as well as gratitude.

5

THE POWER OF WORDS

Real Bullets at Home

1. What words that you've spoken—or had spoken to you—came to mind when you read "Words are never blanks. They're actual bullets, and their impact is absolute. Every time."? (See pages 96–97.)

2. Which words that you've spoken to a child or your spouse do you need to apologize for? Ask your small group to pray for you and hold you accountable for asking forgiveness.

3. Remember Bobbie's dad and his clandestine visit to the skating rink when he was in his teens? What experience taught you the value of speaking truth and only truth? What opportunity have you had—as Bobbie's grandmother did—to teach your child(ren) the importance of being honest and not lying?

4. When has the positive power of words helped you or one of your children stand taller? What positive—and sincere and honest—words of encouragement can you offer each of your children today?

5. Below is a list of suggestions. Which of these potential family policies will you introduce over dinner? What creative approach will help ensure buy-in on the part of the younger generation? And which "parent pointer" will you make a conscious effort to try this week?

   a) No one is allowed to finish "You are" with a derogatory word or phrase.
   b) Children are to refer to their siblings by name, not by *he* or *she*.
   c) Say good things about your kids to others.
   d) Endorse the attitudes and conduct of other children to your kids—but never endorse another child's qualities in areas that your child could never achieve, like physical qualities.

6. Create some spoken word "traditions"—some words that you speak each time certain situations arise. Here's a list of questions to help you brainstorm:

   a) What happy epithet can you give each of your children?
   b) At what points in your regular routine can you remind your kids that they're [fill in your last name here]?
   c) "The Lord be with you" is a wonderful way to say good-bye in a phone call or on the schoolyard. When else could you use it in your family? And what other ways of saying good-bye do you or might you use to be encouraging and supportive?
   d) Which member of your family has the next birthday? What gift of words will you give that person when you describe "what I love about you"?
   e) What "happy thoughts" are the last words you leave with your children when you say good night? (And, parents, a point for brutal honesty: Why can it be such a struggle to spend these valuable, quiet, just-before-sleep moments with our kids? What can we do to resist the temptation of the newspaper,

the to-do list, the office project due the next morning, or our own pillows that seem to be scalling our names?)

What impact can these action steps have on a person? Which will you implement in your home this week?

7. Electronic gadgets can be extremely dangerous to the health of your family. When we're not actually talking to each other, we're not connecting, and we're not acting like a family. What electronic distractions do you have under your roof and in your car? (Yes, cell phones count.) What family rules do you have—or could you institute—to be sure these technological goodies are used by you *and* your kids only in moderation? Sometimes saying "yes" to them is saying "no" to our kids—and letting our kids have unlimited time with their "electronic friends" might be saying "no" to the family and other worthwhile activities. So use extreme caution when operating electronic equipment.

8. As you close with prayer, consider both the wonderful and the terrifying potential of words. In light of James 3:5–7, ask forgiveness for any fires you've started with your tongue. Also, ask God's Spirit to give you the gift of self-control so you can choose your words more carefully.

6

THE POWER OF WORDS PART II

The Family Vitamins

1. Family Vitamin #1 is "I love you," and "I love you" is really "I love you regardless . . . anyway . . . and always." How many doses of Vitamin #1 do your kids get in a typical day? Identify

some moments when you could add another dose—or even two or three! Also, do your kids hear their name after these three magic words? Why is that fourth word so important? (Think about your own experience.)

2. "I need your love" is Vitamin #2, and it's about putting unmet expectations into words. It means daring to tell the ones you love how they can best let you know that they love you. What can you say to let your kids know that doing so is not only okay but it's very important? Be creative!

3. Vitamin #3 is "I'm sorry; I was wrong. Will you please forgive me?"—and like the other four vitamins, it needs to be spoken in its entirety. Review why each of the three components of Vitamin #3 is necessary. Practice explaining it so that your kids will understand when you introduce this new family way of doing things. And, before you move on, to which member of your family do you need to say these words—and when will you do so?

4. "May I help?" is Vitamin #4, and it's an admission that having a successful family can be a lot of work. What might you do to encourage your kids both to ask this question and then to follow through when the person gives a specific response? Yes, setting an example is an excellent idea—as is starting immediately to model this attitude. Anything else? Be creative.

5. "Thank you"—Vitamin #5—is not optional. Gratitude reminds us that we are recipients of blessings rather than demanders of rights. Thank you also lets others know that we notice their efforts. Who needs to hear—or read—"thank you" from you? Make a list of those people—and get to work! Also, what will you do to help your kids develop the heartfelt habit of thank you—both spoken and written? Brainstorm some ideas.

6. Family Vitamins can help healthy families stay healthy, but these vitamins can also be a miracle cure for traumatized clans. In fact, these vitamins can save a family's life. Wherever you fall on that spectrum ranging from good health to 911 trouble, what will you do to remember to take these vitamins every day? What will you do to encourage your kids to take them?

7. Read what Proverbs 12:25, 15:1, and 16:24 say about words and let those verses guide your prayer for you, your children, and these necessary Family Vitamins. Also, since loving someone is something each of us decides to do and it always requires work, ask God to help you love the members of your family with His kind of love—unconditional, forgiving, and steadfast.

7

JUST FOR LAUGHS

The Best Medicine of All

1. A vital piece of the Christian home puzzle is the serious business of laughter. Why do you think laughter is important in a family? What can Christian parents do to be sure that laughter is a permanent resident in their home?

2. Was laughter heard rarely or frequently in the family you grew up in? Why was that the case, and what impact do you think it had on you personally? Did humor have any effect on the way your family functioned?

3. Is laughter heard rarely or frequently in your family today—and why is that the case?

4. Although doing so may feel awkward, planning for laughter may be exactly what you need to do—and here are some tips:

a) Laugh at yourself—and know that stress and pride will keep you from doing so. Okay, I confessed—with a cringe—my bungling of Missy and Jon's wedding rehearsal. Why didn't I just lighten up and enjoy the unexpected fun? What story from either the recent or the distant past can you tell on yourself to spur some laughter in your house?

b) Homemade laughter is more fun than anything store-bought or televised. Does the kissing monster live at your house? Do your kids' ribs regularly need counting to make sure none are missing? What make-believe games ("Mud pudding, grand-daddy?") does your family enjoy? When was the last time you played hide-and-seek with the kids or tussled with them on the living room floor? What clean and funny movie can you watch on a family movie night? Can you track down a Stan Freberg video or recording? With the right snack incentive, could you talk your teenagers into a family-home-video night and watch them grow up again right before your very eyes? Share ideas for homemade laughter with your group.

c) Laugh with your kids, never at them. What might you do, for instance, to help your child create a "laugh with" moment like the one our granddaughter, Harper, enjoyed? What could you do to reinforce this rule—laugh with, not at—among siblings?

d) What did the snail say when he climbed up on the turtle's back? *Wheeeeee.* Why don't oysters share their toys? *Because they're shellfish.* Find a favorite joke to share at the dinner table.

5. "A merry heart makes a cheerful countenance" (Proverbs 15:13), so spend some time asking God to grant you a merry heart that is contagious. Ask Him to not let cynicism, sarcasm, or mockery have any place in your home. Request His help in adding to your family time generous amounts of homemade laughter.

8

DISCIPLINE IS NOT A DIRTY WORD

It's the Stuff of Champions

1. I was seventeen. I was "in love." And I stayed out past my curfew. Then I broke the rules of the grounding (consequences for violation #1) and slipped out at night to visit my girlfriend (violation #2). The pain of the spanking I received was real, but even more painful was the crushing weight of my own rebelliousness. I had disappointed someone who was depending on me, and that made my mutiny unbearable. What scene from your childhood taught you much about discipline? What did you learn and why was that experience so memorable?

2. It is our responsibility as parents to prepare our children for life. Use "discipline" as a verb, and it's something you do. Use it as a noun, and discipline is something you've become. Discipline as a noun is the great reward of discipline as a verb. Yet doing discipline right can be a very difficult and challenging task, can't it? Consider adding to your home—if they're not already present—the following discipline non-negotiables:

   a) **Discipline must be direct.** Why is it important and even helpful to be direct about what the problem is? Do you tend to be direct? If not, why not?

   b) **Discipline must be painful**, but not everyone agrees about the value or appropriateness of spanking. What do you think about spanking in response to open defiance, disobedience, and hurtful actions and words? What do you appreciate about the approach described on pages 167–68: spanking is never done in public; describe the behavior being addressed before you spank; spanking should not be violent, but it should be repetitive; and when you have finished spanking your children, turn them toward you, hug them, and tell them you love them? What are some painful alternatives to spanking? Especially consider what some options are when the children are older.

c) **Discipline must be swift.** A simple, thorough explanation of the rules and your expectation that your children follow them should be met with obedience and, if not, with discipline. What family rules do your children clearly understand? (Ask them!) What have you done—or what will you do—to clarify that you expect your kids to follow the rules the first time? What issues are you stacking blocks on top of instead of addressing? Beware that those issues will be emotionally volatile the next time they arise.

d) **Discipline must be participatory.** The movie director's bullhorn approach may be easier, but why is it not very effective? Give an example of when you were able to add your participation to your spoken instructions and comment on the effectiveness of that combination. What changes in your approach to discipline might this idea of participating, not just talking, prompt? (See pages 171–74.)

3. Think back to a recent time you had to discipline your child. What could you have said to identify and validate his or her feelings? What could you have done to show your availability and to encourage? Now anticipate a likely moment when you could apply "the happy secret" (identify, validate, share) and plan your words and actions now.

4. What if disciplining your kids hasn't been your strong suit? Can that situation change? What might be the first step . . . the second step . . . and the third to take toward introducing discipline into the home? And, yes, that will depend on the ages of your

kids. To whom or to what resource might you turn for help? A word of encouragement: with God nothing is impossible. He can and does redeem our mistakes in every area of life, including our mistakes with our kids. So boldly take the steps that you believe He is directing; you can be confident that God will help.

5. What words, actions, and even attitudes in the lives of some parents suggest that they're so eager to be their kids' best friend that they're afraid to be the *parents*? What kinds of things feed a parent's desire to be their kid's pal? What evidence in your life suggests that your priority is to be a parent, not your child(ren)'s best friend?

6. Doing self-discipline leads to the sheer pleasure of having self-discipline, and self-discipline coupled with self-respect is a fantastic combination for life. So on what day this week will you play a round of "the no game" in your home? Also, what specific and regular chores can your kids do around the house (if they're not doing some already) to gain a sense of self-respect?

7. A conversation about discipline wouldn't be complete without mentioning the "say whens" of life, the discipline of moderation. What are some specific steps you can take to teach self-discipline in the following areas? Brainstorm some ideas together.

   a) Moderation about food
   b) Moderation about other things (TV, spending money, language we use, and so on)
   c) Modesty

   Also talk about how you would approach a family discussion of Romans 7:14–17, 24–25 and 2 Peter 1:3–7. Kids need to know—and parents need to be reminded—that all of us struggle with self-control and all of us can ask Jesus to help us.

8. Spend some time thanking your heavenly Father that He disciplines those He loves (Hebrews 12:6) and that He can give you wisdom, patience, and strength to discipline the child(ren) you love. Ask Him to grant you the grace and humility that will enable you to rely on His help.

9

SAFE AT HOME

The Refuge You Are Looking For

1. I introduced you to Bernie Felstead and his experience in northern France on the morning of December 25, 1914. The fighting of World War I stopped for a few hours; the battle-weary soldiers enjoyed a respite from the struggle. What relentless battles are members of your family (parents included!) fighting? Identifying them might help you better know what to do to make your home an oasis, a place of rest and peace, for the warriors who live there.

2. Safety at home involves the way we treat each other, the way we honor each other. And this kind of safety begins with the freedom to speak. Is it safe to tell the truth—to say, "I broke the vase," "What you said hurt my feelings," or "I'm not as excited about my relationship with Jesus as I should be"—in your home? If you think it is, point to some specific evidence. Talk about what you can do to make your home a safer place.

3. What can we parents do to make sure our kids know and never doubt that we're on their side? Make a list together—starting with "Skip the lecture on physics and give a hug instead when your son crashes on his bike or dents the fender of your new car."

4. What can you do to make your home—a laboratory for life—a safer place to make mistakes? What do you do to communicate to your kids that they are allowed to fail? Before you answer that question, think about how you respond to their failures—when they forget their lines in the school play, strike out in Little League, don't stick a landing in gymnastics, bomb their SAT tests, miss the deadline to register for classes, or find themselves in the wrong place at the wrong time with the wrong people.

5. Your Christian home needs to be a safe place for truth-asking as well as truth-telling. What kinds of parental responses make home such a haven? Consider how you want to respond to questions about drugs, sex, alcohol, or cheating at school.

6. A safe home is a place where people think the best of you. And that's important because family members are likely to become what you think they'll become. (That's also why it's wise to use the phrase, "This isn't like you" when correcting your children's wrong behavior.) So what is on your default screen regarding your kids? Do you automatically think the best of them? What can you do, first, to make sure that it is truth, honor, rightness, and purity—and, second, to make sure that they know you think of them as truth-tellers, honorable people, children striving to do what is right, and young men and women wanting to live a pure life? Be specific.

7. A safe home is a place where people don't play the blame game. Instead, they learn to accept and trust in the mystery of God's sovereignty. Instead of asking "Who's to blame?" people in a safe home ask, "What is God saying to me/us in this situation?" Discuss the value of this approach over the blame game and in what current situation could your family ask this question? You might look back on a past situation that at the time you didn't understand and discuss from the vantage point of the present what God was saying or teaching then.

282

8. A safe home is a place where people express appreciation, where people are treated with tenderness, and where people practice repentance and forgiveness. A safe home is a place of grace, and grace means no more keeping score. What could each of these traits—appreciation, tenderness, repentance and forgiveness, and grace—look like in your home? Describe specific situations and how these traits might be made manifest in your family.

9. What are you doing—or might you be doing—to make your home a place of refuge for your neighbors?

10. Thank God for His power to bring peace to stormy waters—both literal (Luke 8:22–24) and metaphorical—and ask Him to help you make your home a place of peace and safety for your family, your friends, and your neighbors. Ask Him to give you self-control and compassion as you react to kids' mistakes, peace and poise as you respond to kids' questions, and confidence and faith—in Him and in your kids—as you both show them that you're on their side and hold up to them a mirror of your expectations for their lives.

10

PARENTS AS PRIESTS: PULPITS OPTIONAL

Mom and Dad, Why the Robes?

1. Christian parents have been given the right, the privilege, and the responsibility to worship at home with their children, and that worship involves confession of sins, teaching, prayer, and song. The primary responsibility of the Old Testament priest was to conduct worship and be the connecting link between the people

and their God. What were your initial feelings when you read this job description? What might you do to fulfill this responsibility?

2. Speaking through Moses, God was very specific about what priests in that day were supposed to do (Leviticus 22:29, 31–32), and His instructions outline some key things for us parent-priests today:

a) **Sacrifice:** As a priest, you are required to bring your own sin to God in confession, and that involves a sacrifice of time and pride.

b) **Thanksgiving:** A spirit of gratitude—the recognition that God has given to you everything you have—is essential for all priests.

c) **Generosity:** Willingly and enthusiastically serve God and your family. Also, hold everything you have—your treasures, your time, your family—with an open hand.

d) **Obedience:** Your goal is to gradually transfer your children's obedience from you as their parent to God, their heavenly Father. They will learn the importance of obeying God as they see you, the family priest, "keep God's commands and follow them."

e) **Respect God's holy name:** Teach your children about God's holiness and character. When you do, He can shape your kids' hearts.

f) **Hallow His name:** Show your kids deep respect for God.

g) **Music:** Introduce your family to hymns and Christian music.

Which of these dimensions of your priesthood are already in place? Which of the remaining ones are most daunting? Let other group members encourage you (with ideas as well as with prayer) in those pieces of your important role.

3. Now let's consider the organizational chart for our house churches:

a) **God First:** What are you doing to love God most—more than your spouse and more than your children? What evidence in your life—in your daily schedule or your checkbook register, for instance—supports the fact that your primary allegiance is to the Lord?

b) **Your Spouse Next:** Your love for each other is to take precedence over your love for your kids. God commands spouses to live in mutual submission, for wives to submit to their husbands and husbands to love their wives and be willing to die for them (Ephesians 5:21–33). Give an example or two of this kind of mutual submission happening in your married life (remember how Bobbie and I made our career decisions?) or honestly consider what you two could do to better submit to and serve each other in love.

c) **Then the Kids:** Ephesians 6:4 calls us to "bring [our kids] up in the discipline and instruction of the Lord" (ESV)—not command or send. Our kids are coming along with us to the world of "discipline and instruction." What are you doing to be a picture of discipline and learning for your kids?

4. What if your priorities haven't been in order? First, know you're not alone. We all struggle to live according to the priorities we know to be true. Second—as I mentioned earlier—with God nothing is impossible. He can and does redeem our mistakes in every area of life, including our mistakes with our kids. So talk to Him. Tell Him where you've failed . . . thank Him for the forgiveness He offers . . . and ask for Him to bring goodness and strength out of what you see as the bad and the weak of the past. Also ask Him to help you live out His priorities for you so that you can be the parent you want to be.

5. As the priests in the home, parents must be willing to live what they speak, to do what they preach. What are you asking your

children to do that you yourself are not doing? If you're not sure (or if you can't think of anything!), ask your spouse or even your kids. They'll know! Then take steps to be the first in the family to clean up your act.

6. Parenting is not for the fainthearted. It requires dying to self and serving others. Fortunately, God has gone before us on this path of sacrifice and service, and He is available to help us on our journey. Spend some time in prayer, thanking Him for the privilege of parenting, for His ever-present help, and for the hope you find in the fact that He loves your kids even more than you do.

EPILOGUE

1. In the book's introduction, you were encouraged to treat the reading of this book like a visit to a cafeteria—picking and choosing those ideas that looked especially tasty. What ideas have you placed on your tray and found helpful? List them.

_____

_____

_____

_____

_____

_____

2. What ideas do you want to start implementing that you haven't yet? List them here. Circle the one you'll tackle first and describe your plan for making it part of your family's life.

_____

_____

_____

_____

_____

3. What ideas are you saving for later—and what will you do to remind yourself of those ideas when "later" arrives? Why not list them here?

_____

_____

_____

_____

_____

4. In what ways is the family in America under incredible assault? Get past the clichéd part of that truth and identify your specific enemies so that you can pray against them and stand stronger in your home.

_____

_____

_____

_____

_____

5. What encouragement for your parenting do you find in Philippians 3:13–14? Let that be the starting point for a time of prayer for your family and yourself as its priest.

_____

_____

_____

_____

_____

_____

ABOUT THE AUTHOR

Dr. Robert Wolgemuth has spent most of his career in the publishing industry. His credits include executive marketing and management positions in the magazine and book industry in Illinois and Texas, the presidency of a large Nashville book publisher, and the cofounder of a publishing company and literary agency.

Following the sale of his publishing business in 1992, he and his business partner, Michael Hyatt, founded a literary representation agency, for which he served as chairman. In 1998, Robert acquired the agency from Michael. Wolgemuth & Associates shepherds the literary work of more than one hundred authors and writers.

In August 1996, Robert released his first book, *She Calls Me Daddy: Seven Things Every Man Needs to Know About Building a Complete Daughter.* The book became a bestseller ninety days later. In 2014, with more than three hundred thousand copies of the original in print, the book was updated.

Robert is also the author of many other titles, including *Seven Things You Better Have Nailed Down Before All Hell Breaks Loose* and the sequel to his first book, *She Still Calls Me Daddy: Building a New Relationship with Your Daughter After You Walk Her Down the Aisle.*

His latest book is *Like the Shepherd: Leading Your Marriage with Love and Grace.* He is also coauthor of *What Every Groom Needs to Know: The Most Important Year in a Man's Life, What's in the Bible: A Tour of Scripture from the Dust of Creation to the Glory of Revelation,* and *Couples of the Bible: A One-Year Devotional Study to Draw You Closer to God and Each Other.*

His speaking assignments have taken him across America and through several foreign countries.

Robert Wolgemuth has served two terms as the chairman of the Evangelical Christian Publishers' Association. As a layman, he has taught adult Sunday school classes since 1969 in Texas, Tennessee, and Florida.

A 1969 graduate of Taylor University, he received an honorary doctorate in 2005. Dr. Wolgemuth is the father of two adult daughters and their husbands and the grandfather of five grandchildren. Robert and his wife, Nancy DeMoss Wolgemuth, live in Michigan.